Frank Lloyd Wright's Florida Southern College

The Florida History and Culture Series

UNIVERSITY PRESS OF FLORIDA

Florida A&M University, Tallahassee
Florida Atlantic University, Boca Raton
Florida Gulf Coast University, Ft. Myers
Florida International University, Miami
Florida State University, Tallahassee
New College of Florida, Sarasota
University of Central Florida, Orlando
University of Florida, Gainesville
University of North Florida, Jacksonville
University of South Florida, Tampa
University of West Florida, Pensacola

University Press of Florida

Gainesville · Tallahassee · Tampa · Boca Raton

Pensacola · Orlando · Miami · Jacksonville · Ft. Myers · Sarasota

Dale Allen Gyure

FRANK LLOYD WRIGHT'S FLORIDA SOUTHERN COLLEGE

Foreword by Raymond Arsenault and Gary Mormino

15 14 13 12 11 10 6 5 4 3 2 1

Library of Congress Cataloging-in-Publication Data
Gyure, Dale Allen.
Frank Lloyd Wright's Florida Southern college / Dale Allen Gyure, foreword by Raymond Arsenault and Gary Mormino.
p. cm.—(Florida history and culture series)
Includes bibliographical references and index.
ISBN 978-0-8130-3523-9 (alk. paper)
1. Florida Southern College—Buildings. 2. College buildings—Florida—Lakeland. 3. Wright, Frank Lloyd, 1867–1959—Criticism and interpretation. 4. Campus planning—Florida—Lakeland. 5. Lakeland (Fla.)—Buildings, structures, etc. I. Arsenault, Raymond. II. Mormino, Gary Ross, 1947– III. Title.
LD1771.F8335G98 2010
727.'3092—dc22
2010016375

The University Press of Florida is the scholarly publishing agency for the State University System of Florida, comprising Florida A&M University, Florida Atlantic University, Florida Gulf Coast University, Florida International University, Florida State University, New College of Florida, University of Central Florida, University of Florida, University of North Florida, University of South Florida, and University of West Florida.

University Press of Florida
15 Northwest 15th Street
Gainesville, FL 32611-2079
http://www.upf.com

For Daniel C. Gyure,
who taught me everything that matters.
Hiányzol.

Contents

Illustrations

Color plates follow page 112

Foreword

Frank Lloyd Wright's Florida Southern College is the latest volume of a series devoted to the study of Florida history and culture. During the past half-century, the burgeoning population and increased national and international visibility of Florida have sparked a great deal of popular interest in the state's past, present, and future. As a favorite destination of countless tourists and as the new home for millions of retirees and transplants, modern Florida has become a demographic, political, and cultural bellwether. Florida has also emerged as a popular subject and setting for scholars and writers. The Florida History and Culture Series provides an attractive and accessible format for Florida-related books. From avenging hurricanes to disputed elections, from tales of the Everglades to profiles of Sunbelt cities, Florida is simply irresistible.

The University Press of Florida is committed to the creation of an eclectic but carefully crafted set of books that will provide the field of Florida studies with a new focus that will encourage Florida writers to consider the broader implications and context of their work. The series includes standard academic monographs, as well as works of synthesis, memoirs, and anthologies. And, while the series features books of historical interest, authors researching Florida's environment, politics, literature, and popular or material culture are encouraged to submit their manuscripts as well. Each book offers a distinct personality and voice, but the ultimate goal of the series is to foster a broad sense of community and collaboration among Florida scholars.

If only Frank Lloyd Wright could see Florida Southern College now. If only Frank Lloyd Wright could see the architecture that followed his death in 1959! We can only assume that the architectural maestro would be pleased at the former and appalled by the latter, but Wright was notoriously prickly and unpredictable.

Floridians and Americans love the 1930s partnership that brought the unlikely couple of Ludd Myrl Spivey and Frank Lloyd Wright together. They should also enjoy and appreciate the thorough work of Dale Allen Gyure, who has written a book that will please a wide variety of readers and students of architecture, Florida, biography, and mystery. The book addresses many mysterious questions, among them: How did such a world-class architect become interested in the fortunes of a college that had great hope but little fortune?

When Spivey became president of the campus overlooking Lake Hollingsworth in 1925, his vision for Florida Southern College was as bright as the Florida boom. But the immediate collapse of the Florida real estate market, followed by the Great Depression, arrested the dreams of realists and visionaries. But Spivey persevered and kept the faith.

With timely assistance from E. Stanley Jones and his foundation, Florida Southern College eked out an existence during the hardscrabble 1930s. Against all odds, the irrepressible Spivey telegraphed the irascible Wright in April 1938: "Desire conference with you concerning plans for great educational temple in Florida." Gyure patiently details the unfolding relationship and how the campus in Lakeland, Florida, is today home to the greatest collection of Frank Lloyd Wright buildings in the world.

Gary R. Mormino and Raymond Arsenault
Series editors

Acknowledgments

Florida Southern College influenced me to become an architectural historian, and for that I am eternally grateful. I began spending time there in the early 1990s as an attorney with an interest in Frank Lloyd Wright; many trips to the campus fed my growing architecture obsession and roused my curiosity about the campus's creation. Finding no comprehensive published accounts, I started compiling all the information I could find. This process helped me realize what I really wanted to do with my life. Soon thereafter I entered the graduate program in architectural history at the University of Virginia, where I channeled my fascination with Florida Southern. Lynn Dennis was kind enough to let me wander through the buildings and access much of the correspondence that had been organized to that point. Lisa Snyder and Pierluigi Serraino, then graduate students at UCLA, and William Dabars, of the Getty Research Institute for the History of Art and the Humanities, helped me obtain copies of Wright's drawings and correspondence from the Getty Archives. The cogent advice of Richard Guy Wilson, Dan Bluestone, Kevin D. Murphy, and Neil Levine clarified my thinking.

When I turned my attention back to Florida Southern in 2007, I was the beneficiary of even more support. Randall MacDonald and Mary Flekke of Florida Southern's Roux Library were especially generous with their time and resources, and without them I could not have completed this book. James G. Rogers, Jr., and his team of student researchers, and Kathy Ellis—all of Florida Southern—provided valuable information along the way. Likewise, I owe a debt of gratitude to Bruce Brooks Pfeiffer, Oskar Muńoz, Margo Stipe, and Indira Berendtson of the Frank Lloyd Wright Foundation Archives at Taliesin West for their hospitality and gracious assistance.

A Franklin Research Grant from the American Philosophical Society—which Neil Levine, Richard Guy Wilson, and David De Long helped me to obtain—financed my research. Maria Vaz of Lawrence Technological University granted the sabbatical that gave me time to write the book. And the following people were essential in assisting me during the research and writing process: Debra Pickrel; Tom Grafton of the Asbury Theological Seminary Archives; William Offhaus of the University of Buffalo University Archives; Dorinda Garrard of the Polk County Historical and Genealogical Library; Kevin Logan of the Lakeland Public Library; the Library of Congress; Rev. Robert J. Williams, PhD; Kathy Wheeler of the University of Miami; and Leslie Edwards of the Cranbrook Archives. A special thanks to Elizabeth Simmons, Steven Rajewski, Dan Price, Nathaniel Turner, and Mary Power of Lawrence Tech for their efforts regarding images and interlibrary loans.

Thank you also to Meredith Babb of the University Press of Florida for politely listening to my pitch at a Vernacular Architecture Forum conference, to John Byram for granting a deadline extension during a troubled time, and to Sharon Damoff for her incisive editing.

None of my research and writing would be possible without the support and patience of my family—Dan, Jayne, Jan, Matthew, and Jeffrey—to them I owe the most.

Introduction

Florida Southern College in Lakeland, Florida, contains the world's largest unified collection of Frank Lloyd Wright architecture. It was also the longest-lasting commission of his life, from 1938 to his death in 1959, as well as his longest continuous relationship with one client—the school's dynamic president, Ludd M. Spivey. The college contains two of Wright's seven structures for religious worship completed before his death, his only college buildings, and his only completed structures in Florida beyond a house in Tallahassee. Despite these unique qualifications, Wright's Florida Southern College has been relatively ignored compared to his other works.[1]

This critical and scholarly indifference is particularly unfortunate when one realizes the campus's significance. It resonates with some of Wright's deepest beliefs in a way matched by few other projects. Florida Southern is one of Wright's most autobiographical creations, incorporating concepts about nature, democracy, and education that he had developed over a lifetime. Here he weaved together a set of buildings that revealed his philosophy of man's relationship to nature and of the site's importance to architecture, his strong belief in connections between buildings and democracy, and his theory of progressive education. Because of the extent of the campus and the variety of buildings on display in Lakeland—religious, academic, administrative, cultural—it may be the best place to view Wright's genius in action.

Wright's West Campus at Florida Southern also was a milestone in the history of American college architecture. It was the first college designed and built with a modernist architectural vocabulary. Florida Southern was a point of equilibrium between the formal order of contemporary Beaux-Arts-influenced colleges and the architectural chaos that emerged after World War II. The campus plan was unified, but not in a balanced, symmetrical manner like the standard American college. Instead, Wright imposed order through the repetition of basic geometric forms, the appearance of thirty- and sixty-degree angles in plan and buildings, and covered walkways that connected every building on campus.

As the first modernist college in America, Wright's campus undoubtedly caused discomfort for those whose idea of a college campus involved the quaint, ivy-covered quadrangles that conveyed feelings of tradition and stability. Florida Southern was emphatically different; Spivey asked for something that would propel his small school into the public consciousness, and he got it. But Wright's buildings were not modernist in the cubic white box mode of the International Style or the steel and glass skeletons that would appear later in the century. Instead he sought a small-scale modernism, humanized and integrated with the central Florida landscape. The campus is one of the earliest and best examples of Wright's effort to create a type of modern architecture that responded to a specific region. At Florida Southern, he strove for a "Florida form" and "outdoor garden character" that would serve as a guidepost for the future as well as a leading instance of regional modernism.

The story of Florida Southern College is really a tale of *two* men. Wright was able to conceive and construct the college only with the support of Ludd Spivey; together they crafted a dream and doggedly pursued its realization for two decades in the face of economic adversity, war, and frequent disagreements. They were linked by significant commonalities that doubtless strengthened their bond, resulting in a relationship that surpassed that of architect and client. Both men had backgrounds in religion, a shared interest in pragmatic philosophy and progressive education, and a desire to fashion a showpiece of modern architecture. Their mutual beliefs and attitudes certainly helped smooth over the many disputes that arose during the course of this long commission.

This book provides the first detailed account of this important project as it can be discerned from the historical evidence at hand, yet there remains a considerable amount of archival information at Florida Southern that has not been organized and may yield new insights into the story of the Wright campus development. In documenting this story, I hope to clear up some misconceptions and debunk some myths about Spivey, Wright, and the origins of the campus buildings. I also hope that by doing so, I can help raise the status of this composition to its proper place alongside some of Wright's more famous works, for the campus is truly unique, quite exceptional, and deserving of recognition as one of Wright's finest designs and America's most significant twentieth-century works of architecture.

The book took shape during the research, as I discovered a trove of archival information, particularly a rich twenty-year correspondence between Wright and Spivey. Their letters are fascinating reading, and I have tried to include as many of their own words as possible, for these two men were articulate and passionate in their writings about this undertaking that meant so much to both of them. Over the course of their relationship, the letters became less formal (although a degree of familiarity is noticeable from the beginning), often verging on the confessional, and many times veering into conflict as Wright and Spivey conducted an ongoing war over money. In these exchanges one can discern their growing friendship. They had complementary personalities, so much so that it is hard to imagine Wright tolerating so many annoyances with any other client.

Because we know so little about Ludd Spivey, his correspondence was crucial. While conducting the research, I was surprised to discover the paucity of biographical information on him; given his dynamic personality, aptitude for inspiring anecdotes repeated to this day, and crucial role in the college's history, I assumed there would be more material available on his life. Hopefully in the near future some enterprising scholar will engage this fascinating man as a dissertation topic or book.

With Wright, the opposite is true. No other American architect has had more written about him (or her), or has been so analyzed, scrutinized, and lauded. This voluminous scholarship eased the launch of my project, but soon I began to worry about what new angle could be brought to the Wright story beyond a simple recitation of the facts and chronology. But as I spent more time with the buildings and the conditions of their creation, my apprehension disappeared as I recognized Florida Southern's unique position in Wright's long career, in terms of the intense personal beliefs that seemed to permeate its design and the scope of its architecture. I hope that this book helps the reader to appreciate these distinctive characteristics.

Brief Outline

The book follows the history of Wright's Florida Southern campus chronologically. Chapter 1 begins the story by outlining the history of Florida Southern College up to and including Wright's hiring and his first visit to the college. It highlights Spivey's dogged determination first to save the school and then to vault it into prominence, with the formation of the E. Stanley Jones Educational Foundation in 1937 as the chief vehicle to accomplish this goal. Chapter 2 looks at Wright's campus plan in detail, focusing on how his deeply held ideas about nature, education, and democracy shaped its conception. Influences from Wright's past are addressed, and his scheme for Florida Southern is contextualized by examining contemporary college architecture and planning. The third chapter looks at the short period between 1938 and 1941, which included construction of the first new buildings on the West Campus (the main chapel and seminars) and the beginning of the library. During World War II campus growth stagnated, but Spivey's dreams were not dampened, as outlined in chapter 4. Major proposals for a music building and an arts complex involving the same potential donor, Eleanor Searle Whitney, occupied much of Spivey's and Wright's time during the war years, but after an extensive design process and prolonged negotiations, neither project survived. Chapter 5 tells the story of the longest period of campus development, which lasted from 1946 until Spivey's retirement in 1957. During this time five more Wright structures were completed (library, Water Dome, and administration, industrial arts, and science buildings), while other initiatives, most notably the music building, were initiated or resurrected only to fail. The last chapter explains the events surrounding the end of the Wright era at Florida Southern, beginning with Wright's death in 1959 and the school's dispute with his successor firm. It ends with a brief note on the campus's status today.

Frank Lloyd Wright's West Campus at Florida Southern College is one of his most intriguing projects—in the plan, the constructed buildings, and the unbuilt proposals, one can see the extraordinary workings of his creative mind to an extent not found elsewhere. It pointed the way toward a new type of Florida architecture, arising from nature and in tune with the region's environment. It also provided a model for architects who may have sought alternatives to the rigidly ordered and traditionally styled college campuses of the time. And as the largest collection of Wright's architecture ever realized, it served as the best example of what organic architecture might be capable of on a broad scale. Unfortunately, its lead was not followed, and its influence on the architectural profession was minimal. Wright actually predicted this when he told an audience at the college, "I think [the campus] will be regarded in years to come as a missionary, as a thought along the line of a culture which we narrowly missed."[2] This book attempts to recover the campus's missionary status, to stimulate those unfamiliar with it to discover Wright's underappreciated treasure and those who know it well to see it in a new light.

ONE *Florida Southern College, 1845–1938*

The story of Florida Southern College began almost one hundred years before Frank Lloyd Wright agreed to design any campus buildings. The school had a long and tortuous history involving numerous moves and several severe financial challenges. It was mainly through the efforts of one man—President Ludd Myrl Spivey—that the college survived through the 1920s and 1930s and stood in a position to consider America's most famous architect for a campus expansion.

The Founding of a College

The origins of Florida Southern date back to 1845, the year Florida achieved statehood, and to the Methodist church. In that year the Methodist Episcopal Church, South, organized a new Florida Conference to preside over the Florida and South Georgia geographical area, a territory previously under the jurisdiction of the church's South Carolina Conference. Shortly thereafter the young conference's leaders chose Thomasville, Georgia, as the site of its first educational facility, which was named the Fletcher Institute.

In 1852 the Florida Conference decided to open another school, the East Florida Seminary, in Micanopy, the largest settlement in the state at that time. This seminary was a coeducational institution, more like today's high schools than colleges, for prospective ministers and the children of conference members. It struggled along for almost eight years, enrolling as many as thirty students at one time, before closing due to financial problems and the loss of male students to the Confederate army. By 1874, when control of the Fletcher Institute was transferred to the South Georgia Conference, Florida's Methodists were left with only one institution of higher education—Emory College in Oxford, Georgia.

For more than a decade conference leaders made repeated unsuccessful attempts to establish a new Methodist school in Florida. Finally, in 1886, the foundation for the future Florida Southern College was laid when the town of Leesburg successfully bid to attract the Wesleyan Institute, a Methodist-run public high school that had briefly operated in Orlando.[1] The conference chose a board of trustees for the school and changed its name to the ungainly "High School and College of the Florida Conference of the Methodist Episcopal Church, South." Nearly sixty students enrolled for the first semester on the three-building campus, where they embarked on a standard college-level curriculum for the time. Rather quickly, the trustees rechristened the school "Florida Conference High School and College."

Despite fluctuations in enrollment, administrative turnover, and financial difficulties, the college survived and then thrived. At one point near the end of the century, the school could boast of almost 150 students. Inspired by the school's success, the board of trustees decided in 1900 to find a new location that would allow for expansion. The following year the board approved a bid from a company in Sutherland, Florida (now Palm Harbor), a town on the Gulf coast north of Clearwater, and the college moved. A period of financial stability and enrollment growth ensued, marked by successive name changes to "Florida Seminary" and then "Southern College." Then the school's debts began to accumulate, and by 1914 the school owed more than $20,000. When a disastrous fire in early 1921 destroyed most of the campus and uprooted the college, it was saved by the charitable efforts of Edwin Timanus Roux, a college trustee, who allowed the school to use his Clearwater Beach hotel until a suitable new site could be found.

Lakeland

Once again the conference solicited bids from cities throughout Florida, and this time the most attractive offer came from Lakeland, a city located in the heart of Florida's citrus country about fifty miles inland from the Gulf of Mexico. Lakeland offered a sizeable revenue stream, the support of the local business community, and a nearly seventy-acre site of citrus groves on the north shore of Lake Hollingsworth, a circular lake almost three miles in circumference. The proposed land was approximately a mile south of downtown. Trustees Edwin T. Roux, Levi N. Pipkin, and Elliott E. Edge loaned the school $250,000 to finalize the deal. Shortly thereafter a tropical storm and another fire caused further damage to Southern College's temporary accommodations in Clearwater and underscored the need to relocate promptly.

Southern College announced a campaign in July 1921 to raise money for new buildings, envisioning a $300–400,000 cost but without any concrete plans.[2] A few weeks later Frederick H. Trimble, an Orlando architect, was hired to create a master plan for the school.[3] He proposed a monumental campus that was a product of its times, dominated by a prominent domed administration building (modeled perhaps on the early U.S. Capitol designs of William H. Thornton and Charles Bulfinch) flanked by dormitories and classroom structures. The campus featured major and minor axes marked out by walkways across large expanses of manicured lawns, and quadrangles surrounded by matching buildings. This orderly oasis would be carved out of the citrus groves, portions of which were to be left standing on the campus borders. The design took advantage of the site's most salient natural resource, Lake Hollingsworth, by extending an oval-shaped mall to the waterfront, where a boathouse terminated the main axis that began at a gate on the north end of the property and ran through the dome

Figure 1.1. F. H. Trimble, model of a campus plan for Southern College, 1922. Florida Southern College Archives.

Figure 1.2. F. H. Trimble, Dormitory for Women (now Joseph-Reynolds Hall), 1922. Florida Southern College Archives.

of the main building. Trimble's imagination exceeded Southern College's reality, however, and only a few of his buildings would be constructed, and then on a severely reduced scale.

Cornerstones for the first structures were laid in May 1922 in a ceremony described by the school's publicity director as "one of the most notable events in the history of Florida Methodism and of Christian education in this state."[4] The first two buildings to be finished were simple brick buildings of a generic colonial style. The Dormitory for Women (now Joseph-Reynolds Hall) had a large U-shaped form with ground-floor loggias and dormer windows. The Social Hall (now Edge Hall) was smaller and contained classrooms, a library, laboratories, and a dining hall. Both buildings featured hipped roofs, brick walls, and regularly spaced windows, lending them a vaguely colonial air.

Ludd Spivey Takes Charge

In the spring of 1925, college President Rhenus H. Alderman, who had run the school for more than a decade, announced his retirement. He had guided the college through the disastrous Sutherland fire, increased enrollment, decreased the school's indebtedness, and overseen the move to Lakeland. His replacement, thirty-eight-year-old Ludd Myrl Spivey, came to Florida after serving as academic dean and professor of sociology at Birmingham-Southern College in Alabama. When Spivey accepted the job, Southern College's physical plant consisted of the Dormitory for Women and the Social Hall, and its debts totaled approximately $400,000.[5] Spivey would retire thirty-two years later from a campus with more than forty buildings and an operating budget of more than $1 million.

Ludd Spivey was born in 1886, in Eclectic, Alabama, and lived in Alabama, Texas, and Oklahoma while growing up. He attended Epworth University in Oklahoma City and the Vanderbilt University School of Religion between 1909 and 1912, before being ordained in the Methodist Episcopal Church, South. After serving for a time as a Methodist pastor in St. Louis and Cape Girardeau, Missouri, Spivey enrolled at the University of Chicago. This move would prove to be a salient event in his life. When Spivey left that institution, he would be a devoted follower and advocate of two philosophies that would shape the school he later presided over in Lake-

Figure 1.3. Ludd M. Spivey, with Welthy H. Fisher and Clara Spivey, holding plans for the E. Stanley Jones Educational Foundation building. Courtesy of Special Collections, Lakeland Public Library, Lakeland, Fla.

land—modernist theology, with its focus on the reconciliation of science and religion, and pragmatic educational philosophy, with a special emphasis on the interrelationship between education and democracy.

Spivey eventually earned three degrees from the University of Chicago. His first, in 1919, was a bachelor of science. This was followed by a master of arts and a bachelor of divinity. Spivey's master's thesis, "Methodist Education in America Prior to 1820," reflected his dual interests in religion and education. At Chicago he also established a friendship with academic mentor Dr. Shirley Jackson Case. According to a later article in the Florida Southern College student newspaper, Spivey "took every course then offered by Dr. Case" while at Chicago.[6] Case was associated with what has come to be known as the "Chicago School of Theology," a group of like-minded faculty in the Divinity School that espoused a particularly modernist approach to religion. They emphasized the "socio-historical method," which involved using conventional historical inquiry to examine the scriptures as products of particular social settings rather than divinely inspired texts created by miracle. For instance, a Divinity School pamphlet from that period described the department's purpose as "to discover truth. It carries on this search by the utilization of scientific method which has been developed and tested in the University at large and in other institutions of high standing and notable achievement."[7] While Spivey was at Chicago, Case was a professor of early church history and New Testament interpretation; shortly after Spivey's graduation he would become chair of the Church History department and president of the American Society of Church History.[8] Spivey formed a bond with Case in Chicago, and after Case retired from the university, Spivey brought him to Florida Southern as professor of religion and dean of the newly formed Florida School of Religion. Spivey's connections with the University of Chicago also resulted in a number of Chicago faculty lecturing at Florida Southern throughout the 1940s.

Just as influential as Spivey's connection with Case and theological modernism was his exposure to the legacy of John Dewey. Although Dewey had left the University of Chicago in 1904, the philosophy and education departments still bore his imprint when Spivey was there. Spivey was attracted to Dewey's ideas, becoming a lifelong adherent and ceaseless proponent of experiential learning and pragmatic philosophy. When Spivey came to Southern College, he began to integrate Dewey's concept of experiential learning as a way to help students incorporate religious principles into their everyday lives. While he was president, he taught courses in psychology and philosophy, and he regularly presented Dewey's ideas to audiences in lectures and sermons.[9] Biographical bulletins of Spivey, prepared by the college in the 1950s, described him as "a disciple of John Dewey" and claimed that Spivey's "greatest ambition is to make the teachings of Dewey plain to both faculty and students."[10] He edited a collection of writings on Dewey's educational philosophy in 1951.[11] At some point Spivey developed a personal relationship with Dewey and his wife; in their correspondence Spivey often referred to Dewey as "Uncle Johnny" and his wife Roberta as "Robby."[12] He organized a luncheon at the St. Regis Hotel in New York in December 1947 to celebrate the Deweys' one-year wedding anniversary and visited Dewey in the Bahamas. Dewey in turn came to Florida Southern a number of times and received an honorary degree from the school in 1944.[13]

It is intriguing to consider that Spivey also could have been exposed to the architecture of Frank Lloyd Wright while in Chicago. Although Wright was in Japan working on the Imperial Hotel (1915) during most of the period when Spivey attended the university, he nonetheless was a public figure in that city. Even more important, Spivey might have personally experienced two of Wright's best works of the early 1900s. The Robie House (1906) is located across the street from the University of Chicago campus, less than three blocks from where the Divinity School stood during Spivey's tenure.[14] Standing on a corner lot with its dramatic horizontal emphasis and broadly hipped roof, the Robie House is easily distinguishable from the other houses in the neighborhood. Wright's Midway Gardens (1913) was a large structure the size of a city block, clearly visible across the Midway Plaisance from the main university buildings. By the early 1920s, Midway Gardens was no longer operating as an entertainment complex because of Prohibition, but the structure still stood.

Lean Years

When Ludd Spivey arrived on Southern College's tiny two-building campus in 1925, there was little time for thoughts of theological modernism or Deweyan philosophy. Spivey's first priority was clear—he had to raise money. And he proved equal to the task. "The man who preceded me lost his job because he wasn't interested in money," Spivey once told Wright's students. "I have often been in danger of losing my job because I was interested in the money."[15] Within weeks of his appointment as president,

Spivey began a quest for funding to help the small school not only pay its debts but expand, a pattern that would repeat itself over the entire course of his administration. That the campus grew at all is a testament to Spivey's indefatigable efforts. He was able to collect a rather steady stream of money during the lowest point of the collapse of the 1920s "Florida Boom," and most of the Wright buildings would be constructed during the Great Depression and World War II, in the midst of the nation's economic nadir.

Spivey's timing could not have been worse. A rare combination of uncontrollable disasters beset the state and the Florida Conference of the Methodist Episcopal Church, South, on the eve of the nation's descent into economic depression. A financial calamity set the stage. Between 1900 and 1925, Florida went through one of the most intense bursts of economic development in American history. No one factor precipitated this rapid rise, but contributors included extensive additions to the railroad and paved road mileage, increased promotion and interest in the state as a winter tourist destination, and greater awareness of the state's lack of income and inheritance taxes. The boom centered on Miami, whose population almost quadrupled during the twenties. Real estate speculation ran rampant; new communities were hewn out of swamps and scrub lands; and money poured into the Sunshine State at an unbelievable pace. Thousands of buyers, raconteurs, speculators, salesmen, and entrepreneurs migrated to Florida. Some northern banks even failed when too many depositors withdrew savings to purchase Florida land. In the City of Miami, assessed property values rose by 560 percent in four years.[16]

But the real estate bubble burst in 1926, leaving extensive bank failures and a financial crisis in its wake. Nature contributed to the devastation when deadly hurricanes swept through the state in 1926 and 1928, and a lethal combination of severe freezes and the introduction of the Mediterranean fruit fly crippled the citrus industry on which Lakeland relied.

With both the state and the Methodist Conference in dire financial straits, Spivey kicked off his first major fundraising campaign at Southern College, dubbed "the Great Million Dollar Campaign." In the first six months of this crusade, the future appeared bright, with close to $1.25 million pledged. Unfortunately, only a small amount of pledge money was ever collected. The campaign's only tangible result was a small men's dormitory, built for approximately $25,000.[17] This was followed in subsequent years by a heating plant, an athletic field, and a gymnasium.

Seeking money to reduce its debt, Southern College sold twenty acres of land on the eastern edge of the campus to a real estate developer. But misfortune struck the small school again when the developer forfeited the deal, and Southern was forced to pay the accumulated tax bills. By 1927, Southern College could no longer find any creditors to loan money. Spivey later recalled that the faculty "all taught for nothing" that year, and often had to accept chickens from students' parents in lieu of money for tuition.[18] In response to this desperate situation, the Florida Conference of Methodists formed a corporation and authorized more than $300,000 worth of bonds, redirecting its annual appropriations to Southern College to make bond payments. The college responded by pledging an annual repayment of $32,000, secured by college property, until the debts were paid. This creative financing arrangement, which temporarily saved the school from closure but failed to solve the long-term problem, continued until 1933.[19]

Undeterred by the Million Dollar Campaign's failure, Spivey embarked on another scheme. In 1928 he organized the Believers Club, with a $1 membership fee. The Believers Club raised $25,000 for the college in small increments, but this was not enough. The Southern College board of trustees apparently voted to close the school in 1933. By sheer force of personality, President Spivey convinced the board to reconsider; the board members rescinded their decision and approved an indefinite extension of Spivey's contract. Following this vote of confidence, Spivey was able to significantly reduce the school's indebtedness through negotiations with bondholders and a whirlwind of fundraising.[20] The turning point for Southern College came in 1935, when the school finally paid off its debts, changed its name to "Florida Southern College," and earned accreditation. After fifty precarious years, the college had finally managed to achieve stability.

Spivey and the Fundamentalists

During the years of financial instability, Spivey's religious views generated even more trouble for the small school. His modernist approach clashed with many of Florida's hard-line fundamentalists, reflecting a larger battle that raged across America's religious landscape. The clash centered on the modernists' refusal to believe in the literal word of the Bible, but had been fueled at the turn of the century by the theory of evolution and geological discoveries relating to the earth's age. The modernists, like those at the

University of Chicago Divinity School, "tended to look beyond the literal statements of scripture and creeds to 'spiritual interpretations' which kept to the spirit of traditional beliefs while rejecting the letter."[21] According to historian Gary Dorrien, liberal theology like that of the "Chicago School of Theology" is "defined by its openness to the verdicts of modern intellectual inquiry, especially historical criticism and the natural sciences; its commitment to the authority of individual reason and experience; its conception of Christianity as an ethical way of life; its favoring of moral concepts of atonement; and its commitment to make Christianity credible and socially relevant to contemporary people."[22] Although the Methodist Episcopal Church, South, was traditionally conservative, its transition to a more liberal, modern outlook by the early 1930s was relatively smooth. There were, however, some instances of conflict.

Spivey began to feel pressure from the fundamentalists early in his administration. It peaked in 1931 when some Methodist pastors charged him with heresy for claiming the Bible was not the literal word of God. The campaign culminated at the annual meeting of the Methodist Episcopal Church, South, in December. Spivey's accusers succeeded in persuading the attendees to form a Committee of Investigation to determine Spivey's fitness to serve as president of the conference's college. The committee exonerated Spivey and condemned his enemies. On the meeting's final day the attendees gave Spivey a standing ovation. Bishop Rev. John M. Moore, presiding over the meeting, put the matter to rest with a statement of support: "You all know that the church owes something more than $400,000 on Southern college [sic] and you know further, that if it wasn't for the good will of your creditors, you would be shut down before sunset. This conference knows Dr. Spivey has been paying all the institution's bills without calling on us for a penny of assistance and I think that's a pretty big feather in the cap of the college administration."[23]

Spivey's battle with the fundamentalists is enlightening for a variety of reasons. His victory illustrates Spivey's support from both the Southern College board of trustees and the Methodist Conference hierarchy. It also reveals the increasing acceptance of modernist theological views in the Methodist Episcopal Church, South. Notwithstanding sporadic incidents like Spivey's, by 1930 progressive leaders dominated the church hierarchy, smoothing the way for the acceptance of more liberal ideas. The church's leaders had shown an openness to new formulations in scientific thought and an emphasis on pragmatic applications rather than doctrinal orthodoxy. According to historian Robert Watson Sledge, for the Methodist Episcopal Church, South, in the 1930s, "'Modernism' was embraced as a useful ally, leading persons to a more informed and mature faith."[24]

Spivey's triumph likewise might have provided a foundation for him to later consider employing modernist architecture as a way of offering the public a new Methodist image of his school to reflect its more liberal outlook, rather than the staid conservatism that characterized its past. Given his modernist beliefs, Spivey simply could have found traditional architecture inappropriate for a twentieth-century institution. Perhaps his experience at the University of Chicago, where the theologically modernist Divinity School occupied a neo-Gothic building, made him aware of the potential for incongruity between ideology and architecture. In the absence of any records that might enlighten us about Spivey's architectural tastes, however, this is all speculation.[25] What is certainly true is that Spivey was an adept salesman who recognized the marquee value of memorable architecture. He would use that insight in connection with the E. Stanley Jones Educational Foundation.

The E. Stanley Jones Educational Foundation

Ludd Spivey's dreams extended beyond merely stabilizing the financial status of this small southern college; he wanted to turn the school into a nationally renowned center for modern Christian education. A fortuitous meeting would provide him with a great opportunity to begin that process. On a return voyage from a trip to Europe in the summer of 1936, Spivey met E. Stanley Jones aboard the Queen Mary. Jones was an internationally known religious figure on his way to begin an American preaching tour. Known as "evangelist-at-large for India and the world," Jones had made his name through more than three decades of missionary work on the Indian subcontinent, spreading Christianity and helping millions of poor and sick people.

Figure 1.4. E. Stanley Jones, internationally famous Christian evangelist. Florida Southern College Archives.

In particular, Jones founded a number of "Christian Ashrams," or retreat centers that allowed for Christians and Hindus to mutually explore tolerance and cooperation. His prominence was such that he became a close associate of Mahatma Gandhi and Jawaharlal Nehru, and he acted as a mediator between the Japanese ambassador and President Franklin D. Roosevelt just prior to the attack on Pearl Harbor.[26]

Spivey would later recount that he had been deeply moved by seeing the Reformation Monument (1909–17), a 100-foot wall with sculptural depictions of Protestantism's founders, while in Geneva, Switzerland; the experience inspired him to create something "exciting" and "extraordinary" at Florida Southern.[27] Neither Spivey nor his colleagues were ever able to date the Geneva trip accurately, but it appears to have occurred in 1936, so that Spivey's chance encounter with Jones happened shortly after Spivey saw the monument. Spivey seized the opportunity presented to him. Alert to the possibilities that might arise from an association with such a famous person, and always seeking to publicize his school, he invited Jones to rest at Florida Southern during a break in the latter's speaking tour. Jones accepted the offer and visited Spivey with his wife and daughter over the Christmas holiday.[28]

What he encountered in Lakeland is subject to conjecture. Contradictory accounts imply that Jones was either encouraged or dismayed by his exposure to the tiny campus and its students. The local newspaper alleged Jones was "impressed by the Southern campus, and by the academic, social and religious program of the college."[29] Similarly, a publicity film entitled *Insuring Our Destiny*, made a few years later for the Jones Foundation, claimed Jones perceived Florida Southern as a potential model for all of higher education: "At Florida Southern he found that under Dr. Spivey young plastic minds are every day receiving the truth that practical Christianity is a matter of daily personal conduct on the campus . . . At Florida Southern, religious activities are the balancing force of a natural, orderly life, entered upon by the students gladly, without coercion."[30] On the other hand a college-produced pamphlet describing Jones's experience suggested he "sensed that an unhappy change had come over a great many students, something more serious than the usual youthful bewilderment and uncertainty about life. He detected what many of us have seen with concern for a long while—a certain hard religious apathy and cynicism and indifference to everything spiritual that produces the easy and cheap sophistication which has marked an increasing number of college students in recent years."[31]

Whether the experience was favorable or not, it spurred Jones to devise with Spivey a proposal for a new educational foundation to be housed at Florida Southern. By spring 1937 the E. Stanley Jones Educational Foundation was inaugurated. Its goals, outlined in promotional literature, were to combat the religious indifference prevalent among American youth and to create a study center of national prominence for the practical application of Christianity. "The Kingdom of God must be made up of things by which men live," said Jones. "Above all we must find the way to utilize the educational institutions to lead and guide our youth to see its meaning."[32] Jones and Spivey did not, however, intend to create merely a religious curriculum. Instead they sought a synthesis of religion with science, where "with proper guidance, the teaching of science could go hand-in-hand with the building of the Kingdom of God in the hearts and minds of the students."[33]

To accomplish this ambitious task, Jones suggested a "five-point program" involving new college departments. The first, the Department of Comparative Religions, could allow students to learn about the great religions of history. The Department of Christianity would include an intensive study of Christ's "aims, purposes, and ideals." A third department would involve studying the larger implications of Christianity in its worldwide context. In the fourth department, Christianity's real and potential impact on the local community could be examined. And the fifth department, emphasizing personal religion or self-dedication, was not a true academic undertaking but a room for prayer and meditation.[34]

Jones envisioned these departments housed in a single building that would "embody in brick and stone the symbolism of true Christian education," with accompanying statues to explain the foundation's mission.[35] In front of the building, a sculpture *Youth Alone Enters College Eager Uncertain* (as titled in a foundation pamphlet) would depict an anxious boy about to embark on his higher educational career; at the building's rear, facing Lake Hollingsworth, a sculptural group with the unwieldy title *Guided by Religion and Science Youth Enters Life Confident Unafraid* would show the same student leaving school in commencement regalia and flanked by figures representing Science and Religion. A foundation brochure hinted at the broad appeal the proposed building might have: "This spiritual center will be raised not to glorify any denomination or to serve merely a local need . . . It is far greater than the College which will give it shelter."[36]

The Jones Foundation's mission was really an extension of the program already in place at Florida Southern. Spivey had worked to develop a school

Figure 1.5. Proposed statues for the E. Stanley Jones Educational Foundation building, artist unknown, c. 1937. Florida Southern College Archives.

centered on the interplay of modern religion and Deweyan philosophy; the harmonious relationship between science and religion had been stressed at all times. The foundation's film, *Insuring Our Destiny*, underscored this approach, employing Dewey-like language about experiential learning and practical applications to characterize Florida Southern as a place where "practical Christianity is a matter of daily personal conduct . . . Students are taught to relate the larger truths of religion to the everyday facts of the sciences." Since the students encountered religious activities in a natural way, such activities were "Not a dreary business, but a thoroughly enjoyable activity which quickly becomes second nature and of the highest importance of their lives."[37]

Spivey personally used every opportunity to promote the synthesis of science and religion, which he felt offered a path toward the betterment of society. In a published lecture from the early 1940s, he explained the underpinnings of his intellectual position. During the centuries of "conflict between church and state, between individualism and external authority," he stated, a new and better form of authority had arisen—"The scientific method . . . Experimental laboratories were established and a new authority was found. Life was at last its own authority. Tested facts now pointed the way for man and knowledge, which came to man as the result of finding facts, gave him control over his environment." This development affected religion as well. "Religious leaders likewise were forced to reckon with the authority of intelligence. A new study of the Bible, of the church and its doctrines, in the light of the findings of science, brought about a new attitude," Spivey said, alluding to the modern theology he studied at the University of Chicago. "Knowledge, tested knowledge, increased day by day, and this knowledge in turn not only helped to place man's physical world under better control, but it also helped him to control intelligently his social world. The external authority of the church and the state, the so-called authority of the individual, was being gradually supplanted by the authority that comes to man through an understanding of his world."[38] From such statements it is easy to understand why Jones's concept of a program emphasizing the compatibility of religion and science would be so attractive to Spivey.

Building Proposals

By fall 1937 Spivey had traveled to New York, Boston, Chicago, Detroit, and other cities and met with state and local religious leaders to generate enthusiasm and lay the groundwork for a $1 million fundraising campaign for the Jones Educational Foundation. His hard work and natural abilities paid off. The drive officially began in Lakeland in February 1938, and within months more than half of the statewide goal of $400,000 was pledged.[39] A national campaign targeting fifteen eastern and midwestern cities kicked off in the fall.

The fundraising aspect of the foundation proved to be easier than the decision on what the material outcome of the campaign would be. It is difficult to date much of the foundation's literature, but the earliest pamphlets included conflicting visions for the foundation building. What appears to be the earliest conception showed an English-type cathedral of rather monumental scale for the small school, largely neoclassical in style but with a blunted, spire-less octagonal tower over the crossing. A now-lost aerial drawing of the project revealed a cruciform shape. Jones's proposed sculptural group *Youth Enters Life Confident* was depicted near an entry in the only known drawing of the building.[40]

Another foundation pamphlet, which dates from 1938, contained a full-page elevation and small floor plan by architect L. Alex Hatton of nearby Bartow, Florida. The plan depicted a cruciform building with rooms for seminars, classes, administration, and a library, and one arm of the cross devoted to a chapel. It seems to have been designed pursuant to Jones's idea for the five departments. The façade is in a Georgian Colonial style, dominated by an extremely tall spire. Awkward elements in the proposed

Figure 1.6. Proposal for the unbuilt E. Stanley Jones Educational Foundation building, possibly by L. Alex Hatton, c. 1937. Florida Southern College Archives.

drawing suggest the work of an inexperienced architect.[41] Although this drawing appeared in an article in the *Southern*, the Florida Southern student newspaper, in February 1938, it is unclear whether the proposal had the full backing of all parties involved or if there was agreement on what form the foundation building should take.[42]

Four months earlier the Florida Southern College Alumni Council had voted to appropriate $50,000 for a library building as part of the Jones Foundation, yet Hatton's Georgian-styled building was not a library.[43] And in a March 1938 speech on campus, Dr. Frederick Bohn Fisher, pastor of Central Methodist Church in Detroit and close friend of E. Stanley Jones, predicted that the foundation building "will be unique in America," and for that reason "ought to have an oriental flavor . . . Perhaps a group of minarets, an oriental dome, tapestries and carvings, and certain niches for statues from India, China and Japan."[44] Fisher was revealing his own tastes as well as proposing Jones's Indian background play a part in design.[45] The student newspaper reported that "[Fisher's] suggestions are being seriously considered." Whether this is true or not, it does reveal that influential persons associated with the foundation might have continued to search for the right design.

Both of the early conceptions of the Jones Building imagined structures much larger than the five rooms Jones originally implied. The new buildings depicted in the drawings would add needed space to the college, including a library, chapel, administration offices, and academic departments. At the same time, they symbolized Jones's and Spivey's conflicting goals for the endeavor. Spivey had great ambitions for the development of his campus, and the Jones Foundation provided the springboard. From the beginning he promoted the new building beyond Jones's rather limited recommendations. Before fundraising even started, Spivey expanded his conception of what the foundation could do for the college. He campaigned for an extensive list of new structures and programs, including "library, chapel, carillon, sculpture, endowment of professorships in religion, endowment of fellowships in religion, establishment of student loan fund, endowment of library, endowment of special lectures and endowment for special library collections, works of art and similar projects."[46] A few months later the local newspaper reported that the Jones Foundation leaders now saw their building as "a national shrine for Protestantism," while the *Southern*, no doubt with Spivey's prompting, predicted "the huge three-story building, with its tower and chimes, is expected to head Florida's list of attractions."[47] The following month, the paper reported that "Dr. Spivey repeated with new emphasis his recent statement that the Foundation would soon cause the college to expand into a large university with international fellowships."[48]

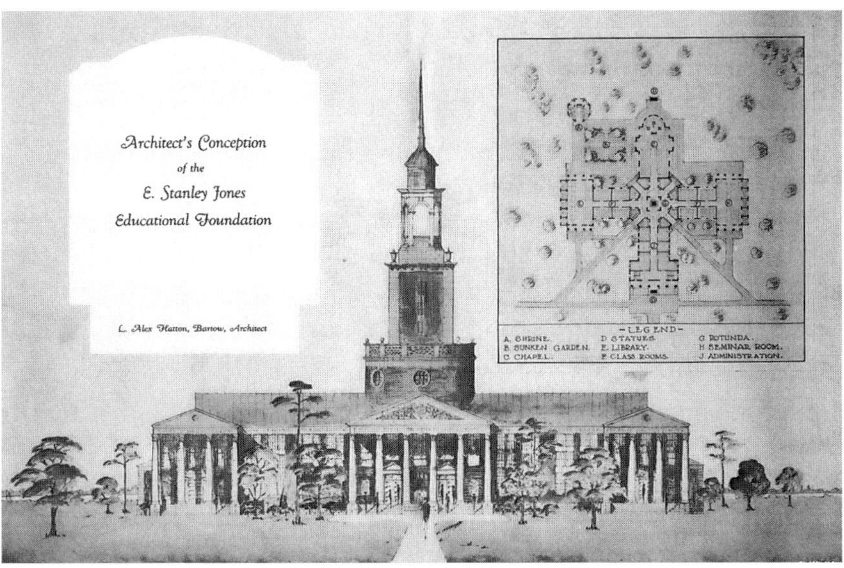

Figure 1.7. L. Alex Hatton, proposal for the unbuilt E. Stanley Jones Educational Foundation building, c. 1937. Florida Southern College Archives.

Conflict

Spivey's grand plans, and his handling of the Jones Foundation's finances, caused friction that eventually led to the organization's demise. Jones began to feel his modest proposal was being distorted by Spivey's extravagant vision. At some point in early 1939, he ordered Spivey and Florida Southern to stop using his name to raise funds. He explained his decision in a revealing letter to Methodist Bishop Paul Kern. "I did feel that I was being exploited and requested them that no more money be raised in my name for this Foundation after June 30, 1939," Jones wrote. "I have received no reports of the program of the scheme and have had no accounting. During my last visit to the States I was at the corner stone laying of the chapel and was then told that $400,000 had been pledged on the scheme. But I have no record or written account of anything concerning the scheme." Jones further outlined how the foundation had grown far beyond his modest original idea: "During a visit to Lakeland, Florida, Dr. Spivy [sic] asked me how I would visualize Christian education on a College campus. I suggested two simple monuments depicting a youth going into College and that same youth emerging. Between these two monuments I suggested four rooms where the study of Christianity could be carried on, the details of which I need not put before you. The whole scheme as I outlined it would probably not have involved more than $25,000 at the most. Dr. Spivy took this and enlarged it into the present E. Stanley Jones Educational Foundation. During a hurried visit to me at Harrisburg, Pennsylvania, I consented to some of his plans. This, I see, was a mistake."[49]

The reply to this letter came from R. E. Diffendorfer, the corresponding secretary for the Board of Foreign Missions, Methodist Episcopal Church. Diffendorfer wrote that Bishop Kern's first reaction was "I am not surprised." "I then discovered that Bishop Kern is well acquainted with this situation at Lakeland and has felt like some of the rest of us that your name was being exploited for the general purposes of the school," wrote Diffendorfer. In closing, he added, "Our Board has had long and difficult negotiations with Dr. Spivy [sic] over the settlement of an estate in Florida. We could have given you some sound advice!"[50]

Jones's complaints could have been attempts to downplay his role in the foundation's development after the fact. But it does appear evident that Spivey used Jones's fame to raise money for his college and to further the monumental dream first conceived in Geneva. In a speech to Methodists in Orange County, Florida, for example, Spivey referred to the fact that "Jones has millions of friends, and they will come to Florida to see this ideal of his take form in brick and mortar." He also claimed the foundation "will be the greatest movement not only in the State, but the nation, it will not be for Methodists alone, but for every person in these United States."[51] While he spoke of the foundation's mission and relation to his students at the beginning of the campaign, his more grandiose ambitions soon became apparent. Newspaper articles and promotional literature demonstrated the two men's different emphases. Jones liked to talk about how the foundation would promote Christian faith and help reconcile science and religion, while Spivey often predicted how the foundation would become a powerful force in America's spiritual life and a major tourist attraction. In Jones he had found a means to realize his fantasy of a larger campus and more prominent school.

After the rift the Jones Foundation name appeared less frequently in newspaper articles describing campus construction, although as late as 1941 it still occasionally surfaced. And Jones never attended the dedication of the first building erected with the funds gathered in his name; after helping to lay the cornerstone for the chapel in late 1938 and attending Spivey's "Democracy Day" two years later, his next trip to Florida Southern came in 1942, after the chapel was completed, and then only to speak about the relation between democracy and religion.[52] By then, however, a great campus expansion had begun, and Ludd Spivey had found another famous name to attract attention to his school.

Spivey Finds Wright

In the absence of any memoirs or verifiable accounts, it is difficult to determine the decision-making process that led Spivey to contact Frank Lloyd Wright. There is no evidence that Spivey was aware of Wright before 1938. According to Corning Tolle, former business manager and dean of men at Florida Southern, the process began when Spivey encountered dissatisfaction with L. Alex Hatton's design as he traveled around Florida promoting the Jones Foundation. "Even though the proposed buildings had been designed, the question of the architect and architecture arose in many cities as we moved around the state," wrote Tolle. "The general feeling of many people was that, if the college was really going to honor so unique and outstanding a leader as E. Stanley Jones, the buildings associated with his name should likewise be unique and outstanding."[53] Administrative discussions soon centered around high-profile architects, and, according to Tolle, Frank Lloyd Wright's name was broached by Harris Sims, a journalism professor who had read about Wright, and two other faculty members who had ties to Wisconsin. "These three urged the name of Mr. Wright upon Dr. Spivey if he were really seeking the most outstanding architect in the world," wrote Tolle.[54] Spivey also might have seen Wright's picture on the cover of *Time* magazine in January 1938.

While Tolle's account is reasonable, fantastic legends arose regarding the first contact, with stories ranging from the plausible (someone suggested Wright as an architect, but Spivey was initially unfamiliar with Wright and confused him with the popular novelist Harold Bell Wright; or Spivey telephoned the Chicago office of an architectural magazine and asked who was America's finest architect, then phoned Wright on their recommendation) to the improbable (Spivey was inspired by reading Wright's *Autobiography* and flew to Taliesin to meet him) to the ridiculous (Spivey and Wright met as seatmates on a train to an unknown destination).[55]

Spivey's unawareness of Wright prior to early 1938 casts doubt on another popular tale about Spivey's and Wright's initial meeting. In later years Wright frequently asserted that Spivey specifically chose him "as much for my philosophy as for my architecture."[56] While the two men certainly found common intellectual ground over the years, nothing indicates that Spivey knew much about Wright or his philosophy before making his offer; Spivey's recollection after Wright's death that he originally approached Wright because he "wanted to do something very extraordinary" with Florida Southern but "couldn't find anybody who would do something exciting" seems more plausible.[57]

What is known is that Spivey sent a telegram to Wright in Arizona on April 11, 1938, that bluntly stated: "Desire conference with you concerning plans for great education temple in Florida."[58] After that events moved rather quickly. Wright's reply suggested a meeting in Wisconsin. Spivey scheduled a trip the following day. The two men met on April 21 at Taliesin, and in a few hours a deal was reached with a swiftness that would stand in sharp contrast to the speed of actual construction. Each man apparently impressed the other at this initial meeting with his forceful personality and visionary ideas.

At the time, Frank Lloyd Wright, approaching seventy-one years of age, was enjoying a professional renaissance. The period between 1926 and 1932 had marked Wright's nadir. He entered his sixties with virtually no work on the heels of a second failed marriage. Only a handful of Wright's designs were constructed, and most were for himself or family. He was regularly involved in litigation over financial matters. No longer considered much of a practicing architect, Wright spent most of his professional time criticizing modernist architecture (and fellow architects) in speeches, lectures, and articles.[59]

Things began to change for Wright in 1932. In that year, a series of events occurred that would stimulate Wright's architectural renewal. Wright founded the Taliesin Fellowship at Spring Green, Wisconsin, to train young architects and to provide a steady means of income through tuition payments. Since Wright retained a certain amount of respect in the architectural world, he had no trouble attracting students. The Taliesin Fellowship proved to be a key factor in the revitalization of Wright's career by providing him with an inspiring atmosphere in which to create—similar to his Oak Park, Illinois, office in the early 1900s, where many of the Prairie School architects trained.

Wright further established himself in the public eye with two books in 1932. The first was *An Autobiography*, which has been perceptively described as "a difficult, revealing, inaccurate, but compelling book" about Wright's life and philosophy.[60] *An Autobiography* was reviewed and praised in many leading journals. The second book, *The Disappearing City*, was Wright's tirade against urbanization; it contained his first discussion of Broadacre City, the agrarian utopia that he intended as the replacement for the modern city.[61]

In the next five years, Wright reemerged on the national architectural scene with such renowned designs as the Kaufmann "Fallingwater" House (1935), the Hanna "Honeycomb" House (1936), the Johnson Wax Administration Building (1936), and Taliesin West (1937). His star was shining brighter than ever, and more commissions began to arrive at Taliesin. Wright would continue to work on a seemingly endless stream of projects until his death in 1959 at the age of ninety-one.

In addition to the *Time* cover in January 1938, Wright appeared in nearly thirty articles during that year, from such popular fare as *Life* and the *New Yorker* to a remarkable special issue of *Architectural Forum* (also in January) devoted entirely to his architecture.[62] And the Museum of Modern Art in New York opened an exhibition on Fallingwater in January, the first time that institution ever held a major one-building exhibit on a living architect.

So when Spivey visited Wright at Taliesin, the office was already extremely busy. Why, then, would Wright be attracted to a commission for a small, unknown college with little money in the middle of Florida?

The simple answer is that Wright rarely, if ever, turned down a prospective commission. Like H. H. Richardson, the famous nineteenth-century architect whom Wright admired, his philosophy was that no job was too small. In 1932 alone he designed a standardized service station, a standardized prefabricated roadside market, and a combination cinema and shops; in 1937 designs for a gift booth, a car garage, and a dress shop came off his drafting board. What Spivey did not know was that Wright constantly needed money to support his extravagant lifestyle, along with the Taliesin Fellowship, and could be retained quite easily by a prospective client. And while the story was often recounted that Spivey told Wright he had no money, but would get some if Wright would produce some plans, shortly after their first contact it was reported that the E. Stanley Jones Educational Foundation had raised $225,000 in pledges in just over two months, with more Florida cities targeted, and a national fundraising campaign ready to begin.[63] Wright would later claim that "I understood we had some $365,000.00 pledged" at the beginning of the project.[64] So there appears to have been enough proven financial interest to make Wright feel comfortable, although Spivey and the college were quite familiar with discrepancies between monies pledged and collected—for example, out of more than $10,000 in subscriptions for a pre–Jones Foundation fundraising drive in the late thirties, only slightly more than $5,000 was ever paid.[65]

The challenge of creating a multiple-building ensemble—which Wright undoubtedly imagined from the beginning, rather than the single structure of the Jones proposal—probably intrigued him. He may have been primed by seeing Stanford University during a recent visit to clients Paul and Jean Hanna—who lived in a Wright house adjacent to the campus—a mere seven days before Spivey's first telegram arrived. Further, it is not difficult to assume that Wright viewed the commission as an opportunity to compete with Eliel Saarinen. The two men met in 1931 as judges of an international design competition in Rio de Janeiro and became adversarial friends. Saarinen, who was in the midst of a twenty-five-year building campaign at the Cranbrook educational community in Bloomfield Hills, Michigan, invited Wright to speak at Cranbrook in 1935, and thereafter Wright made almost yearly trips to see the Saarinens. Wright wrote about his Finnish colleague in *An Autobiography*, even admitting—in a rare move for Wright—to professional jealousy over Saarinen's luck in landing large-scale, well-paying commissions. "I had always resented Saarinen a little, regarding him as our most accomplished foreign eclectic," Wright claimed in his autobiography. He was "a little jealous too of [Saarinen's] easy berth, bestowed by the hand of American riches, while I had to wait and work and scrape for mine, the hard way."[66] Given these circumstances and Wright's inclinations, he could very well have viewed the Florida Southern job as his chance to respond to Saarinen's Cranbrook campus, albeit on a reduced scale.

And finally, Spivey probably did not know it, but he had an inherent advantage by nature of his ministerial credentials. Frank Lloyd Wright demonstrated a lifelong fondness for men of the cloth, likely a result of having a minister father and the noted Rev. Jenkin Lloyd Jones, an uncle, on his mother's side of the family. Wright's relations with minister clients were among the best of his career.[67] For many reasons, then, Wright was inclined to accept the Florida Southern commission. He agreed to visit the school, and Spivey returned to Florida to resume his fundraising activities for the Jones Foundation, with high hopes that another famous figure was on board.

Spivey's decision to offer the Jones Foundation commission to Wright encountered no apparent opposition from the hierarchy of the Florida Conference or the Methodist Episcopal Church, South—further evidence of their open-mindedness, at least in architectural matters. Florida's Methodists rallied behind Wright and his proposal, just as many of them had supported Hatton's designs, although some dissatisfaction with Hatton's scheme seems to have motivated Spivey to explore other options.

Wright's First Visit

Wright visited Lakeland in early May 1938. Upon arrival he sent a quick telegram to his wife, Olgivanna, back in Wisconsin: "Here safe and sound. Tedious journey through America's back yard—college genial and promising."[68] Spivey, obviously pleased to have engaged such a high-profile architect, presented Wright at a banquet for more than 300 guests in Lakeland and also arranged for Wright to speak the following evening in nearby Tampa. Thus began a process where Spivey used Wright's celebrity status to attract potential donors. Wright later described his relationship with Spivey to the students at the Taliesin Fellowship: "I never go down there that the Doctor doesn't impress me into service and stick me on a platform and talk when he can. He started me that way . . . So now he makes me shell out whenever I come around."[69]

Despite his insincere protest, Wright was always willing to take the podium. He summarized his architectural philosophy for the eager Lakeland crowd, touching on the need for an American architecture and espousing some of his core beliefs. "We ought to help the indoors to go outdoors and the outdoors to come inside . . . We do not need a French chateau for a firehouse nor a Greek temple for a bank. We have had educated architects who never faced reality, an escapist architecture that has never faced reality," Wright said. "My book has been the book of nature . . . Education has been too willing to read out of other books. We need to get on speaking terms with culture. I believe we are now ready for a culture of our own, something indigenous to America. We have the 57 varieties in architecture. All my life I have longed for something we in America could call our own."[70]

Such language was standard fare from Wright. He had offered another version of it earlier that afternoon, when speaking to a student guide chosen to escort him around the tiny campus and proposed site. "Every building is out of the ground into the light—a child of the sun," Wright supposedly claimed. "Buildings should seem to grow from the earth and belong as a tree belongs."[71] But what is more interesting is what Wright said at the evening banquet specifically about his new commission. Less than a month after his first meeting with Spivey, and after a few hours on the site, Wright had already begun to formulate a design approach. "This is a great opportunity here because you have a beautiful piece of ground," said Wright. "I shall be very proud indeed to give the Foundation a fresh form, a Florida form. No real Florida form has yet been produced. Most of you here have simply built here as you built back home."[72]

What Wright would have seen on his brief tour of the proposed location at the college was essentially a thirty-acre citrus grove filled with more than 1,000 trees.[73] From the north end of the property along McDonald Street to the south-end shoreline of Lake Hollingsworth, a distance of about one-third of a mile, the land gently dropped nearly eighty feet. Passing glimpses of the lake may have been visible through the abundant rows of citrus trees.[74] To the west, the site was bounded by a residential neighborhood along Johnson Avenue; the eastern limit was the small group of buildings that made up the campus at the time. Approximately ten buildings of various sizes were scattered through the citrus groves. Like the first campus buildings, most were generally utilitarian brick structures with

Figure 1.8. Frank Lloyd Wright speaking in the Annie M. Pfeiffer Chapel. Florida Southern College Archives.

no pronounced stylistic tendencies other than a general air of Georgian-Colonial. The college's full-time student population was just over 700, with around 70 faculty members.[75]

Lakeland's population in the late 1930s approached 18,000, making it the eighth largest city in Florida.[76] The local topography beyond the Florida Southern campus is characterized by gently rolling hills and small- to medium-sized lakes. Lakeland is located on the Lakeland Ridge, part of the Polk Upland, which contains some of the highest ground in Florida.[77] There are thirteen natural lakes within the city limits. Originally covered with oak hammocks and pine savannahs, by the 1930s the landscape had been changed by human intervention, and citrus groves dominated the region, providing the bulk of the local economy.[78] In 1939 one-third of the state's citrus crop was grown in the Lakeland region. Appropriately, the Florida Citrus Commission headquarters was located in the city. The semitropical climate in this part of Florida ranges from mild winters with rare frosts to hot, humid summers when the temperature can remain in the nineties for months. The summer heat is punctuated by short, violent rain showers that occur almost every afternoon. Hurricanes are a yearly threat. The most dominant feature of the Lakeland climate is abundant sunshine.

Wright apparently experienced as many of the region's natural qualities as possible during his three-day sojourn and was impressed by what he saw. According to Spivey, Wright visited the proposed expansion site and "let the sand go through his hands," then had Spivey drive him "all over the country to see the various parts of Lakeland and the county."[79] A college professor later recalled how Wright admired the landscape during a subsequent trip: "As we walked along, Mr. Wright talked about the natural beauty of the campus in terms of the lake, citrus trees, and rolling terrain, and he actually stated that it could not be found any place else on earth. It was this natural beauty of the site which had appealed to him so much."[80] Spivey probably did not realize at the time that Wright was surveying the surroundings for clues to their natural tendencies, which he would attempt to reveal in his campus design.

Anticipating the Plan

While Wright might have formed ideas for the new campus during that first trip, the first drawings would not appear for months. Until those drawings arrived, there was much speculation about what the architect had in mind for the small campus. In fact, there was no consensus in the spring of 1938 on whether Wright would be designing one building or an ensemble. On May 16, shortly after Wright returned to Taliesin, the local newspaper related Spivey's description of the project: "Dr. Spivey explained that *the building*, with a series of courts and gardens, will extend for two blocks across the campus to Lake Hollingsworth, where a swimming pool will be constructed" (emphasis mine).[81] The story also contained another reference to a singular "building." A week later a similar article in the *New York Times*

Figure 1.9. Aerial view of the Southern College campus, c. 1920s. Florida Southern College Archives.

by Harris Sims, the college's journalism professor, referred to a "$500,000 building" containing, according to "the suggestion of Dr. Jones," the five religious departments set up for the foundation, a library, an auditorium, scientific laboratories, administrative offices, "a little theater," a music conservatory, and space for the home economics and manual training departments.[82] Once the single building was completed, wrote Sims, the remaining foundation money was to be used as an endowment to support the foundation's work.

Such statements might have merely reflected the assumptions of the people at Florida Southern in the absence of further information from Wright. The pre-Wright design for the foundation building was indeed a solitary structure housing the various elements that Sims listed. Alex Hatton's drawing had been publicized for months. For some unknown reason, the college had even displayed it at Wright's speech in Tampa during his first Florida visit—and, as might be expected, Wright criticized the colonial confection.[83] Nor was he impressed with Florida Southern's existing buildings, which he described as "boxes with holes punched in them."[84] During his first campus tour Wright allegedly explained the contrast between the school's colonial-influenced structures and his own modern vision to a student in colorful terms: "Oh, after all, every princess must have her maids in waiting and they must be ugly to enhance the beauty of hers. I'll just leave those buildings and mine will be more beautiful than any of them. I'll circle the whole place with buildings."[85]

In early 1938, however, Wright's plans remained a mystery. Wright did not attend the Jones Foundation's groundbreaking ceremony on May 24, but his name was mentioned liberally during the gala, even if he was overshadowed by E. Stanley Jones, another absentee. The ceremony was part of a grand pageant, specifically timed to fall on the 200th anniversary of Methodist founder John Wesley's Aldersgate conversion experience. It featured a cast of 500 actors recreating salient episodes from the lives of both Wesley and Jones (including a "Foundation Gift Scene," which presumably re-enacted Jones's and Spivey's decision to create the Jones Foundation—with Spivey playing himself).

No drawings or plans from Wright could be displayed at the event because none existed—the celebration had been scheduled before he became involved with the project. At the time this lack was probably a minor concern, but as the months passed with nothing from Wright, Spivey grew nervous. A week prior to the groundbreaking he optimistically told an audience of potential donors to expect a rough draft of the building within days. Three months later, shortly after he had traveled north to Madison, Wisconsin, for another brief meeting with Wright, Spivey wired a fretful message to the architect: "Am anxious to hear from you please wire me."[86] A few weeks after that Spivey tried a different approach: "Just as soon as you have the plans ready, I know that you will advise me."[87] By the end of September, Spivey could barely control his exasperation: "I have been looking for the picture of the chapel every day since I returned home. I really need it very much. I hope that you see that we get the plans for the foundation of the chapel in a few days. It is not possible for me to do much here financially until you send the picture of the chapel."[88]

Wright was working the entire time, though not quickly enough for Spivey, and as the last message demonstrates, he and Spivey had determined by September that the first building for the new campus would be a chapel and not a multipurpose structure as previously proposed. Spivey's fears would be assuaged when the earliest chapel drawings and campus plans arrived in late October or early November 1938, and he could finally see Wright's vision for the new campus.

TWO *Wright's Campus Plan*

Wright probably began to think about the project almost immediately after his initial meeting with Spivey. He developed the West Campus plan and several building designs during the summer and fall of 1938. By November 8, Wright had shipped the first set of drawings for Spivey's review. But before then Wright outlined his concept for the campus in a remarkable letter to Spivey, worth quoting at length:

> The plans for Florida Southern are taking shape rapidly and I can assure you that we shall have a college unequaled in the beauty of use or the use of beauty anywhere on earth.
>
> The general plan is a pattern of terraces and arbors connecting the various buildings—a free pattern in itself the most important single feature of the design, I think. And then, each separate building finds a better way of doing the thing to be done in it than has been seen elsewhere as you will see.
>
> Each building is individual in character—practical in effect—yet contributing its share to an occult symmetry—delightfully informal and easy as a whole.
>
> The reflex enters into architecture in these plans for Florida Southern as against the regimentation characteristic of the classic or Gothic architecture which have become a college habit in America.
>
> A spiritual catharsis in design—I should say, and a structural example of the freedom needed very much at this time in our national life.

> We are making the ground, trees, buildings, the young people inhabiting them, and even the instructors themselves—all living factors in one comfort giving, protective, sympathetic building, divided into special buildings for special activities. What I am most proud of having done in this effort is to have succeeded in making all units into the one gracious pattern—a complete whole for college work.[1]

In these few paragraphs Wright was able to capture in words the salient ideas that would inform the final design: the integration of architecture and site, the desire for "a Florida form," his lifelong engagement with progressive education, and his fervent belief in democracy.

The First Plan

Surprisingly, what seems to be Wright's first draft of the plan revealed few if any of these themes. None of the earliest plan renderings Wright made for Florida Southern is dated, but it is safe to presume he began working on the design shortly after returning to Wisconsin from his Florida trip. He would not visit Lakeland again until the plan had been created, relying on his memory and impressions, a topographical map, an aerial photograph, and sixteen ground-level photographs sent to him over the summer by the college.[2]

An intriguing drawing in the Frank Lloyd Wright Foundation Archives appears to be Wright's first formulation of the Florida Southern plan; we can assume this is the initial attempt because it is so different from the other versions. The undated drawing shows an orthogonal arrangement of structures, ordered by a grid system, occupying the school's West Campus property, bounded by Johnson Avenue on the west, the existing buildings on the east, McDonald Street on the north, and Lake Hollingsworth on the south. Most of the proposed buildings are aligned along two conspicuous north-south axes, one at the property's western edge and the other about halfway between that border and the Women's Dormitory. These parallel spines created a large, rectangular open space in the new campus's center, terminated by a large circular pool and fountain (the Water Dome) to the north. Wright placed a group of structures along the lakeshore at the campus's opposite end: a semicircular outdoor theater attached to an oval swimming pool and a boat dock stretching into the lake.

Although much of the central rectangular area has been cut out of the

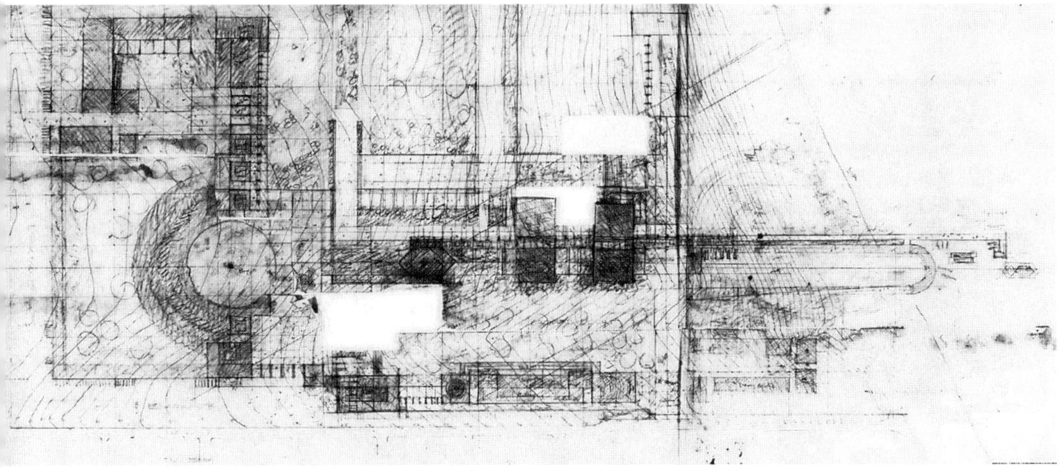

Figure 2.1. Frank Lloyd Wright, Florida Southern College plan, orthogonal version, 1938. Copyright © 2009 The Frank Lloyd Wright Foundation, Taliesin West, Scottsdale, Ariz. 3805.007.

drawing, the remaining portion depicts a space filled with trees, presumably the preexisting orange groves. Wright obviously felt the groves were valuable, and early in the summer he had telegraphed a quick note to Spivey: "Suggest trees be located so all possible be saved."[3] Other than a hexagonal structure near the ensemble's center (probably the main chapel), the oval swimming pool, the semicircular outdoor theatre, and the circular Water Dome, the buildings depicted are rectangular or square in plan.

These characteristics seem to indicate that when he was confronted with the challenge of designing a multibuilding campus for the first time, Wright actually responded conservatively: the plan evoked the Ecole des Beaux-Arts tradition in its orderliness and linear arrangement of buildings. More specifically, the plan resembled Thomas Jefferson's University of Virginia (1817–26), right down to the large circular feature occupying one end of an elongated courtyard lined with buildings. And the sympathetic relationship with nature that would characterize subsequent plans was missing. In general, this inaugural effort was cautious and conventional and did not represent Wright at his creative best.[4]

Subsequent Plans

Wright's experiment with an orthogonal plan was short-lived, and soon he embarked on an alternate version that took the main features of that initial

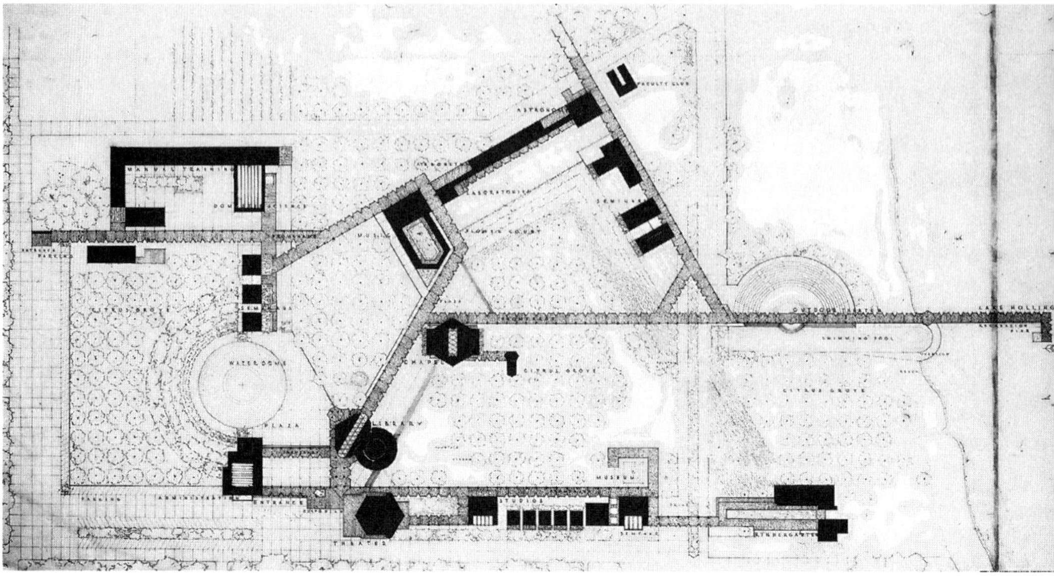

Figure 2.2. Frank Lloyd Wright, Florida Southern College plan, 1938. Copyright © 2009 The Frank Lloyd Wright Foundation, Taliesin West, Scottsdale, Ariz. 3805.017.

attempt and redistributed them along the site in a manner more consistent with his previous work and design tendencies. The new plans appear at first glance to consist of a random arrangement of uniquely shaped buildings scattered along the sloping landscape, attached by covered walkways called "esplanades." The buildings' purposes were determined by agreement between Spivey and Wright as outlined in an extraordinary thirteen-page document in the Frank Lloyd Wright Foundation Archives with the handwritten title "Programme for University."[5] This undated document, on stationery with the Florida Southern College letterhead (that corresponds to the type used before 1941), combines typewritten items with Wright's handwritten notes and may have emerged from one of the earliest meetings between the two men, either at Taliesin or Lakeland. The "Programme" lists seventeen structures, with the titles "Administration," "Little Theatre," "Library," "Chapel," "Art Museum," "Music Studio," "Manual Training and Home Economics," "Nature Study," "Seven Seminars," "Experimental Childgarden," and "Outdoor Theatre and Games." For each proposed unit there is an estimated cost and a list of rooms or requirements; Wright's notes elaborated on these necessities or recorded his own thoughts.

Wright's succeeding plan drawings slightly altered the basic units listed in the "Programme": a "Small Chapel" was added to the library; the art museum became the "Studios, Art Exhibition, and Exposition" building; the music studio became "Music Study and Performance"; the children's building was renamed "Child Culture Group"; and an "Arboreal Hemicycle and Water-Dome Pool," "Pools and Barges," and "Sculpture" were added to the list. Furthermore, many of these structures now displayed a different spatial relationship to each other. While Wright retained his original north-south orientation, defined by the same two axes and a grid system of six-foot square modules, he overlaid it with two alternative grids. The first rotated the main grid thirty degrees toward the southeast from an imaginary line that extended north from the center of the proposed Water Dome. Wright anchored one end of the music building along this new axis and also used it to define the length of the science ("Nature Study") unit. The thirty-degree angle mirrored the northeast wall of the hexagonal main chapel. Using one of the two north-south axes as the hypotenuse and the new diagonal as one leg, Wright then created a thirty-sixty-ninety-degree triangle, with seminar buildings aligned along the other leg.

Wright created a second alternate grid by rotating the north-south axis along Johnson Avenue sixty degrees to the southeast, using the library as the pivot; the new axis bisected the book stack section of the library structure, passed the main chapel, and connected to the music building. And like the other new grid, its new angle was reflected in the buildings—in the wall of the theater next to the library and the prow-like end of the music building. These manipulations left the campus with three grids, all of them visible at ground level. The original north-south axis could be seen outlined in the concrete plaza between the Water Dome, library, and administration buildings (as well as the perimeter parking lots and courtyard of the manual arts and domestic science unit); the thirty-degree grid was etched into the terrace in front of the science unit; the sixty-degree grid was visible in the plaza connecting the library and main chapel; and all were reinforced by the directions of the esplanades.

Wright's introduction of these alternative axes created a new relationship among the structures. Diagonal esplanades now dominated the scheme, and many of the buildings were skewed from strict north-south lines. Except for the plazas mentioned above, trees filled almost every space between the buildings and esplanades, in keeping with the "outdoor garden character" that Wright would use to describe his design. When one consid-

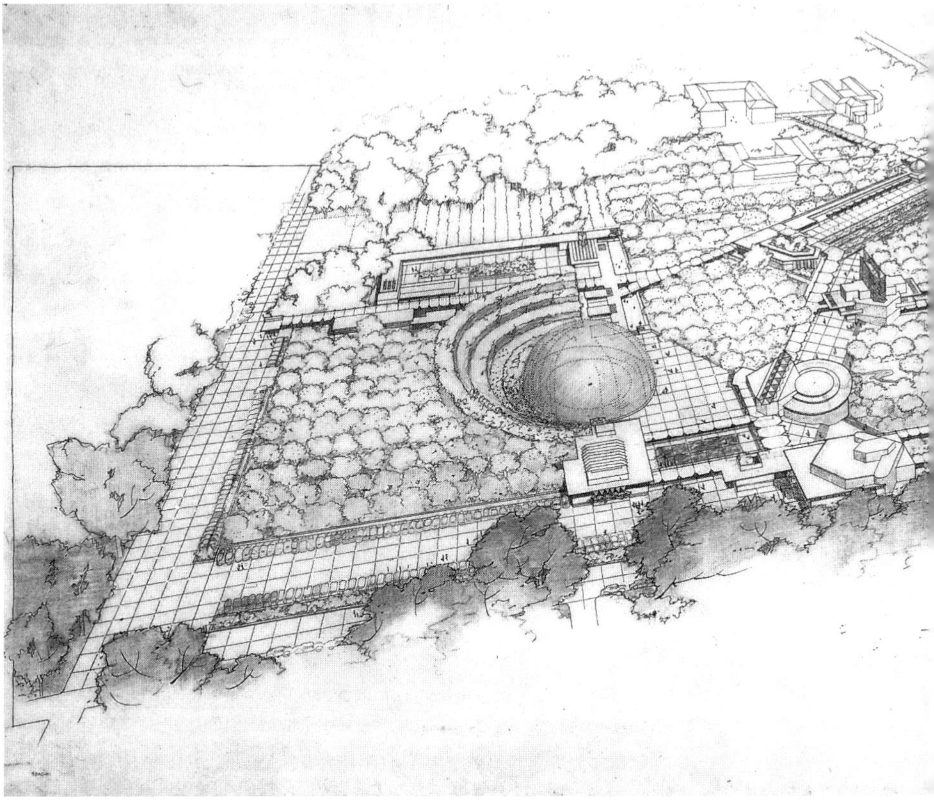

ers that the citrus trees were only slightly taller than the proposed esplanades, the effect would have been one of mystery and surprise since most buildings would be largely hidden from view at a distance. These trees, in combination with the hillside site, would have made it nearly impossible for a visitor to grasp any organization to the buildings' arrangement because of the blocked sight lines and lack of large open spaces.

Adding to this elusive quality was the fact that there was no main entrance. Wright designed the school for pedestrians, restricting vehicles to parking lots along the new campus's perimeter, although the early plans show a rerouted Lake Hollingsworth Drive passing through the south end of the site beneath elevated esplanades. He envisioned access points from the parking lots at the manual arts and domestic science unit and the administration building, but neither was privileged in the renderings.[6] An-

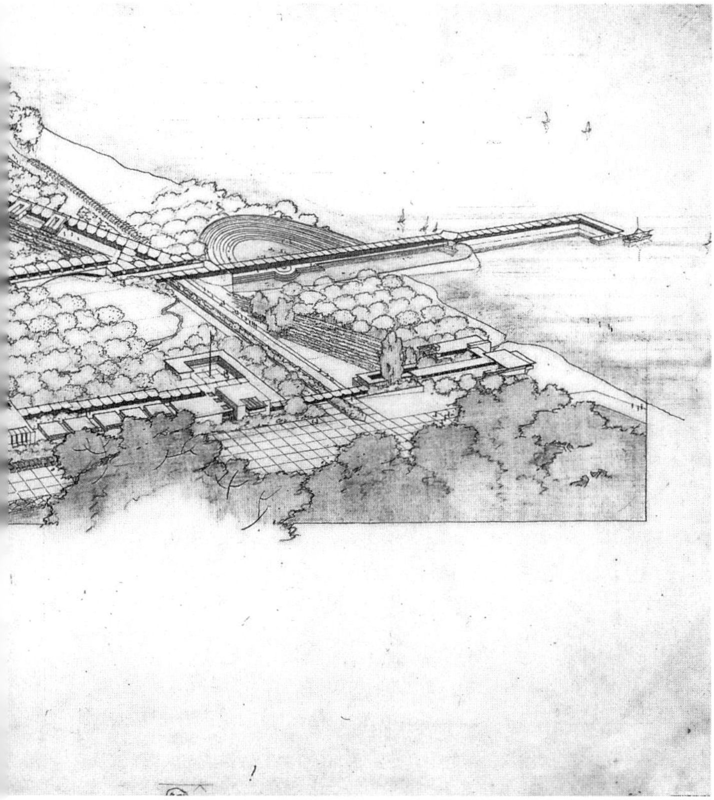

Figure 2.3. Frank Lloyd Wright, Florida Southern College plan, aerial drawing, 1938. Copyright © 2009 The Frank Lloyd Wright Foundation, Taliesin West, Scottsdale, Ariz. 3805.001.

other pedestrian access would occur between the old campus and the new science building.

Wright also altered the individual building plans from the orthogonal drawing. While many of the structures retained square or rectangular footprints, others now contained the same thirty- and sixty-degree diagonals of the new plan axes, and the library combined a diagonal stack section with a circular reading room that echoed the circles found in the Water Dome and the semicircular outdoor theater.

Wright intended the Water Dome, the chapel, and the library to be the most important structures, and their placement formed the core of the plan. He kept the chapel and library in close proximity in every version of the plan, connecting them with a short esplanade and plaza. This arrangement emphasized the prominent role religion and scholarship would play in the college. It also personified E. Stanley Jones's notion of a place where the teaching of science and religion could coexist in harmony. Wright linked the chapel and library by their close visual and physical relationship and by the hexagon that appears in both of their floor plans. One could even imagine that the hexagons might also symbolize Jones's "five-point program." Wright included a small chapel in the library's basement to further emphasize the bond.

Wright also incorporated the Water Dome in a triangular relationship with these two salient buildings. The triangle was one of Wright's core geometric symbols and design elements, and his use of it to relate these three structures meant that this central area of the plan contained triangular, circular, and hexagonal shapes—all demonstrating Wright's tendency at the time to move away from strictly orthogonal designs such as his initial Florida Southern proposal.

The arrangement of buildings and esplanades produced a dynamic plan unlike the typical static collegiate layout; instead, the drawings were imbued with motion and activity. The diagonals introduced a sense of movement that countered the stationary buildings. Wright's concept of the "reflex" informed the entire composition. By that term he meant a diagonal that was more natural and therefore fitting to human behavior than the right angle. "The obtuse angle is more suited to human 'to and fro' than the right angle," he argued. "That flow and movement is . . . a characteristic lending itself admirably to life, as life is to be lived in it."[7] Reflex angles humanized buildings and provided the kind of flexibility and functional emphasis that distinguished modern architecture. And they counteracted the severely linear character that ruled architectural planning of the time. "The reflex enters into architecture in these plans for Florida Southern as against the regimentation characteristic of the classic or Gothic architecture which have become a college habit in America," he wrote to Spivey.[8]

A consequence of the many diagonal angles would be a constant shifting of views as a visitor moved around the campus. The school was meant to be experienced from multiple points, unlike the rigid, controlled Beaux-Arts ensembles of the period, and since most of the buildings were partially or totally hidden within the citrus groves, movement through the campus along the esplanades' path would be the only way to get a feeling for the totality of Wright's creation.

Over the ensuing years Wright's changes to the master plan mainly related to two areas: the positioning of additional buildings and the location and structure of the outdoor pool and theater complex on Lake Hollingsworth. The most extensive alterations occurred at the meeting between campus and lake. The earliest plans showed a Greek-style theater and swimming pool at the water's edge. These structures faced each other at the terminal point of a continuous esplanade that led from the main chapel down the hill to the lake. This esplanade marked one of the north-south axes. Alongside this pool-theater complex the relocated road that passed beneath the north-south esplanade created a secondary east-west axis. This line balanced a similar east-west axis at the other end of campus, which ran through the administration building, the Water Dome, the seminar buildings, and the manual arts and domestic science unit.

Later renderings of the master plan revealed changes to the pool-theater arrangement. The theater and pool were pulled out into the lake instead of resting on the shore. Wright reduced the theater's size and reshaped the pool so that the two structures combined to form a full circle. He then created a lagoon to encircle the pool. The two buildings were moved slightly west so that they were in line with the Water Dome at the north end, thus forming a balanced composition with circular water shapes at each end.

Several aspects remained invariable during these modifications, including the site of the Water Dome; the triangular relationship between Water Dome, main chapel, and library; and the connecting framework of esplanades. And though the abundant citrus trees throughout the site appear on Wright's aerial renderings, their arrangement changed from a natural scattering to a regimented order, as if to reinforce the hidden order—or "occult symmetry"—of the plan.

The Buildings

Wright designed the Florida Southern College buildings as variations along a similar theme. Although the building plans were dissimilar, stressing their individuality by their distinctive footprints, there was an overall harmony to the campus through the use of common design elements and motifs. Wright called for all of the new buildings, and the covered walkways that connected them, to be constructed with the same materials, providing a visual continuity among the buildings that balanced their formal differences. "I intend the whole to be as splendidly correlated as it is conceived," he wrote to Spivey.[9] The main construction materials were concrete blocks, poured concrete, steel, copper, glass, and Red Tidewater Cypress. Wright told a local reporter, "They will make much of the association with the round and thorough-going harmony, each to each and each to all."[10]

Except for the main chapel, which rose skyward as the campus's spiritual centerpiece, the buildings were low to the ground, emphasizing their relationship to the land and human scale. The proposed landscaping would have enhanced the feeling of buildings growing from the ground. As Wright said to a Florida Southern student during his first visit: "Every building is out of the ground into the light—a child of the sun. Buildings should seem to grow from the earth and belong as a tree belongs."[11] In a promotional

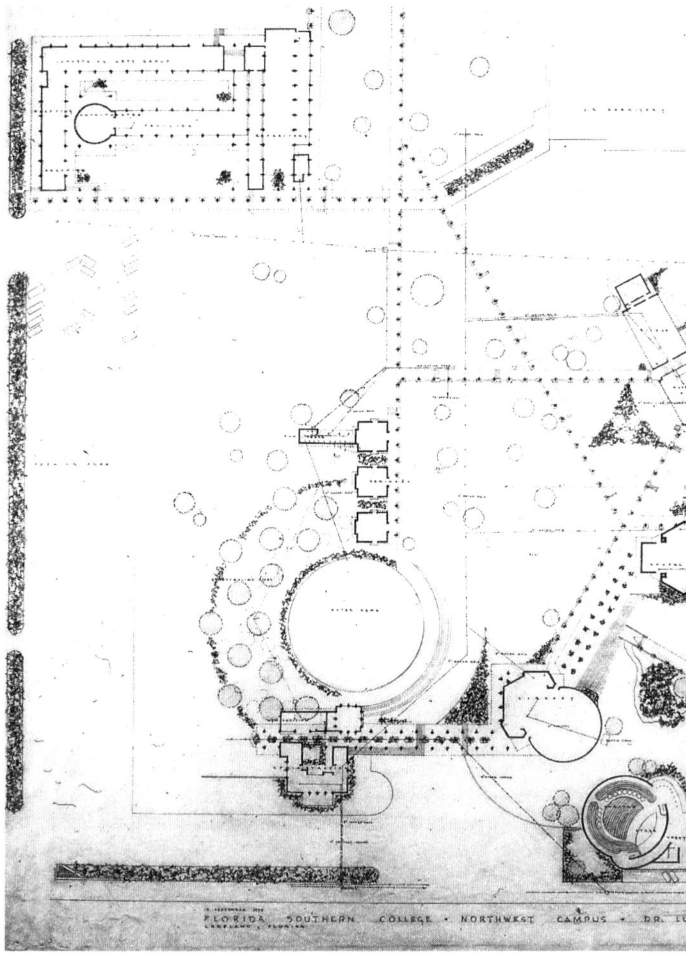

Figure 2.4. Frank Lloyd Wright, Florida Southern College plan, 1955. Copyright © 2009 The Frank Lloyd Wright Foundation, Taliesin West, Scottsdale, Ariz. 3805.003.

brochure for the E. Stanley Jones Educational Foundation, printed in May 1939, Spivey used similar Wrightian language: "He has designed each structure so that it will appear to grow out of the ground in harmonious relationship with vibrant nature."[12]

Despite the buildings' ground-hugging quality and small scale, Wright's use of a concrete block system added a monumental quality to the buildings; without this system, they might have appeared insignificant and lost in the citrus groves. The monumental references in these relatively small buildings, however, created a visual imbalance. From a distance, many of

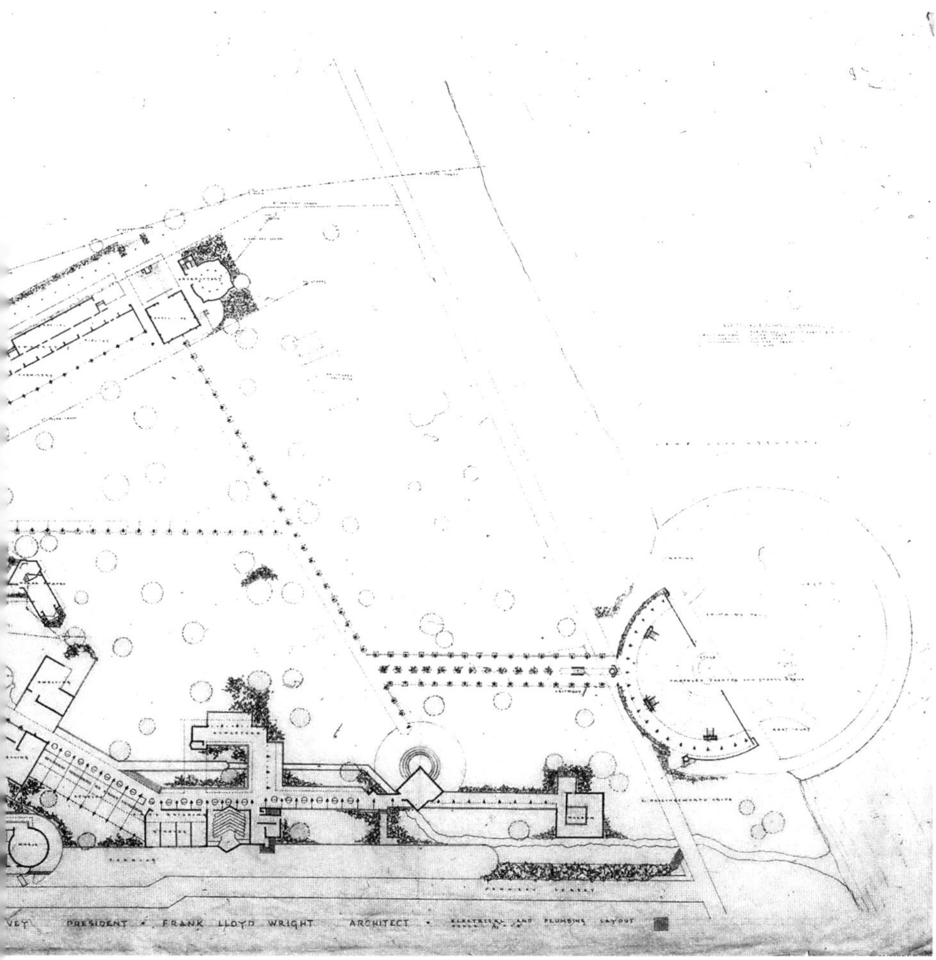

the Wright buildings look larger than they are. In this sense, the Wright buildings at Florida Southern symbolize the inherent modernist tension between a distrust of monumentality (as symbolic of power and authority) and a desire to dignify certain types of architecture.[13] Wright attempted to solve the problem by scaling the buildings to the human body, while constructing them with materials that carried monumental associations from a distant land and culture—in this case, the Mayan temples of Meso-America.[14] Wright's designs provided an impressive public face for a school that had often struggled to exist for almost one hundred years; his plans would certainly be in keeping with Spivey's request for a "great education temple."

The individual buildings carried Wright's diagonal geometries from the plan into three dimensions. It was the first collection of American college buildings designed in a modernist mode. Wright rejected the standard fashions of the day—Gothic, Georgian/Colonial, or Classical—opting instead for his own idiosyncratic vision of how higher education should look. Wright's buildings were distinctive in the way they utilized an extensive array of geometric forms. He had created a plan and a group of buildings that would give the college the "exciting" and "extraordinary" image Spivey wanted. "We have the ideals, we know what we are trying to do," Spivey had explained back in May, "but we need a symbol of those ideals lest they be lost." While Wright promised "a shrine to both idealism and religion," he undoubtedly had more than the Jones Foundation in mind as he developed his designs.[15]

Nature

The overall layout and individual forms of the Florida Southern buildings embodied many of Wright's deeply held convictions about architecture's relationship to nature; they may also reflect his interests in progressive education and democracy. One can read in his buildings and plan the experiences, influences, and theoretical concepts of a lifetime. In many ways, this was one of Wright's most autobiographical works.

Wright's belief in a modern architecture arising out of nature is well known to those who have even a passing acquaintance with his buildings. Evidence of his notion of an organic architecture existing in harmony with nature is visible throughout the course of his career in his emphasis on natural materials, his efforts to remove barriers between interior and exterior (e.g., the extensive glass window-walls in the Prairie style and Usonian houses), his integration of building with site (e.g., Fallingwater), or even his use of nature as literal model (e.g., the Johnson Wax Research Tower's emulating the structure of a tree). Wright's attempts to explain organic architecture to a reading or listening audience, however, were often unsuccessful. Statements such as "Architecture already favors the reflex, the natural easy attitude, the occult symmetry of grace and rhythm affirming the ease, grace, and naturalness of natural life. Modern architecture—let us now say *organic* architecture—is a natural architecture—the architecture of nature, for nature," did little to help others understand his philosophy.[16] Wright's difficulty articulating the theory of organic architecture may be due in part to its nonarchitectural roots in the spiritual worldview of nineteenth-century romantic idealism; beneath the discernible architectural features that literally connected a building to the natural world was an obscure mixture of religion, art, and philosophy. It is necessary to grasp this foundation in order to fully comprehend Wright's achievement at Florida Southern.

Wright's attitude toward nature was immensely influenced by the Unitarian religious beliefs of his mother's family and their interpretation of Ralph Waldo Emerson's writings and speeches.[17] For the Lloyd-Joneses, the notion of unity infused every aspect of their lives. "The Unitarianism of the Lloyd-Joneses . . . was an attempt to amplify in the confusion of the creeds of their day, the idea of life as a gift from the Divine Source, one GOD omnipotent, all things at one with HIM," Wright recalled in his autobiography. "UNITY was their watchword, the sign and symbol that thrilled them, the UNITY of all things! This mother sought it continually."[18] The family believed everything in the visible world—mountains, lakes, people, animals—revealed an underlying spiritual harmony. As a result, man and nature mirrored each other. Emerson alluded to this relationship when he asked, "What is man but nature's finer success in self-explication?"[19] Furthermore, Emerson taught that natural objects correspond to spiritual ideas; things experienced in the visible world are "emblematic," and "Every natural fact is a symbol of some spiritual fact . . . The visible creation is the terminus or the circumference of the invisible world." "[B]ehind nature, throughout nature," Emerson wrote, "spirit is present."[20]

Emerson was an intellectual hero of the Lloyd-Joneses, and Wright's sister Maginel later recalled "one's mother, father, aunts and uncles . . . always quoting Emerson."[21] Wright's exposure to Emerson as a youth had a formative effect; his adult attitudes toward art, nature, and their interrelation were profoundly Emersonian. For example, Emerson, and later Wright, considered art vitally important to human existence. Emerson believed art served to disclose the relationship between the natural and spiritual worlds. Art can create beauty, or, in the case of existing objects, can "educate the perception of beauty."[22] According to this formulation, although wild nature is beautiful, it is not as beautiful or as meaningful as the spiritual idea that lay behind it. As historian William Cronon has pointed out, "raw nature was much less compelling for most nineteenth-century romantics than it is for modern nature-lovers. The romantics regarded plants and animals and the rest of creation as the outward manifestation of an all-encompassing spiritual unity whose name was God."[23] But that unity or order is not immediately observable—it requires the artist to expose it. "Thus in art does Nature work through the will of a man filled with the beauty of her first works," wrote Emerson.[24] The artist's creation, if done properly, will be beautiful because it illuminates the spiritual unity of all things.

Following Emerson, Wright also believed architecture can connect people to nature, to make them aware of the spiritual world beneath it and the hidden unity that ties everything together. Emerson argued, "Every appearance in nature corresponds to some state of the mind, and that state of the mind can only be described by presenting that natural appearance as its picture."[25] Similarly, Wright stated that "architecture is simply a higher type and expression of nature by way of human nature where human beings are concerned."[26] He felt that built forms can reveal patterns in the landscape that will reinforce this connection. "[A]rchitecture . . . is the organic pattern of all things," he wrote in 1937. "This remains the hidden mystery of creation until the architect has grasped and revealed it . . . It is the significant structure of all created things as the mind may know them. It is at least the geometric pattern of things, of life, of the human and social world. It is at best that magic framework of reality that we sometimes touch upon when we use the word *order*."[27] Wright used the word "pattern" to describe the means by which abstraction, or spirit, is personified in material forms. Patterns can exhibit "cosmic laws," which are "the physical laws of all man-built structures as well as the laws of landscape."[28] Patterns are present in all things to the extent that "plant, animal creature and earth and man resemble each other for purpose malign or beneficent."[29]

This all-encompassing unity means that the patterns the architect needs to translate into buildings can be found in natural forms. "Herein is especially apprehended the unity of Nature,—the unity in variety,—which meets us everywhere," Emerson famously wrote. "A leaf, a drop, a crystal, a moment of time is related to the whole, and partakes of the perfection of the whole. Each particle is a microcosm, and faithfully renders the likeness of the world."[30] So architecture, too, can expose this hidden harmony by reinforcing associations between spiritual and material worlds. The land provided this nexus. When designing, Wright believed, "We start with the ground . . . In any and every case the character of the site is the beginning of the building that aspires to architecture."[31] The ground can disclose appropriate architectural patterns to the knowledgeable designer. "The ground already has form. Why not begin to give at once by accepting that? Why not give by accepting the gifts of nature?"[32] By incorporating the patterns of nature in the building, the architect achieves a unity between structure and site that symbolizes the all-inclusive unity that links nature, humans, and human activity.

Wright's design philosophy matured during the 1920s, when a number of projects in the American West exposed him to a grander, more sharply defined natural landscape, full of dominant mountains and vast deserts, and much different than the midwestern geography he was familiar with. Wright tellingly said of this experience: "The spiritual cathartic that was the desert worked—[it] swept the spirit clean of stagnant ways and habitual forms ready for fresh adventure."[33] In proposals for the Lake Tahoe Summer Colony (1923), the Doheny Ranch Development (1923) and the A. M. Johnson Desert Compound (1924) in California, and San Marcos in the Desert (1928–29) in Arizona, and in the built forms of the Ocatilla Desert Camp (1928), Wright attempted to reveal nature's underlying order through architectural form. The system he developed to do this, later expanded in the 1930s, made extensive use of diagonal lines and thirty-sixty-ninety-degree triangles.

It is possible to imagine that Wright saw in the gentle slope of the Florida Southern site, in the circular shape of the lake, and in the regimented orange groves the patterns he needed to translate the inherent order of nature as divulged in the landscape into built forms. Diagonals dominate his campus plan; they appear in individual building plans and in the footprints of the esplanades that link the buildings together. Wright could have found the diagonal on the site, either in the cross section of the hillside slanting down to the water, or in the angle created where the land and lake intersect in plan. This would not be the first time he appropriated a geographic cross section for a design; much of his work in the American West during the

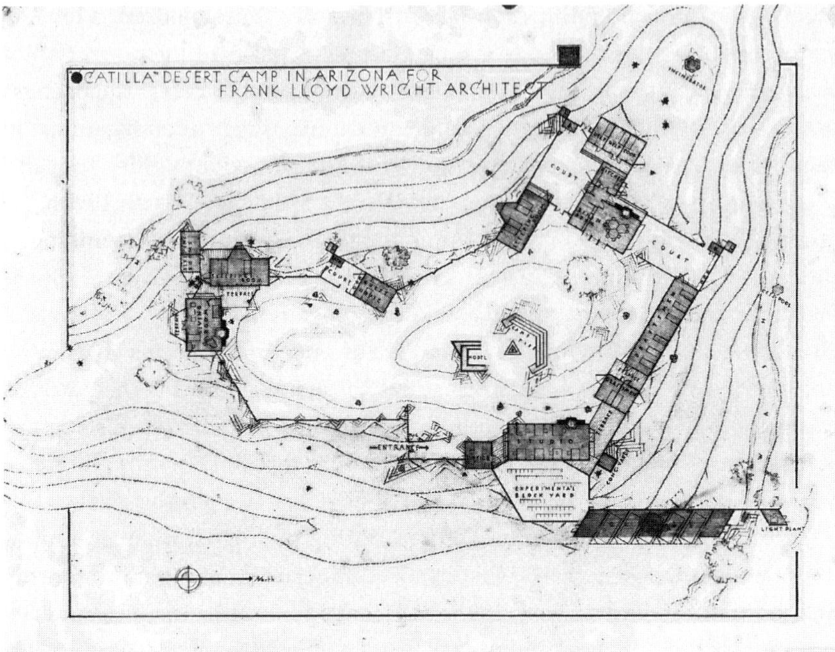

Figure 2.5. Frank Lloyd Wright, Ocatilla Desert Camp plan, Arizona, 1928. Copyright © 2009 The Frank Lloyd Wright Foundation, Taliesin West, Scottsdale, Ariz. 2702.004.

1920s was a response to his encounter with the invigorating topography of flat valleys and prominent mountains. "The one-two triangle we used in planning the camp is made by the mountain ranges around about the site," he wrote about the Ocatilla camp. "And the one-two triangle is the cross section of the talus at their bases. This triangle is reflected in the general forms of all the cabins as well as the general plan."[34] While the angle of Florida Southern's hillside might not have directly inspired the thirty-sixty-degree diagonals, the mere presence of a slope might have justified the use of such angles in Wright's mind.

It is also possible to assume that Wright appropriated the water and circular form of the lake, the trees' shape and repetitious order, and other natural elements to make campus buildings and esplanades that were both aesthetically attuned and site specific. "Architectural features of true democratic ground-freedom would rise naturally from topography, which means that buildings would all take on the nature and character of the ground on which in endless variety they would stand and be component part," he once said, and Florida Southern would be a perfect example of his philosophy in action.[35] The circle reappeared in the plans of many proposed buildings, the water was used for a symbolic sculptural program and the Water Dome, and the trees were abstracted into esplanade piers.

In Wright's September 1938 description of the plan in his letter to Spivey, the meaning of the phrase "Each building is individual in character—practical in effect—yet *contributing its share to an occult symmetry*" (emphasis mine) becomes clearer when viewed in the context of his design philosophy, particularly the use of the word "occult." Wright's choice is ingenious, touching on the varying definitions of "occult" as mystical or supernatural, inscrutable, and hidden from view—all of which describe a campus plan that could be seen as signifying the philosophical ideas of Unitarianism and Emerson. Similarly, Wright's statement "What I am most proud of having done in this effort is to have succeeded in *making all units into the one gracious pattern*" (emphasis mine) discloses his ongoing attempt to extract patterns from the landscape and insert them into plans, sections, and elevations to tie structures to their site and to each other. One can see this at Florida Southern, where diagonals govern the plan and appear in the individual buildings.

Florida Form

Another key to interpreting Wright's campus lies in understanding his desire to create "a Florida form" for the college, expressed in his first public speech in Lakeland after accepting the commission. Over the course of the next two decades, Wright made repeated references to his design's "Florida character" or "outdoor garden character."[36] This aspect was an integral part of his attempt to create a regionally specific modern architecture.[37]

Wright thought Florida lacked an architectural heritage and needed a modernist architecture that could provide some connections to the region's distinctive environment. In the 1930s it was still a relatively young state; the central and southern regions had been extensively populated for only a few decades, and Florida's greatest period of growth had just occurred in the twenties. The closest thing the state had to an architectural tradition was the Mediterranean Revival or Spanish Revival recently popularized by Addison Mizner in the Palm Beach area. Mizner's use of Spanish motifs was largely based on personal taste, but he also felt it meshed with the area's distant history and climate. Similarly, architect Thomas Hastings of the prominent New York firm Carrère and Hastings, which designed the influential Ponce de Leon Hotel in St. Augustine for famed developer Henry Flagler in the late 1880s, claimed that the "logical expression of the semi-tropical climate and historical background was in some form of Spanish Renaissance style."[38] The Florida economic boom of the early 1920s spread Mizner's preferred manner across the southern part of the state. But that popular style was based on a romantic image rather than any built legacy; almost nothing remained of the Spanish colonial era, and the subsequent centuries had not seen the development of an indigenous alternative.

Meanwhile, modernistic architecture had made some inroads into the region, particularly in the Miami area. A district of Tropical Art Deco hotels and public buildings had begun forming in Miami Beach in the mid-1930s, while throughout southeast Florida a tamer version was becoming popular. As illustrated in the December 1938 issue of *Architectural Forum*, these new Florida buildings were marked by their flat roofs, bright colors, stuccoed concrete-block construction, simplified façades, and rounded corners—in other words, they were regional variations of what was labeled "Streamline Moderne" style.[39]

Wright refused to acknowledge the legitimacy of Florida's borrowed Spanish style and dismissed the state's architecture for its provincial quality. "Most of you here have simply built here as you built back home," he said to a Florida audience.[40] For him, Florida was the architectural equivalent of a blank slate, perfect for a grand experiment in regional modernism. A modern architecture true to organic principles would necessarily reference the area's special characteristics. "I am a great believer in so-called regional development," Wright told the Fashion Group of Miami. "I don't believe you should have the same things in Miami that you have in the streets of New York City . . . Look at the flowers. Look at the trees. Look at the beauty of your coral reefs. Look at these outcroppings of your wonderful stone. Look what you've got!"[41] For Wright, a "Florida form" would necessarily incorporate shading and plantings. This view implied that Florida weather allows, or even encourages, year-round outdoor activities, but they must be mitigated by the need for protection from heat and sun. "If Florida means an environment that is something arising out of the ground, then this is Florida at Florida Southern College," he would later profess. "This is what

Figure 2.6. Mediterranean Revival house, Florida, c. 1920s. Postcard, author's collection.

Miami should have. Shaded walkways. Trees. Beautiful plantings instead of what's down there."[42]

Defining a regional modernism could involve considering such aspects as climate and geography, but also local flora and fauna and indigenous traditions. In his proposal for the Arizona state capitol (1957), for example, Wright incorporated symbols of Native American culture, references to state history, and abstracted date palm trees. For Florida, a place with little regional heritage, he sought to create an assembly of buildings that responded to the hot and sunny climate, the topography and lake, and the surrounding citrus groves. This intention can be seen in a number of design elements. Covered walks provided shelter from the sun and frequent summer rains. Except for the two chapels, Wright's buildings had few instances of large glass expanses or direct lighting. Sand from the site and coquina, a Florida limestone made of crushed seashells, were used to make concrete blocks used in all the buildings, further tying the structures to their locale. And Wright included water, which has symbolic meaning in Florida—particularly in citrus country—throughout the campus. Wright blended all of these components to create an architecture unlike any other ever seen in the state—a model of a Florida form to guide future generations.

Education

While nature and the search for a Florida form clearly shaped Wright's overall plan, it is not difficult to assume that his deeply held views about education also found their way into the design for Florida Southern. It was, after all, the largest educational commission he would ever receive, and it provided him with an unprecedented opportunity to put into action principles of progressive education that he had absorbed since childhood.

Wright was surrounded by and involved with education for most his life. His activities with the Taliesin Fellowship are well documented, but his contact with education actually began much earlier. Wright's mother, Anna Lloyd Jones, had been a teacher before her marriage to William Cary Wright, and education was extremely important to the entire Lloyd Jones family. Wright recalled, "Education was Sister Anna's passion even while very young. All this family was imbued with the idea of education as salvation."[43] According to Maginel Wright Barney, Wright's younger sister, "Education obsessed [Anna], and she would teach anyone who showed even the vaguest desire to learn."[44] His other sister, Mary Jane, followed in her mother's footsteps and taught elementary school in Wisconsin and Illinois.

The real foundation of Wright's educational experience, however, was formed through the family's connections with the Hillside Home School. His aunts Jane and Ellen Lloyd Jones—nicknamed "Aunt Jenny" and "Aunt Nell"—were lifelong teachers who organized and ran the school on the Jones property at Taliesin in Wisconsin. The sisters formed the Hillside Home School in 1887 as an early experiment in progressive education for children ages five to eighteen. Hillside differed radically from standard educational practices by promoting active rather than book-based learning, utilizing subject matter correlated to children's interests, and teaching that nature was the primary source of all human knowledge.[45] The school's built environment and general atmosphere were very homelike and at the same time agrarian, with great emphasis on outdoor activities. Two notable American educators—Francis Parker and John Dewey—influenced the Lloyd Jones sisters in these pursuits.

In his *Autobiography*, Wright described Aunt Nell and Aunt Jenny as "disciples of John Dewey by way of Francis Parker under whom they once taught school."[46] Francis W. Parker was a seminal figure in late-nineteenth-century educational reform. His fame rested on his work as a school principal in Quincy, Massachusetts, where he implemented one of the nation's first curricula based on the child's natural curiosity. Parker rejected the typical pedagogical methods of his day, such as recitation and memorization, and refused to use standard textbooks. Instead, his child-centered schools emphasized the use of materials developed by the students themselves that corresponded to their own interests. Parker further encouraged children to actively explore their environment as a means of providing experiences for learning. His success in Quincy eventually led him to Chicago, where he established a teacher training school that John Dewey's children later attended.

John Dewey, in addition to being a famous philosopher, is a monumental figure in American education. He was the most prominent individual in the field for almost sixty years and a leading educational reformer. Like Parker, Dewey rejected any form of systematic instruction or fixed methods of presenting knowledge. He believed in an educational process that cultivated individuality, stressed learning through experience, and advocated the freedom to question antiquated ideas and teaching techniques. Dewey also felt the school was the preeminent training ground for democracy, since it was at school that children were instilled with the spirit of democratic participation in civic life. "Experience" and "growth" were Dewey's watchwords. Education should be a process of eternal growth, with no particular end or goal. He believed a person must continue to grow in response to the ever-changing experiences of life. This growth was accomplished through experience—"learning by doing." Education for Dewey, like Parker, was a process initiated by an active child rather than a passive recipient.

Parker's and Dewey's educational theories resonated with Wright's aunts. At Hillside they created a coeducational school of small, informal classes and emphasized activity and contact with nature. The curriculum covered standard subjects like languages and geography, but the methods involved the faculty "looking upon each child as an individual and centering all its efforts on his reasonable growth, activity, and self-expression."[47] Wright's sister Mary Jane and many of his cousins taught at the school, and he would send his two eldest sons there even when the family resided in Oak Park, Illinois. Since Wright was emotionally close to his aunts, he undoubtedly absorbed their radical educational philosophy to some extent; he also would have been influenced by his mother, Anna, the former teacher who guided young Frank and his two sisters through Friedrich Froebel's "Gifts" early in life.

Wright's engagement with educational reformers continued when he left Wisconsin and moved to Chicago in 1887. Within a few years he was either directly or indirectly associated with the city's main progressive educators. For example, he was involved with Jane Addams's Hull House by the 1890s. Hull House was a social settlement dedicated to various community causes, including the education of immigrant women and children. It was also a haven for arts and crafts enthusiasts, and the site of Wright's famous 1901 speech, "On the Art and Craft of the Machine." Wright might have met John Dewey at Hull House, given that Dewey was a close friend of director Jane Addams and served as a Hull House trustee from 1889 to 1903. The two men clearly moved within the same circles of Chicago's social reformers and arts and crafts supporters until Dewey's departure for New York in 1904. Correspondence in the Frank Lloyd Wright Archives to and from Dewey later in life confirms that the two men knew each other. For purposes of Wright's architecture, what is important is the degree to which the two men shared similar ideas about education and its place in American society.

Constant exposure to progressive educators from birth through young adulthood affected Wright. There is evidence that he fancied himself an educator in the family tradition: a 1910 letter between two of his clients included a comment that Wright "Says his work in life will be to educate his children."[48] Even his scandalous affair with Mamah Cheney was based in part on a mutual interest in education. When the pair traveled to Europe together in 1909, the trip was partially intended to give Cheney time to translate the writings of Ellen Key, a Swedish child development pioneer.

Wright prominently displayed his passion for progressive education when he created the Taliesin Fellowship. Opened in 1932, although dating back several years as a concept, the fellowship provided a means for Wright to produce income during the doldrums of the Depression while training a new generation of architects in the principles of organic architecture. Not a school in the traditional sense, the fellowship was more akin to a commune, with Wright as the leader. Students, or "apprentices," paid tuition to live at Wright's property at Taliesin in Wisconsin (later they would divide the year between Wisconsin and Taliesin West in Arizona, a tradition continued to this day by the Frank Lloyd Wright School of Architecture). They spent part of their time studying design and working on Wright's commissions and much of the rest working in the farm fields and gardens, cooking, cleaning, doing laundry, or making repairs to the property and equipment. Every apprentice was also expected to specialize in some craft, in the tradition of the Arts and Crafts and the German Bauhaus. And participation in the fine arts was encouraged, with music and drama performances occurring on a regular basis.

The fellowship arose in part from Wright's desire to revive his aunts' Hillside Home School, which had fallen into financial distress and closed in 1915. He later claimed in his autobiography that he had promised his aunts he would "see their educational work go on at beloved Hillside on the site of the pioneer homestead. That filial promise would go along with me wherever I went."[49] Wright continued his aunts' progressive educational ideals in the fellowship, eschewing a formal curriculum or traditional instruction methods and instead emphasizing "learning by doing." This activity-based approach later provided some senior apprentices the opportunity to supervise construction projects away from Taliesin.[50]

Despite the prominence of education in his development, Wright had few opportunities to create educational buildings. Prior to the late 1930s he designed a handful of elementary-level school buildings, but only three were built—the Hillside Home School for his aunts (1887 and 1909; 1933), the Coonley Playhouse (1911), and the Jiyu Gakuen Girls' School in Tokyo (1921). While all three were schools, none genuinely expressed Wright's personal approach to education. And when he expanded Taliesin East (1933) and created Taliesin West (1937) for his fellowship, he was designing for an atypical situation that was more of a community than a traditional school.

It may be that a single building could never exemplify Wright's complex educational philosophy. His ideas, which were a mixture of family traditions and individual beliefs, would rightly be characterized as "progressive." For instance, Wright absorbed one of Parker's and Dewey's salient lessons—the idea that education should not be the highly regimented study of standard courses but rather a free exploration of a person's physical, social, and personal environment that would lead to continuous growth. Like Dewey, Thomas Jefferson, and Walt Whitman before him, Wright equated education with self-expression, and self-expression with democracy. He believed that individuality should be the driving force behind a proper education, resulting in more intelligent citizens who could fully participate in civic life. Wright adopted the progressive educators' beliefs that education should be a process of "learning by doing." Wright also interjected an Emersonian reverence for nature into this formulation. Emerson once said,

"The land, with its tranquilizing, sanative influences, is to repair the errors of a scholastic and traditional education, and bring us into just relations with men and things."[51] Architecture also entered into the equation, playing a pivotal role in everyone's education because it formed a bridge between man and nature, the true source of all knowledge.

A story contained in Wright's autobiography illustrates much about his educational ideas at the time and also provides a possible intellectual foundation for the Florida Southern College master plan. In the prelude to the book, Wright told of a childhood walk through the snow with one of his uncles. The uncle forged ahead on a straight, unwavering path, while young Frank wandered to and fro behind him, gathering weeds. At the crest of a hill, the uncle gazed back admiringly on his trail but was disturbed to see young Wright's tracks had formed a "wavering, searching, heedful line embroidering the straight one like some free, engaging vine as it ran back and forth across it." The uncle was not pleased. His message was clear: "NEITHER TO RIGHT NOR TO LEFT, BUT STRAIGHT, IS THE WAY." According to Wright, he was troubled that his uncle "had left out something that made all the difference."[52] Wright illustrated his story on the book's cover with a dashed line dancing at angles over a dark, heavy, straight line.

The story might be taken as a metaphor for Wright's attitude toward education. The boy follows his own natural, instinctual path, while his uncle attempts to impose a regimented course on him. If we interpret the boy and his actions as representing the free and active nature of progressive education, the uncle symbolizes the traditional system. Wright's assertion that the uncle "left something out" reveals his opinion of American education.[53]

Wright disliked the American educational system. He attacked it as being unresponsive to the needs of "free people." The system had not provided "enlightenment"—i.e., a proper awareness of nature. Wright, displaying his Unitarian and Emersonian background, believed man was "a phase of nature, and only as he related to nature does he really matter."[54] Consequently it was only through studying nature that humans could learn what they truly needed to know about themselves and their world. This would be accomplished by using art, religion, and science as spiritual guideposts on the path to an understanding of "truth."

Wright outlined in broad strokes his ideal education system in the book *The Living City*. His plan essentially called for establishing a series of schools modeled on the Hillside Home School operated by his aunts

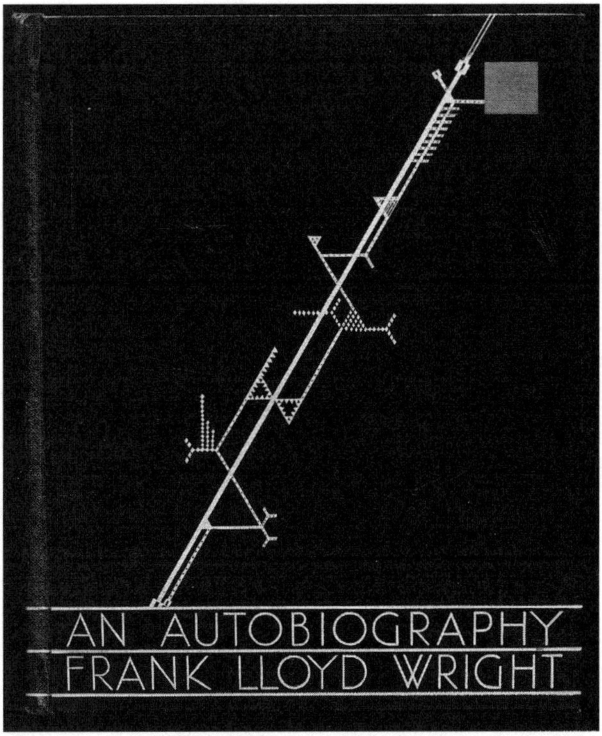

Figure 2.7. Cover, Frank Lloyd Wright, *An Autobiography*, 1932. Copyright © 2009 The Frank Lloyd Wright Foundation, Taliesin West, Scottsdale, Ariz.

a half-century earlier. He envisioned small schools with approximately twenty-five students each. Their curricula and facilities would assimilate ideas derived from pioneers like Parker and Dewey, guided by the principle of experiential learning. Nature study—through drawing—agriculture, and cooking figured prominently in his conception; children would cultivate flowers and vegetables, learn to draw and model, and prepare food. "Eye and hand, body and mind, and what we call the soul thus becoming more sensitive to Nature and appreciative of integral rhythm," he claimed. "The very synthesis of being would appear."[55] This type of education, Wright believed, would have the bonus value of preparing children to understand, appreciate, and even create organic architecture because they would acquire the fundamental skill of learning to see properly.[56]

The correspondences between Dewey's and Wright's educational philosophies are readily apparent. Both men felt the ideal school should be located in a natural setting. "The school building has about it a natural environment," wrote Dewey. "It ought to be in a garden, and the children from the garden would be led on to surrounding fields, and then into the wider country, with all its facts and forces."[57] Wright agreed: "Any culture center called a school in the universal city would be set in a natural park in the choicest part of the whole countryside . . . Enough ground for flower and vegetable beds would be planted."[58] Both Dewey and Wright thought learning occurred when the learner was actively engaged rather than passively exposed. Dewey described his famous Laboratory School at the University of Chicago as a place where "the child comes to school to *do*; to cook, to sew, to work with wood and tools in simple constructive acts."[59] Wright believed "general education by and for life in the free city should be had by doing—by life-experience."[60]

The methods for exposing children to those situations where they could learn from experience were equivalent in Dewey's Laboratory School, in Jane and Ellen Lloyd Jones's Hillside Home School, and in Wright's proposed schools. Dewey outlined "how the school may be connected with life so that the experience gained by the child in a familiar, commonplace way is carried over and made use of there, and what the child learns in the school is carried back and applied in everyday life, making the school an organic whole, instead of a composite of isolated parts."[61] Wright, using an example that Dewey also favored, noted that children would learn to grow, prepare, cook, and present food as an educational activity. Dewey often explained how the simple act of cooking a meal presented an opportunity to teach students about food groups, geography, chemistry, anatomy, physics, and mathematics, and it was all presented in a very natural way, just as a child might learn at home from his or her parents. Mary Ellen Chase, a former teacher at Hillside Home School, similarly recounted how Wright's aunts "insisted that the life in studies be made interesting and as alive as the life outside them, in fact, that the play elements within books seem as natural as play itself . . . they knew that things in books have meanings only as they are associated with other things, either in books or outside them."[62]

While Wright's ideas about basic education were firmly rooted in progressive philosophy from earlier in the century, his view of higher education was unique and eccentric. According to Wright, American higher education was particularly ill-adjusted to the proper educational mission. He referred to college as "the four year loaf," and famously claimed, "Were I a Rockefeller—Ford—or Du Pont, I mean as rich, I would buy up our leading universities—close them and hang out the sign—closed by the beneficence of one, Frank Lloyd Wright."[63] Universities were merely "Highly specialized trade-schools" conditioning students to be specialists.[64] He considered the higher education system misguided, as its real goal should be to cultivate an understanding of, and passion for, the truth.[65]

In Wright's view, universities should be "noble storehouses where all that mankind has produced in science, art and philosophy would be a matter of record, or model available for free study." There would be no professors and no curriculum—instead, the collective fields of science, art, and philosophy in each state would gather to elect representative "father confessors." These three experts would be joined by a statesman—"if one could be found." Everyone else would fall into the broad category of "privileged students" to be employed in research, but only those "having some proof of inner human experience in some one of these qualities of human life" (science, philosophy, or art) could formally be accepted to the university. Wright specifically stated that vocational training would be gradually discontinued, in keeping with his belief that "No preparation for teaching or practicing anything should be a feature of these 'universities.' "[66]

Ideally, this utopian institution would inspire citizens to "deeper study of nature's organic laws," not as an end in itself but as a means of pursuing truth and thus strengthening democracy. In this atmosphere, students would be free to learn at their own pace and according to their own interests. Nature, of course, would be central to the university's physical environment. The new campus would exist "in quiet retreats made beautiful and appropriate for reflection and concentration."[67] And architecture could model beauty and truth for the students. Wright alluded to this idea when he told Florida Southern students in a 1951 address: "Here at Florida Southern College you will be educated in an atmosphere of *truth*. And if you can only see it, you have a better chance of growing into something fine spiritually as you are being educated in a good atmosphere."[68]

Although Ludd Spivey's ultimate educational goal seems to have been to unite the teaching of religion and science as proposed by the E. Stanley Jones Educational Foundation, in his thirteen years at Florida Southern, he had been able to shape the institution according to his passion for Deweyan philosophy to some extent. The college's official language, as well as Spivey's own writings and lectures, often alluded to Dewey's pragmatic approach, including judging actions by their results, focusing on practical applications, and learning through experience. In the same manner that Spivey encouraged experiential learning as a way to merge progressive educational philosophy with religious education, Wright infused the campus architecture with progressive notions. A careful analysis of the Florida

Southern design uncovers two salient ideas Wright had been exposed to through his contacts with progressive education: freedom and activity.

Both Parker and Dewey had emphasized the importance of letting children have a say in the subjects and activities of their own education; they also stressed the need to let students explore their environment as a means of gaining valuable experiences that would enrich their educational development. Although this approach was impractical within the traditional higher education system that Florida Southern used, Wright could at least reference it in the built environment. He imbued Florida Southern with a sense of freedom in the way he laid out the buildings and esplanades. Wright rejected the traditional orthogonal plan and the popular quadrangular formula used at other colleges. Instead of controlling symmetry and neat courtyards lined with nearly identical buildings and crossed by major and minor axes, Wright's college plan arranged differently shaped buildings along thirty- and sixty-degree angles in what Wright called "a free pattern." One might imagine the campus as having broken free from the restraints of orthodox design. Upon closer inspection, the plan's resemblance to the illustration on the cover of Wright's autobiography may be more than a coincidence.

Wright's plans also demonstrated the educational principle of activity or movement. Parker, Dewey, and Wright's teacher-aunts had all advocated an educational process that emphasized active participation—children moving rather than passively sitting. At Florida Southern, Wright conveyed a sense of movement through the arrangement of the esplanades. He once wrote that the esplanade "runs all over and finally gets together and makes a building."[69] In the course of this "running," the diagonal walkways provide the campus with a dynamic quality—an energy that is not found in the static quadrangular layouts of contemporary schools. The esplanades beckon the visitor to move forward and explore the grounds. And as one moves around the campus, the views constantly change. The school was meant to be experienced from multiple vantage points, unlike the rigid Beaux-Arts-influenced campus that controlled how the buildings should be seen.

Democracy

Wright's Florida Southern plan also provided a means for him to model a democratic architecture. This would have been a key consideration, for democracy, like education, had been a vital component of Wright's intellectual maturation. Emerson, whose significance to the Lloyd-Jones family was outlined above, was a prominent advocate of democracy. Walt Whitman, "The Bard of Democracy" and another family favorite, may have been even more meaningful to Wright's understanding of democracy.[70] Whitman wrote often of democracy, and one of its outstanding aspects for him was personal freedom. "The second principle [of democracy] is individuality, the pride and centripetal isolation of a human being in himself-identity-personalism," he claimed. "Whatever the name, its acceptance and thorough infusion through the organizations of political commonality now shooting Aurora-like about the world, are of utmost importance, as the principle itself is needed for very life's sake. It forms, in a sort, or is to form, the compensating balance-wheel of the successful working machinery of aggregate America."[71] The idea of "rugged individualism" even entered his poetry: "I am for those that have never been master'd . . . For those whom laws, theories, conventions, can never master."[72]

For Whitman, the individuality and freedom at the heart of democratic society required a corresponding expression in the arts, for "democracy can never prove itself beyond cavil, until it founds and luxuriantly grows its own forms of art, poems, schools, theology, displacing all that exists, or that has been produced anywhere in the past, under opposite influences."[73] Wright's interest in Whitman helped him bond with Louis Sullivan, whom Wright called his "Lieber Meister." Wright spent many hours as a young architect listening to Sullivan explain his idiosyncratic theory about the need for an individual American architecture that integrated democracy and organic growth.[74]

For Wright, like Whitman and Sullivan, a democratic society more than anything else accommodated and encouraged individuality. This understanding formed the basis for his lifelong quest to forge a true *American* architecture. His view of democracy remained remarkably consistent over the span of his life. In 1910, for example, he wrote: "[America's] ideal is democracy . . . This means that she places a life premium upon individuality—the highest possible development of the individual consistent with a harmonious whole—believing that a whole benefited by sacrifice of that quality in the individual rightly considered his 'individuality' is underdeveloped."[75] Compare these words with this statement, written almost half a century later in 1958: "Democracy should bring freedom for the individual to realize himself as an individual—creative, unique, free. The validity and the dynamics of democracy lie in a continued insistence upon man's free will and the right to follow his own mind and his conscience."[76]

To Wright, any architecture that professed to represent true democracy should personify the individuality and freedom at the heart of a democratic society. According to historian Narciso Menocal, Wright felt the words "democracy" and "organic" were synonymous, both "signifying a harmony with nature."[77] In nature, as Menocal pointed out, since each specimen's appearance is unique, nature can be said to foster individuality. Nature is also a mirror of human existence according to Wright's Emersonian beliefs. So this individuality can be considered a natural human attribute. Organic architecture, which encouraged individuality in design in response to the unique features of the site, was therefore not only a natural architecture, but *the* natural architecture of democratic society. "Organic (or intrinsic) architecture is the free architecture of ideal democracy," Wright claimed.[78] He would accomplish the task of manifesting the abstract principle of democracy in his work by emphasizing individuality—and this would be easiest to demonstrate in multibuilding ensembles where qualities of individuality and unity could more readily be explored. Florida Southern offered an unprecedented opportunity to do this.

Wright's belief in democracy as "the highest possible expression of the individual as a unit not inconsistent with a harmonious whole" was noticeable in his campus design.[79] In the long September 1938 letter to Spivey describing his vision for Florida Southern, he asserted that in his proposed plan "each building is individual in character—practical in effect—yet contributing its share to an occult symmetry."[80] This sentence reveals the design's democratic underpinnings. The master plan exhibited democracy in the way it fit a group of heterogeneous buildings into a unified whole. The buildings had dissimilar plans and elevations, but they shared a common vocabulary of materials. So while buildings like the library, chapel, and science building differed in size, form, and expression, their shared architectural lexicon of textile blocks, smooth stucco surfaces, and copper trim helped create a "harmonious whole." And all were interconnected by esplanades, imitating the way America's democratic society assimilates individuals with widely varying backgrounds, opinions, and beliefs. In a sense, Wright gave the buildings the freedom to exist as individuals within a framework that embraced them all. Wright explained the effect to Spivey in his September 20 letter, calling his design "a structural example of the freedom needed very much at this time in our national life" and "one comfort giving, protective, sympathetic building, divided into special buildings for special activities."[81]

Beyond personifying democracy through the free plan and diverse buildings, the campus design in its entirety also can be construed as Wright's declaration of the inherent democracy of regional modernism. As historian Joseph Siry observes, for Wright "democracy in architecture meant not only a modern rather than a historically derived style, but also a modernism that exhibited the regional variety of organic architecture, not the uniformity of the International Style."[82] The troubling world events of the 1930s provided the immediate context for this interpretation—the same developments that prompted Spivey to denounce Germany, Italy, Japan, and the Soviet Union in speeches and chapel talks. Wright had found the rise of International Style modernism out of Europe in the 1920s equally disturbing and had been explaining its deleterious effects to audiences and readers for almost a decade. Just as Spivey warned of the dangers totalitarianism posed to democratic societies, so Wright cautioned against the blind acceptance of European artistic modes, which he equated with totalitarianism and communism. "The 'International Style' is neither international nor a style. Essentially it is totalitarianism, an old totalitarian cult made new by organized publicity," he wrote. "The nature of the freedom prophesied by the Declaration of Independence originally made by our nation is antipathetic to an international level either of style or of life. That 'style' would be the communistic shadow descending over our own tradition, disgracing the great individualities that gave us our traditions in all their bewildering and wonderful fascination, color, and variety."[83]

The remedy for growing universal tendencies in modern architecture was Wright's organic design, derived from the land and the character of society and therefore capable of producing an infinite variety of architectural solutions. Because it was free, individual, and voluntary, organic architecture—"the sovereign Architecture of Democracy"—was the natural architecture of America. Its benefits, however, could be reaped anywhere in the world. "Because of our increased techniques, organic architecture could easily afford *all* nations new means of realization, on their own soil, along lines of character and development already peculiar to themselves," Wright maintained.[84] At Florida Southern, his largest nonurban, multi-building commission since the appearance of the International Style, he had a chance to fashion an exemplar of democratic architecture. Using the innate freedom and individuality of organic architecture, Wright created a new modern expression for Florida based on the distinctive characteristics of the region.

Sources

Along with the formative influences of nature, education, and democracy, other considerations shaped Wright's Florida Southern design. For instance, diagonal motifs that later would be worked out in the campus plan can be traced as far back as the 1910s, having their origins in Wright's decorative designs for buildings like the Midway Gardens. By the 1920s, the diagonal emerged from the decorations and began to appear in Wright's plans and elevations. Early examples of Wright's nonrectangularity in unbuilt projects include the Little Dipper Kindergarten (1923), floating cabins for Lake Tahoe (1923), the Johnson Desert Compound (1924), the Nakoma Country Club (1924), and the San Marcos in the Desert resort hotel (1928–29). All of these schemes either included some form of diagonal axis running at thirty or sixty degrees from the plan's main axis or incorporated a unique geometric form, thereby differing from Wright's square or rectangular Prairie and California houses.[85] The Little Dipper building, for example, combined a circle and square. Some of the Tahoe cabins and part of the Nakoma Country Club were hexagonally shaped. The Gordon Strong Automobile Objective project (1924–25) was circular.

Figure 2.8. Frank Lloyd Wright, Taliesin Fellowship/Hillside Home School remodeling project, 1932. Copyright © 2009 The Frank Lloyd Wright Foundation, Taliesin West, Scottsdale, Ariz. 3301.010.

The bold use of diagonal planning and geometry in Wright's designs existed mainly on a conceptual level at that time. Few of his nonorthogonal proposals had been constructed. The Hanna House (1936), with its hexagonal module, was an exception. An immediate predecessor for Florida Southern among Wright's built designs, as mentioned above, was the Ocatilla Desert Camp (1928, fig. 2.5). Wright and his assistants established the camp as a temporary headquarters while working on projects in the Arizona desert. He placed the camp buildings in a pattern encircling the crest of a hill; the wood and canvas shelters stood apart from each other but were connected and united by a wooden fence around the perimeter. The nearby mountain forms and the contours of the site inspired Wright to adopt a series of thirty- and sixty-degree angles for the fence plan and the cabins' roof structures. In fact, the entire camp was designed on a thirty-sixty-degree, "one-two triangle" system.[86] This layout allowed for a freely arranged group of buildings unified by diagonal planning. The Ocatilla camp anticipated Florida Southern in the way the buildings were connected by a unifying line, in its prominent diagonals in plan and elevation, and in the manner in which it used those same diagonals in the designs for the buildings and their decorative details. Both plans included a variety of building shapes, and both adapted to the contours of a sloping site.

Wright continued to explore the diagonal through the 1930s in the Taliesin Fellowship/Hillside Home School remodeling (1932), Taliesin West (1937), and the Stevens plantation "Auldbrass" (1938), the latter conceived just months after Florida Southern. He also introduced thirty-sixty-ninety triangles into his Usonian houses in 1938 and 1939. By the time Spivey contacted him with an offer to design the college, Wright had firmly established the diagonal as a design motif.

The Florida Southern drawings also reveal Wright's personal symbolism. In the 1920s and 1930s he engaged in a series of formal experiments arising from a belief in the power of "pure form." The genesis of Wright's attitude toward geometric shapes has been the subject of much speculation and is far from clear. But by at least 1912, Wright's philosophy regarding the symbolism of forms had crystallized. "It would carry us far from our subject if we should endeavor to render an accurate, convincing account of the reason why certain geometric forms have come to symbolize for us and patently suggest certain human ideas, moods, sentiments—as for instance: the circle, infinity; the triangle, structural unity; the spire, aspiration; the spiral, organic progress; the square, integrity," he wrote. "It is nevertheless a fact that more or less clearly in the subtle differentiations of these elemental geometric forms, we do sense a certain psychic quality which we may call the 'spell-power' of the form, and with which an artist freely plays, as much at home with it as the musician at his keyboard with his notes."[87] Wright later came to believe in the triangle as a symbol of aspiration (due to its similarity to praying hands) and the circle as an emblem of universality.[88] He felt the appropriate use of such forms had the power to change society. Before this could happen, however, the society had to discover the proper forms, derived from these elemental geometries, to express its cultural identity. This reasoning lies at the heart of Wright's lifelong search for a "democratic" architecture to express the ideals of the American people.[89]

Although the search for a proper expression of his ideas led Wright to fall back on some of his own previous work for inspiration, he also appears to have looked elsewhere, to existing college design and established precedent, and maybe even to antiquity. One historical reference might be found in the cloisters attached to Christian churches in Europe beginning in the middle ages. Wright would have recognized the cloister's significance to a church-sponsored institution. But his modern version—the esplanade—was pulled away from the buildings and made to serve as the campus framework, alluding to traditional religious architecture while adopting it for a new purpose.

Another possible inspiration was mentioned above—Thomas Jefferson's University of Virginia, one of the nation's most famous collegiate designs.[90] Jefferson was one of Wright's heroes; he once described Jefferson as "one of my patron saints."[91] The similarities in their attitudes toward cities, for example, are obvious. Both Jefferson and Wright disliked urbanization and envisioned the ideal society as agrarian. And both spent much of their lives seeking appropriate architectural forms for America. Speculations about Jefferson's possible influence on Wright's designs, however, are difficult to prove. While Wright certainly would have had access to published information on the University of Virginia, it does not appear that he ever visited Charlottesville.[92] Further, Wright's admiration of Jefferson tended more towards the latter's philosophy than his architecture.[93] But there is no denying the formal similarities between the two plans. Both include a conspicuous circular, domed structure at one end of the campus (the Water Dome at Florida Southern, the Rotunda at Virginia) and covered walkways attaching to buildings that are dissimilar but share the same general decorative vocabulary and materials.

Yet there are also significant differences in the ways Jefferson and Wright used these elements. Where Wright detached the esplanades and used them to give form to the campus, the colonnades at Virginia act only to visually unify Jefferson's ensemble. Without them "the Lawn" would remain an organic whole because of the spatial organization of the buildings behind them. Wright's design also resists analogies to Jefferson's use of the central dome or "center." The University of Virginia Rotunda overwhelms the rest of the Lawn and clearly establishes itself as the dominant component of the design. There is no comparable structure at Florida Southern. While it is true that the Water Dome, if it had worked, would have been an imposing presence, it was challenged by the nearby chapel's tower. And from certain locations on the campus, the Water Dome would barely have been visible. In the final analysis, the affinity between Florida Southern and the University of Virginia was stronger in Wright's first attempt at the plan and diminished thereafter as he added diagonals to enliven the arrangement of campus buildings. The motifs of the circular feature and covered walkways, however, remained.

Stanford University is a less obvious influence that might be more immediately linked to Wright. He visited clients Paul and Jean Hanna, who lived next to Stanford, on at least two occasions: in 1936, prior to designing their "Honeycomb House"; and in 1938, after the house was completed.

Figure 2.9. Thomas Jefferson, University of Virginia, Charlottesville, Virginia, 1819–26. Photograph by author.

Paul Hanna wrote that when Wright first toured Stanford, he was very impressed. According to Hanna, "Mr. Wright strolled meditatively through the quadrangles . . . It was clear that he was in a thoughtful mood. He would murmur, 'Magnificent. The hand of that master, Richardson. Nothing matches this architecture in quality on any campus that I know.'"[94] Perhaps more interesting is the fact that Wright's second visit to the Hanna house, where he doubtless saw the Stanford campus, occurred on April 4, 1938—only *seven days* before Ludd Spivey sent his initial telegram. Stanford University would have been fresh in Wright's mind when he received word that someone wanted him to design a college. He could have recalled how Stanford's Romanesque-styled buildings were organized around courtyards and connected by cloister-like arcades. The similarity between Stanford and Florida Southern, with their covered walkways connecting individual buildings, may therefore be more than coincidental. But like the University of Virginia, Stanford's inspiration seems more conceptual than formal.

Perhaps more interesting is historian Vincent Scully's claim that Wright's campus plan was inspired by Hadrian's Villa (early second century). Scully based this attribution on similarities between plan drawings of the two sites: "Florida Southern College would seem to have derived its pivotal circular pool, its long opening and closing diagonal axes with their colonnades, perhaps even its outdoor theatre and top-lighted buildings of many

Figure 2.10. Shepley, Rutan, and Coolidge, Stanford University Inner Quad, Palo Alto, California, 1887–1891. Postcard, author's collection.

shapes—such as the chapel and the library—from the published plans of Hadrian's Villa at Tivoli, of the early second century A.D."[95] The correspondences are indeed suggestive. Scully might have also noted the specific resemblance between Wright's first version of the outdoor swimming pool and the "Canopus" or "Canal," both of which share the same shape, or the integral role that water plays in both designs. Wright certainly knew of Hadrian's Villa and might have visited the site during his six-month stay in Italy in 1910; even if he did not, published plans of the villa were readily available in America. However, Scully's assertion has been challenged, and the authors of an authoritative history of Hadrian's Villa called the evidence of such influence "ambiguous."[96]

The Plan and the Buildings in Context

Wright's Florida Southern College design starkly contrasted with contemporary and traditional college architecture and planning, deviating from accepted stylistic standards and reformulating the orderly Beaux-Arts plans that dominated higher education.[97] His vision represented a bold step in the introduction of modern design to the traditional bastion of the American college. He was in the vanguard of a modernist infiltration of higher education that began at roughly the same time in the late 1930s.[98]

Prevailing attitudes toward collegiate architecture favored the Gothic, Colonial, and Georgian styles, which reflected the "conservative tendency" of academic architecture according to the author of a popular 1928 book on American architecture.[99] Architects Jens Fredrick Larson and Archie Palmer, in *Architectural Planning of the American College*, similarly suggested new campus buildings could find a suitable expression only in the "Early American," "Classic Revival," "Hispanic or Mediterranean," or Gothic styles.[100] The first three styles were considered "native" to America. Larson and Palmer spoke for many architects and college administrators when they claimed, "If there is any institution in modern life which cannot cast off the past, which must be built upon the treasures of its rich heritage, it is the college."[101] They gave no specific advice regarding campus planning—despite the book's title—but the many examples the authors used to demonstrate appropriate planning all contained similar arrangements of dominant and secondary axes, bilateral symmetry, and orderly quadrangles surrounded by comparably styled buildings, much like Trimble's early plan for the Southern College campus (see fig. 1.1).

Plans for higher education facilities were addressed rather extensively in a 1929 book by Charles Klauder and Herbert Wise intended to "register at its best the present-day theory and practice of college architecture."[102] After acknowledging the debt owed to the World's Columbian Exposition of 1893 and the Senate Park Commission's 1902 Plan for Washington, D.C., the authors imparted their principles for the college plan. First and foremost was *order*—"Heaven's first law." According to Klauder and Wise:

> Order, then, is the guiding star under which a development plan is desired, conceived and followed. That the group of buildings shall not be a motley jumble of structures so located as to be at odds with each other, displaying discordant styles, erected at haphazard, confusing to beholders and irritating to occupants, but rather that it should be a homogeneous, clearly apprehended scheme, in which there is a studied and happy balance of things, of buildings located with regard to their functions, importance and architectural effect, of natural views conserved and topographical advantages skillfully exploited.[103]

Klauder and Wise celebrated the strictly regulated, orderly Ecole des Beaux-Arts campus design through numerous examples. They believed the architectural style of college buildings should relate to the campus plan. Interestingly, they admitted such a formal plan was not *always* ideal. Formal plans called for styles such as "Classic or Renaissance, Georgian, Colonial, regular, symmetrical, rectilinear." Informal plans were best suited to "Gothic, or picturesque and irregular, unsymmetrical" buildings.[104]

These examples, along with others from leading practitioners of and commentators on college architecture, demonstrate the conservative aspect of academic design and planning in the thirties.[105] College planning remained heavily influenced by the Columbian Exposition and the City Beautiful movement. Educators and designers favored formal, rectilinear plans, relying heavily on the type of order advocated by Klauder and Wise. A rediscovery of Jefferson's University of Virginia by architects of the late nineteenth century inspired numerous imitators and affected planning well into the 1900s.[106] For campus buildings, administrators held fast in their belief that only the traditional historical styles properly expressed the ideals of higher education. In 1937 *Life* magazine opined, "There is scarcely an institution of higher learning in the U.S. which does not subscribe to the belief that it is not complete until it has a row of columns somewhere on its campus."[107] And as Wright formulated his Florida Southern design, an article in the *Architectural Forum* recognized that "in government and institutional buildings the influence of tradition, so-called, has been decisive, and purely utilitarian problems are generally subordinated to other factors . . . thus colleges are now Gothic, now Georgian, with side excursions from Byzantine to Spanish. There can be no doubt that this group, almost the last trench of the old guard, will move toward modern only over their dead bodies."[108]

In the spring of 1939, less than a year after executing the first drawings of the Florida Southern plan, Wright was invited to London by the Royal Institute of British Architects to give a series of lectures. In one of those lectures, he explained his approach to planning in a manner directly related to his work in Lakeland. "So modern architecture rejects the major-axis and minor-axis of classic architecture," Wright said, alluding to designs like Trimble's 1921 master plan for Southern College. "It rejects all grandomania, every building that would stand in military fashion heels together, eyes front, something on the right hand and something on the left hand." He argued instead for an organic architecture that "favors the reflex, the natural easy attitude, the occult symmetry of grace and rhythm affirming the ease, grace, and naturalness of natural life," invoking language similar to that employed in the letter to Spivey the previous fall, when he boasted, "The reflex enters into architecture in these plans for Florida Southern as against the regimentation characteristic of the classic or Gothic architecture which have become a college habit in America."[109]

Wright was able to synthesize old and new ideas in creating a plan at Lakeland that exuded a tension between order and irregularity. Instead of copying the "ideal campus," using Klauder and Wise's "delightful vistas projected between rows of buildings and ending at an imposing architectural mass embellished with entrance, tower, or dome," Wright created an arrangement that, at the deepest level, was governed by order, but was not balanced, symmetrical, or axial.[110] Florida Southern had no main entrance—it could be accessed anywhere. The buildings did not face each other in ordered rows across a lawn or quadrangle, as was the 1930s custom, but were scattered about the sloping lakeside, sliding toward the water. There was not one single focal point but three—the Water Dome, chapel, and library—in a triangular relationship. The buildings' angled relationships to each other and the plan's multiple axes countered the formal symmetry then in vogue. Yet the plan was not chaotic—there was order in the consistent use of thirty- and sixty-degree angles, in the connections between buildings, and in the use of the same materials for all structures. In this sense, Florida Southern revealed a kinship with twentieth-century neo-Gothic campuses like Duke and Princeton, which likewise sought unity through style.

The buildings, like the plan, were a bold deviation from the norm. When Wright criticized Florida Southern's existing buildings as ugly "boxes with holes punched in them," he expressed a deeply held conviction that American collegiate architecture was badly done. In a 1931 lecture at Princeton, Wright had attacked the neo-Gothic buildings of the University of Chicago as characteristic of an unfortunate trend in higher education: "If environment is significant and indicative, what does this highly reactionary, extensive, and expensive scene-painting by means of hybrid collegiate Gothic signify? . . . why should an American university in a land of democratic ideals in a machine age be characterized by secondhand adaptation of Gothic forms, themselves adapted previously to our own adoption by a feudalistic age with tools to use and conditions to face totally different from anything we can call our own?"[111] Two decades later he would tell Florida Southern's students, "No one can refer to the buildings of colleges today as architecture. They are hang-overs. No longer indicative of our times. That's why we are high and dry today."[112] Wright hinted at an appropriate college environment when he described the ideal university in *The Disappearing City*. "Here in quiet retreats made beautiful and appropriate for reflection and concentration," he wrote, invoking Emerson.[113] And when construction of his vision for Florida Southern was under way, he implied that it would exemplify this idea. "Students here will go out with a better sense of beauty than those at Harvard and Yale and other Gothic designed colleges but it should be so, by all that's holy," he told them.[114]

Unfortunately, the fantastic, nontraditional scheme Wright presented in the campus drawings would never exist in the real world in the form he imagined, and many of those prospective buildings would be changed or disappear even before working drawings were made. Spivey and Wright undoubtedly knew the process of creating a new college would be slow and arduous, but in all likelihood neither expected that two long decades later the project would remain unfinished. They might have found clues, however, in the first few months.

THREE *"Out of the ground and into the light"* A Campus Struggles to Grow, 1938–1941

A contract between Wright and Spivey, dated the same day that Wright sent Spivey the letter describing his "gracious pattern" for the campus, cemented a relationship that would last two decades. But the first years of that relationship would bring distress and disappointment to both men as the school struggled through the economic depression while trying to construct Wright's extraordinary plan.

The Pfeiffer Chapel

The contract probably did little to alleviate Spivey's anxiety over Wright's working pace. For months Spivey had unsuccessfully prompted Wright for the first drawings. By the end of September, four months had passed since Wright's visit without any concrete indication of his ideas for the school. However, Wright had a reason for his deliberate pace; his letters to Spivey clarify that he did not want to rush the process of designing the chapel, because it was part of a larger ensemble. "I think the need at the present moment is not so much the chapel building as to make available a suitable presentation of the whole project for campaign purposes—and this is expensive business—taking more time than you might imagine because I intend the whole to be as splendidly correlated as it is conceived," he wrote in an effort to appease Spivey.[1] Two months later he added, "You should remember that it is not just a chapel we are designing but the first unit in an aggregation of buildings—and what we work out now decides the fate of the whole. We can save you many tens of thousands of dollars by faithful preparation now."[2] Wright finally sent the initial drawings in late October or early November.

While the campus plan featured a trio of focal points, the clear architectural highlight, from the very beginning of the design process, was the chapel. Wright conceived it as a modern alternative to the neo-Gothic religious architecture prevalent at the time, while also retaining the spiritual nature of the traditional church. The finished chapel would be a superb example of Wright's ability to create a space that is both intimate and grand at the same time.

The college desperately needed a new chapel, not only to embody the Jones Foundation but also as a practical necessity. For years chapel ses-

Figure 3.1. Frank Lloyd Wright, Annie M. Pfeiffer Chapel, preliminary drawing, 1938. Copyright © 2009 The Frank Lloyd Wright Foundation, Taliesin West, Scottsdale, Ariz. 3816.003.

sions and gatherings on campus had been conducted in a minimal outdoor chapel with folding chairs beneath a Spanish-moss-covered wire frame. When inclement weather interfered, services were often moved into the gymnasium. Large convocations took place in a neighborhood Methodist church.

The "Programme for University" document contained few specific requirements for the new chapel: 750 seats, a nonsectarian nature, and a "new form" with "simple materials." Wright's handwritten additions to that page were far more revealing, indicating the direction of his thinking at an early stage. His impressionistic notations included "Integrated sound and lighting"; "Light effects—concerted with sound"; "Vistas of garden and trees—earth and sky"; "Taking the place of cloistered interior effects"; and "Correlative of form, color, sound."[3] It is significant that Wright was already thinking in aesthetic terms about the chapel because such notes are absent from the other sections of the "Programme." This indicates that Wright approached the chapel differently from the rest of the campus.

The "Programme" also included a hasty sketch by Wright at the bottom of the chapel page. This sketch, in the nature of a traditional Ecole des Beaux-Arts *esquisse*, established the motif that would guide the design through to the finished building—a horizontal base supporting a tall vertical tower.

The existing drawings show the chapel followed the same pattern of development as the overall campus plan, evolving from orthogonal to diagonal forms. What seems to be the earliest version of the campus plan—the orthogonal design described in the previous chapter—depicted the chapel footprint as a rotated square overlaid with a rectangle, creating a main body and angled, prow-like lateral arms. That may have been the second incarnation, however, because two undated drawings show a less sophisticated chapel plan with two rectangles superimposed to make a cross.[4] One of these undated drawings also indicates the tower structure that could be found, with some alterations, in the final building: a gabled roof over the center of the auditorium, and rising out of it a tall tower with two parallel concrete walls connected by five triangular "bow-tie" braces whose thirty-degree angles echoed the gables and mimicked diagonals later found in the campus plan. In this central area of the building, Wright wrote "caryo," most likely an alternate spelling of "karyo," which means a kernel or nucleus of a biological cell, implying the organic quality of the tower growing out of the base as a flower blooms from a seed.[5]

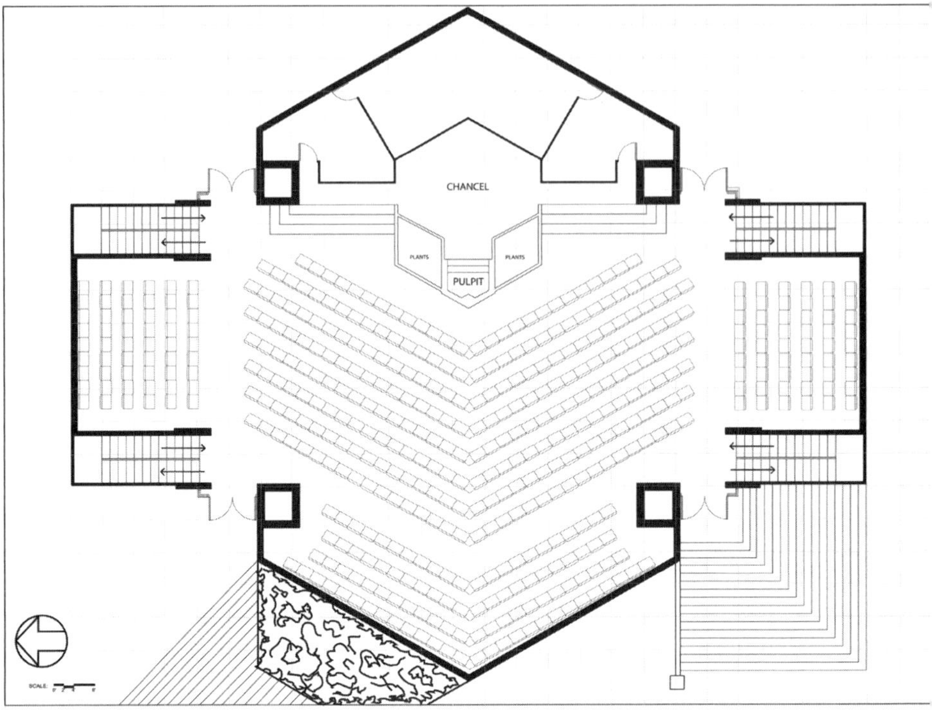

Figure 3.2. Pfeiffer Chapel plan, based on original drawings. Courtesy of Dan Price and Nathaniel J. Turner.

In later drawings Wright changed the chapel's rectangular main block into an elongated hexagon with lateral arms, and it is in this form that the building appeared in the next group of campus plans. Wright rotated the hex so that a main axis ran from one corner to its opposite to establish directionality. He followed this by placing the stage, pulpit, and choir loft at the "top" (east) side of the hexagon. These moves produced a design closely related to Wright's unbuilt proposal for the New Theatre, Woodstock, New York (1931). The floor plans of the two buildings were almost identical. Both structures were hexagonal in plan, with continental-style seating arrangements (no center aisle), and exteriors with smooth, unadorned surfaces and trellises over side balconies. Wright also repeated the hexagonal form for the interior space of his proposed Model Theatre project for the Florida Southern campus (as described in chapter 4).

Wright placed entries and stairways in the chapel's four corners, where the hex met the rectangular arms. The main entries were behind and to the sides of the pulpit, a strategy Wright borrowed from his Unity Temple

(1904). Seating on the main floor and balconies would be intimate, with none of the nearly 1,000 seats more than 50 feet from the speaker. The interior mezzanine extended outside at the lateral wings to become exterior balconies—a move that emphasized the unity of interior and exterior, and one that Wright would repeat in his designs for the administration building and a later version of the unbuilt music building. At the mezzanine level, Wright put a choir loft above the stage, partially shielded by a ninety-foot concrete block screen perforated with hexagons that suggest the chapel's plan.[6]

Wright wanted all attention in the interior directed to two places: the pulpit and the overhead skylights. The massive pulpit emphasized the importance of the sermon in the Methodist service, while the skylights illuminated the interior, made the building's fascinating tower structure visible, and directed one's eyes skyward.[7] Wright placed the pulpit on a stage in the building's eastern angle. It was made with a concrete block base and overlapping cypress planks above, taking the form of a ship's prow, which further reinforced the diagonal motif. Large planters flanked the pulpit, which contained seating behind the speaker's lectern. The audience seats

Figure 3.3. Pfeiffer Chapel, original interior. Florida Southern College Archives.

faced the pulpit at thirty-degree angles, echoing the angle of the pulpit's peak; the seats were individual rather than bench seats, made of cypress in the Florida Southern shops.

Above the auditorium, glass skylights gave the audience a prospect of the fantastic carillon tower while bathing the interior in natural light. There were five skylights in total—two smaller ones over both the choir loft and

Figure. 3.4. Pfeiffer Chapel, skylights. Copyright © 2009 The Frank Lloyd Wright Foundation, Taliesin West, Scottsdale, Ariz. 3816.073.

Figure 3.5. Pfeiffer Chapel, 1990s. Photograph by author.

west balcony, and the central light well. This meant that the most rewarding view out of the chapel for visitors in their seats would be up—there were no traditional windows (except for the doors behind the seats in the mezzanine arms) and, apart from the entry doors, no place within the seating area from which the ground outside was visible. The tower's design magnificently displayed Wright's engineering talents. He cantilevered the superstructure over the auditorium so that no supports would block the audience's sight lines. The tower's weight was carried on four hollow piers, six feet wide, standing at the hexagon's corners near the entries, leaving the interior free and open.[8]

The steel and concrete tower would become the most identifiable object on campus. In his original conception Wright intended the tower to be eighty-five feet tall with chimes or bells inside. Its two parallel walls would meet each other at only five points. These pyramidal bow-tie forms would allow the forces of the tower walls to counteract each other and thereby achieve balance. Running throughout the tower was a metal latticework intended to support plants and vines, in keeping with the outdoor garden theme; flower boxes above the skylights and trellises on the outdoor balconies reinforced this motif.[9] The great openness of the interior, which is totally unexpected from the outside, correlates with Wright's notation on the "Programme for University": "Taking the place of cloistered interior effects."[10]

During the design process Wright reduced the tower's height to sixty-five feet and removed two of the bow ties. In its overall form the tower recalled a similar structure he once proposed for the unbuilt San Marcos in the Desert project (1928). In addition to being a daring way to expose the tower's innovative structure, the open space between the concrete tower walls provided resonating space for chimes. Three spherical bronze bells were hung above each pyramidal connection. Their sound would reverberate in the tower and travel across the campus and its neighborhood. The carillon had been one of the salient elements of the chapel design even before Wright became involved. The school's desire to include bells may have been a response to the nearby Bok Tower in Lake Wales, which opened in 1929 and quickly become a tourist stop with its fifty-three-bell carillon.

The chapel's final form stayed true to Wright's hasty sketch in the "Programme." The structure balanced both directions and textures. A horizontal base of three layers—consisting of patterned concrete blocks at ground level, smooth plastered surfaces above, and a third level of concrete blocks on top—supported the vertical tower, which combined smooth surfaces, coffered squares, and diagonal supports.[11] Most of the blocks on the lowest level contained colored glass—more than 50,000 cubes of red, amber, blue, green, and white glass inserted, by hand, into the freshly molded blocks. These colored jewels were intended to sparkle in the light and add to the church's ethereal quality. Approximately 6,000 blocks in 46 different designs were used in the chapel, including perforated blocks with colored inserts, unperforated blocks, and blocks that were plastered over to obtain a smooth, even surface.[12] This example of individuality and unity in detail provided a microcosm of the campus as a whole.

The original color of the chapel's plastered sections matched the golden or light straw color of the concrete blocks in an effort to establish continuity. The three distinct exterior levels of the chapel's horizontal base may have been intentionally created by Wright with the surrounding citrus grove in mind. Distant photographs of the chapel during and after construction show that the height of the leaves and branches of the citrus trees corresponded almost perfectly to the blank middle zone of the chapel's base, so viewers would see the patterned blocks above and below but the stuccoed center surface would largely be blocked by foliage. If one considers how many trees Wright envisioned around the chapel, it is fair to assume that Wright made those parts of the building that would be most visible more visually interesting than those that would be covered. While there is no documentary evidence to support this assertion, it is not implausible given Wright's sensitivity to natural features and his determination to link buildings to their surroundings.[13]

Wright's intentions in creating the chapel can be read in two statements he made during and after construction. Late in 1938 he told a Florida Southern faculty member and reporter for the local newspaper that the chapel "will be perhaps the most spirited and spiritual expression of all the buildings . . . It will be free from the drawbacks of heavy stone masonry. After all, a chapel building is a thing of the spirit, and best serves its purpose when the body is comfortable, which it never was in Gothic architecture."[14] And in a March 1941 letter he sent to Spivey to be read at the chapel's dedication, Wright claimed, "When the flowers are in the boxes and climbing

Figure 3.6. Pfeiffer Chapel, showing the abundant citrus grove that originally covered the site. Florida Southern College Archives.

up the metal trellises, and the round bronze bells are ringing above them Florida will have found an expression in building of her proper name."[15] In these statements we see Wright promoting a religious architecture that uses modern principles and materials to evoke both the unique character of its location and the spirit of beauty that has infused religious structures of the past.

Despite the reference to the discomfort of Gothic architecture, he did not feel that all aspects of the Gothic heritage—which was actually alive and well in the form of a neo-Gothic revival headed by architects like Ralph Adams Cram—should be discarded. In fact, the Florida Southern chapel is probably best understood as a new modernized form of Gothic. Like its medieval predecessors, it used structural innovation combined with an interest in verticality and light to create beauty. Inside the chapel one's eyes are instinctively drawn upwards to the light pouring through the glass roof, inviting contemplation of the heavens. Meanwhile, the twinkling colored glass in the pierced block surrounding the first floor brings to mind the great religious tradition of stained glass, but in an abstract way. Those walls, despite their concrete construction, are actually screens, since the building's weight is carried on the four corner piers; in that sense, they are comparable to Gothic construction yet also represent the dynamic possibilities of modern architecture. Years later Wright would acknowledge the value of these qualities and explain his approach to designing religious architecture in an article entitled "Is It Good-By to Gothic?" In the text Wright answered the question of its title affirmatively: "as a style. But not to its spirit of reverence for beauty. That should be expressed in new styles attuned to the new day, using steel, concrete, glass, and other modern materials." He elaborated, "All forms of religion have a basic desire to function in harmony with their beliefs and I try to help them—to materialize their ideas in something beautiful for all humanity."[16]

Wright's creation certainly represented a departure from contemporary Methodist churches. In the late nineteenth century many Methodist congregations had favored an auditorium plan—a square, circular, or octagonal building with inclined rows of seats and radiating aisles focusing attention on a pulpit placed on a stage or in a corner. These churches helped highlight the sermons and musical performances that dominated the Methodist liturgy at the time. Romanesque and Renaissance Revival were the most popular exterior styles, with Gothic Revival also common. By the twenties and thirties the popularity of auditorium plans began to wane, and a new configuration called the divided chancel plan appeared more frequently. Divided chancel churches looked back to religious tradition by moving the altar and choir seats farther from the congregation, enlarging the chancel area, and centering attention on the altar rather than the pulpit. This plan was often combined with a long nave and center aisle to form a rectangular building. Simultaneously, the Methodists were caught up in the same Gothic Revival craze that swept through other Protestant denominations. Although the Gothic style was favored, many congregations instead opted for neo-Georgian or generic Colonial churches.[17]

Wright's chapel is closest in spirit to the auditorium, or pulpit-centered, plan. Against the fashionable trend, he designed a structure without a nave or center aisle, and with an extremely close proximity of congregation to the chancel, an inconspicuous altar, and an emphasis on acoustics. Wright used the word "sound" three times in his notes on the chapel in the "Programme for University," indicating the importance in his mind of creating a space to accommodate the traditional Methodist emphasis on the spoken word delivered from the pulpit. In some small ways the chapel did follow the advice of Elbert Conover, director of the Methodist Episcopal Church's Bureau of Architecture, in that it had a level floor and colorful light (although not from stained glass windows), and it attempted to make "the Divine Presence appreciable" through the building.[18] But Wright's methods for doing so contrasted with normal Methodist architectural principles. He was oriented toward the future rather than the past or present, and his notation on the "Programme" document that the chapel should be "Suitable for new rituals wherein all there will be one" is revealing.[19]

Wright completed the drawings for the chapel in October 1938. Spivey responded positively to the first images, saying they were "very wonderful" and that "Everyone is highly excited."[20] On November 20 the local newspaper published a drawing of the chapel that emphasized the tower's height and the extensive greenery overflowing the building throughout the exterior. The reporter stated, "The chapel is expected to become an architectural monument of major interest in the south, attracting thousands of visitors here each year."[21]

Florida Southern held a cornerstone ceremony for the chapel a week later. Wright was unable to attend that event but sent his regards. E. Stanley Jones, the main attraction, roused the crowd with a speech about the future of Christianity and the relationship between science and religion. "I lay this cornerstone, not in my honor, but that you may lay your lives upon the altar of Christianity," said Jones. "Christianity is within one generation of extinction always. You must always get the next generation. Christians must out-think pagans, out-live them and out-die them."[22] He also explained how science and religion complement rather than conflict with each other; while science "weighs and measures," religion "evaluates" and adds spirit to scientific findings. His remarks illustrated his ongoing interest in promoting the reconciliation of the two fields, as well as the thorough religious emphasis that first motivated the Jones Educational Foundation, an emphasis that disappeared over time as Spivey steered the campaign more toward campus improvement and promotion and away from Jones's original intentions.

But trouble loomed behind the scenes of the festive occasion. Florida's citrus crop was threatened by an impending natural disaster in the fall of 1938, and this crisis directly impacted Spivey's ability to raise money for Wright's buildings. "I have been at a loss to tell you what to do about continuing with the plans for the other buildings right now," wrote Spivey. "I just do not know how our funds are going to come in. Up to now, they are not coming in very rapidly. As you likely know, Florida depends largely upon her citrus fruit. This year we are getting absolutely nothing for the fruit. Practically everybody who is interested in this project is in the fruit business, and since we are not getting anything for the fruit it is difficult to get money."[23] Money would become a constant source of friction, with Spivey and Wright taking the first steps in what would be a continuing dance of begging, cajoling, threatening, and stalling that lasted almost twenty years. Wright responded to Spivey's concerns about the citrus situation with patience—at first. "I understood we had some $365,000.00 pledged to begin with and could go right ahead so I was a little disconcerted to find we would have to proceed so slowly," he wrote. "But I've made the readjustments and realize the part I must play to help you get the necessary money together . . . I am keeping toes and fingers crossed, also, hoping your pledges come through."[24]

The chapel's financing was in better shape. In May 1938 Spivey had persuaded wealthy philanthropist Annie M. Pfeiffer of New York City to donate $50,000 "to erect a library or any other unit you care for in honor of Henry and Anne Pfeiffer."[25] Pfeiffer became associated with the Jones Educational Foundation through her friendships with Methodist bishop Rev. W. F. Anderson and Mrs. Charles Hawkins, the wife of a Florida Southern faculty member.[26] Shortly thereafter Spivey convinced her to put the money toward the new chapel; in recognition of her generosity, the building would be called the Annie M. Pfeiffer Chapel. Annie Pfeiffer and her husband, Henry, eventually contributed more than $40 million to various American colleges, lending their names to Pfeiffer College (now University) in North Carolina and buildings at Bennett College for Women, West Virginia Wesleyan College, and Illinois Wesleyan University, as well as endowed chairs at several institutions.[27]

Block-making

The Pfeiffers' largesse was helpful but not enough to pay for the entire chapel, and by early 1939 pressure built as the project inched forward at a glacial pace. The lack of money contributed to somewhat strained relations between the educator and the architect. The year began with workers clearing sites for the new chapel, esplanades, and plazas. But this initial activity was not enough for Spivey's tastes: he wanted swifter progress, and he wrote to Wright in January, "The psychology of this affair here is pretty bad. The report is spread everywhere that the whole project has fallen through. I must tell you that it is highly important that we lay some blocks pretty soon. I hope you will keep this in mind."[28] The concrete blocks, however, would take almost eight more months to perfect.

These concrete blocks were the crucial element in Wright's construction system. He started using concrete "textile blocks" in his California houses of the 1920s.[29] By the late 1930s Wright had refined the block construction system. The Florida Southern buildings employed blocks of 36 inches by 9 inches, 4 inches thick, laid together without mortar and connected by ⅜-inch metal rods running in a grid pattern of grooves behind the blocks. (This netting of metal rods also acted to translate the grid system used to create the campus plan into the vertical dimension.) The grooves were then filled with cement grout. Each wall was essentially a double shell, with a space in between the blocks for air circulation. Some of the blocks would contain perforations filled with colored glass inserts. In other places the block was stuccoed for a smooth, contrasting surface. Often this surface treatment is indistinguishable from poured concrete. The completed campus would require more than forty versions of the block design.

Wright originally conceived the textile block system as a way to save money by eliminating the need for skilled craftsmen, and this rationale was particularly appropriate for Florida Southern. Early in the project Spivey

Figure 3.7. Concrete blocks, Florida Southern College. Photograph by author.

and Wright agreed to use student labor for construction. Spivey devised a program where students could reduce their tuition by working on the buildings. In the beginning, students worked three days a week—mixing and pouring concrete for the foundations and walkways and making concrete blocks—and attended classes three days.[30]

Workers made the blocks by mixing coquina, a soft limestone formed from coral reefs and seashell fragments (and a traditional Florida building material), with sand, cement mix, and water, and then pouring the mixture into wooden and aluminum forms that created the block shape and imprinted an appropriate design.[31] After molding, the blocks were set out to harden for two to three weeks before being ready for use.

The idea of using local soil as a construction material was not new for Wright. The idea originated in the 1920s with his work in California. There he encountered a culture that, like Florida, had no real architectural tradition apart from an imported Spanish colonial heritage. Wright set about creating a new image for the state, an early exemplar of the regional modernism he would emphasize later in his career. He described his work on the Alice Barnsdall complex at Olive Hill in Los Angeles as "a new type in California, a land of romance—a land that, as yet, has no characteristic building material and no type of building except one carried there by Spanish missionaries in early days." That new type involved the textile block. Wright instructed workers to use the "gravel of decayed granite" from the area in the cement used to form the blocks; this assured a relationship between the building and the land it sat upon.[32]

Block-making efforts in Lakeland occupied much of the first year of construction. While leveling the site and pouring the chapel foundation went smoothly, it took considerable time to find the right mixture of ingredients, in terms of color and compressive strength, for the blocks. As he often did, Wright suggested on-site materials to lessen construction costs and connect the buildings with the site. On his second visit to Florida Southern in December 1938, he supervised attempts to make blocks by combining sand from the orange groves with cement, but these blocks crumbled to pieces, probably because of accumulated fertilizers. After that, sand was trucked in from other Florida locations and mixed with coquina from the St. Augustine area. Testing of various formulas for the concrete blocks began in January and would continue through the summer without success.

In February 1939 the student laborers finished pouring the chapel's foundation, but work stopped to await the blocks. Spivey grew anxious. He had a potential donor interested in the chapel but felt that unless construction

Figure 3.8. Student laborers constructing esplanade. Florida Southern College Archives.

resumed by early March, the opportunity would pass. Wright responded with a call for patience: "Please be patient. We may seem slow but we will be faithful and we do know our stuff."[33] A month later Spivey begged Wright to come for a campus visit for fundraising purposes and to assure those who had already donated that everything was all right. Wright came, and might have assuaged some fears, but his appearance had no effect on the pace of construction. By May, Spivey was alarmed. "Things are moving along pretty slowly here at the college. No blocks have been made as yet," he wrote to Wright's chief assistant and son-in-law, William Wesley (Wes) Peters.[34] In June he grew desperate. "You know why I am having such a hard time getting money. The basement has been standing here for more than six months without anything being done about it. The people are not going to pay their pledges until they see some work going on here on the campus."[35]

Meanwhile the block-testing process continued. Correspondence indicates that the first blocks included a white lime base and local sand; by spring a type of cement called "Santa Cruz Hi Silica" had been added to the mix. In April the blocks were still not the proper color, which Wright described as "light flesh colored."[36] By May a flesh-colored "Master-Builder Mix" was being added, and strength tests were ordered; experiments were performed using the Master-Builder Mix for the facing and not the entire block. The blocks failed the strength tests, and the process reached a standstill despite Spivey's protests.

In early August 1939 C. W. Palmore, a local banker who was supervising the block-making process, made some important suggestions to Wright. First, Palmore advised removing rock from the mixture because it was creating an odd appearance and weakening the blocks. And he also suggested Wright try "a beautiful golden sand" he had seen a few weeks earlier at Daytona Beach. That sand was crushed from coquina rock, the soft limestone with seashell fragments. Palmore speculated that the sand would produce the proper color without the need for artificial color mixes, thus saving thousands of dollars.[37] A few test blocks were made and sent to Wright; he felt the color was "too muddy" at first and suggested mixing the coquina sand with white California cement.[38] This mixture apparently worked. By the end of August 1939—after almost eight months of experimentation—Wright was finally satisfied with the strength and appearance of the blocks.

Two articles from the Florida Southern student newspaper described the block construction system in early September, as work proceeded on the chapel, the first Wright building on campus. H. M. Contner, a contractor in charge of mass-producing the blocks, explained that the blocks were made of two different dry mixtures: one cement and sand, the other cement and ground coquina rock with a little water. A former worker later recollected that the first mix—or facing—into the wooden mold was damp coquina sand and cement, and on top of that was added a mix of gray cement for the parts of the block that would never show. The 30,000 blocks to be used in the chapel were shaped into molds, then placed on pallets to harden for twenty-four hours, then stacked in the open air and watered daily for seventeen to twenty days (although Wright requested the blocks be damp cured for at least thirty days). Contner's work crews were averaging five hours per day at that point and turning out 125 blocks per day; their goal was 2,000 blocks per week.[39]

Faculty Housing and Dormitory Projects

Although clearly frustrated with the project's sluggish pace, Spivey pushed forward during the work stoppage with his plans for the campus. He had asked Wright to design two dormitories, each capable of holding fifty men, along McDonald Street at the campus's north end, and twenty faculty houses on property adjacent to the school. Wright designed the faculty houses later that year as simple two-bedroom structures similar to the Jacobs House (1936), the first of Wright's Usonian houses. The faculty houses borrowed the Usonians' simple internal design, with the living room and bedrooms radiating out from a centralized "workspace" (kitchen). However, the faculty houses did not share the overall floor plan of the later Usonians, which were generally designed in an L or I shape. The faculty house plans more closely resemble the cruciform room arrangements of Wright's Prairie houses of the early century.

In response to Spivey's request for two dormitories, Wright proposed a complex of three identical buildings, each with two wings of two stories. He designed the buildings using a three-foot-square module, and according to the plans they would have been approximately 210 feet long and 19 feet wide. Each dormitory wing could accommodate between forty and fifty-five men. The two wings were angled away from each other but were joined by an esplanade and a short, screened pergola. Perspective drawings show the buildings to be constructed with the decorative textile blocks used in

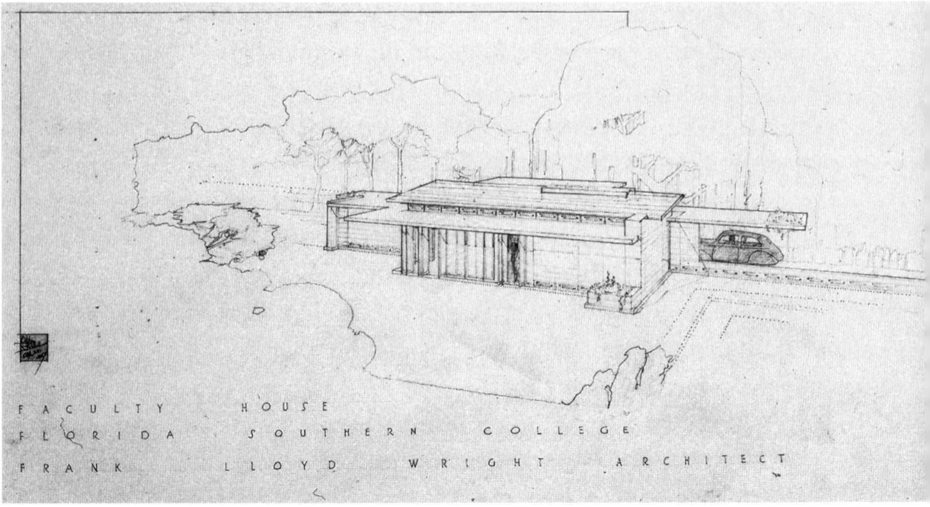

Figure 3.9. Frank Lloyd Wright, proposal for unbuilt faculty house, 1939. Copyright © 2009 The Frank Lloyd Wright Foundation, Taliesin West, Scottsdale, Ariz. 3922.003.

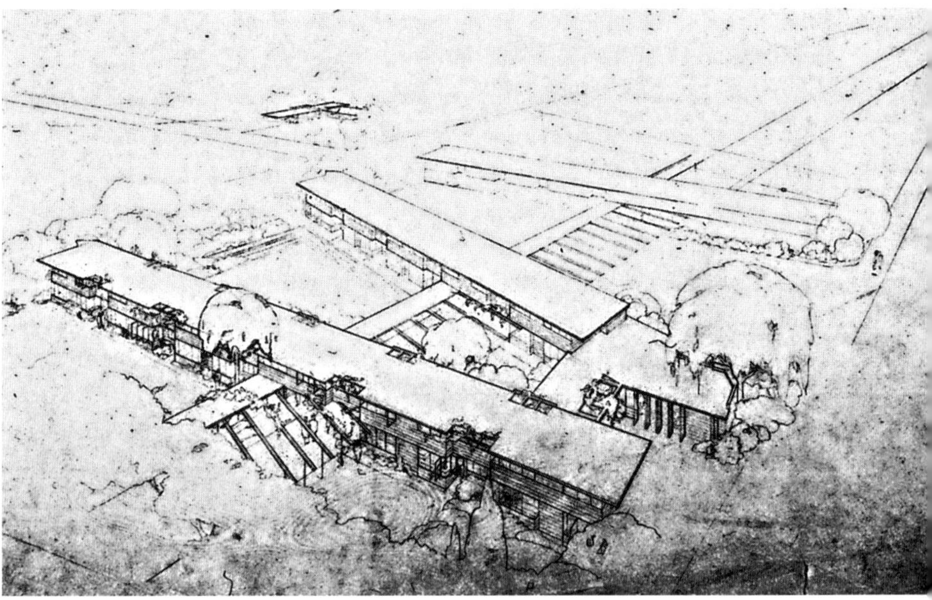

Figure 3.10. Frank Lloyd Wright, proposal for unbuilt dormitory, 1939. Copyright © 2009 The Frank Lloyd Wright Foundation, Taliesin West, Scottsdale, Ariz. 3922.008.

the rest of the campus. Each dormitory had a flat projecting roof. All student rooms had balconies, and a continuous walkway on the upper floors along one side of the buildings served as a passage to the individual rooms in lieu of an interior corridor.

The last plans Wright drew for the faculty houses showed only fourteen of them, and they were relocated to be on campus, on two large tracts of land immediately south of the proposed boys' dormitories. Although Wright prepared working drawings for the faculty houses, and met with Federal Housing Administration (FHA) officials in Washington, D.C., to discuss the project, they never materialized. Their fate is shrouded in mystery. In February 1940 Spivey reported that the FHA had requested changes to the houses, mainly concerning the need for pitched instead of flat roofs; however, correspondence between FHA administrators reveals that they were more concerned with the proposed wall system and the failure to meet FHA Standards of Minimum Construction regarding painting of woodwork, ceiling heights, fireplace masonry, and other small details.[40] The FHA administrators also disliked the houses' proposed "extreme modernistic architecture," and in one letter a "Senior Valuator" in the Tampa, Florida, office was encouraged to try to convince Spivey that "if he will change his program to a more conventional type of house that will be more in keeping with the surroundings of the neighborhood," the project would stand a greater chance of approval.[41] Wright responded testily that the technical changes would "senselessly add seven hundred dollars per dwelling," but agreed to make them.[42]

The record is then mute until the fall of 1941, when Wes Peters sent two messages to Spivey, inquiring about the progress on the faculty houses. Spivey's response is not known, nor is it clear whether Peters specifically meant the Wright-designed faculty houses. Wright's versions were never constructed. And the dormitories never advanced beyond the planning stage; their proposed site was occupied in the late forties by residence halls and fraternity houses designed by Miami architect Robert Law Weed.

Democracy and Dictatorship

As the chapel walls began to rise, Spivey's attention was drawn to nonarchitectural matters. The first had to do with his campaign to establish Florida Southern as a center for the study and propagation of American democracy. During the previous fall semester Spivey had announced the creation of the country's first "Chair of Democracy" as part of the E. Stanley Jones Educational Foundation. The chair would be used to "combat Communism, Fascism and other un-American trends."[43] The program started with a visit and speech from Dr. William E. Dodd, formerly a University of Chicago professor and U.S. ambassador to Nazi Germany. Now Spivey was ready to fully implement his plan. In November he organized a "Congress on Democracy," which included the formal dedication of the Chair of Democracy. The three-day event brought various political and religious dignitaries to campus, culminating in a speech by the head of the new Federal Security Agency, Paul V. McNutt.

Spivey's interest in issues of patriotism and democracy was long-standing. In the late 1930s the Lakeland newspapers regularly reported his warnings about the dual threats of communism and fascism and his opposition to Japan and Germany.[44] In 1939, when organizing the Congress on Democracy, he was the Florida State Chairman of the American Civil Liberties Union.[45] Spivey was also involved with the Freedoms Foundation, an organization formed to promote awareness and appreciation of democracy. At about the same time, he instituted a Department of American Culture at Florida Southern, a kind of proto–American Studies program, designed to instill national pride and "combat Socialism and Communism on the College Campus."[46]

Spivey's belief in democracy as an antidote to the communist and totalitarian forces threatening the western world was bolstered by his opinion that democracy and religion were equivalent. His personal opinions could be discerned in a précis for a course titled "Christianity in America," prepared by a faculty team charged with developing the proposed Department of American Culture. "Growth of respect for individual personality. Democracy borrowed this conception from religion," stated the course description. "The genius of Christianity is Democracy. Democracy is nothing but the political name for the ideals which Christianity brought into the world as religion. These ideals, whether one indicates them by their religious or their political name, are threatened today."[47] Spivey probably felt the interrelated nature of religion and democracy made his school, which already emphasized the connections between religion and science, a perfect location for spearheading the campaign to revitalize the democratic spirit of America's college students.

Issues of democracy and dictatorship also engaged Spivey in November 1939 for altogether different reasons than the Congress on Democracy.

That month a faculty rebellion of sorts arose at Florida Southern, creating a challenge that would distract Spivey for more than a year. The crisis was instigated by Gordon Halstead, a disgruntled sociology instructor. Halstead accused Spivey of acting as a dictator over the college, among other things. In a letter to E. Stanley Jones, Halstead asserted that Spivey, despite his professed love of democracy and freedom, stifled it among students and faculty. The letter began with a claim that Florida Southern students had very little interest in the Jones Educational Foundation "because they were convinced that the Foundation and your name were being used merely to erect some new buildings." Halstead then launched a litany of complaints about Spivey, including heavy-handed control of student organizations, intimidation and extortion of faculty members, forcing teachers to award credit to undeserving students, and extramarital affairs. According to Halstead, the students viewed Spivey as "a dictator. He disregards their views. Intimidation is practiced. Many of the students live in constant fear of losing their jobs or being dismissed from the College if they cross him in any way." And his relations with faculty were worse. "Frankly I have never seen such a group of cowed people," wrote Halstead. "They seem to live in constant fear of him. He has forced them to change grades of students, to pass students who really should fail, to contribute money to this, that and the other thing, including the Foundation."[48]

Halstead also made his grievances public. The Florida Southern College archives contain a letter to Spivey from Dana F. Robinson, the college's dean of women, which suggests that a faculty meeting was held to discuss these accusations. The meeting apparently included a petition of some kind, for Robinson professed shock at the situation and assured Spivey that she "did not sign the paper, for I believe I can do you a greater good by talking and writing to you."[49] After Spivey fired Halstead upon learning he was fomenting rebellion in meetings with student fraternities, Halstead disrupted the weekly chapel gathering, charging Spivey with tyranny, "immoral practices with female students," and embezzlement. The board of trustees immediately gathered for a special meeting. They listened to Halstead's indictments and rejected them, fully supporting Spivey.[50]

The matter seems to have settled down within a few months, only to be reignited by Thomas P. Chalker, a Florida Southern professor of religion also fired by Spivey, evidently as part of the Halstead case. In August 1940 Chalker notified the Florida Conference of the Methodist Church and the Southern Association of Colleges and Schools, the body responsible for accrediting the college, of Spivey's alleged offenses. He charged Spivey with coercion of grading, irregularities in granting degrees and reporting salaries, using unqualified instructors and creating a phony graduate program in religious studies, dismissing faculty without just cause, and financial improprieties.[51] The matter was serious enough that Chalker was allowed to present the charges to a Florida Conference committee in September, and Spivey was forced to respond at a Southern Association meeting in December. In both cases he was exonerated, but the Chalker affair, along with the Halstead controversy before it, impinged on Spivey's time for a year and a half and doubtless added further stress to an already strained work environment.[52]

Spivey

By January 1940 the chapel's block walls were constructed to about twelve feet, but Spivey was not pleased. "I stay 'sore' practically the whole time because the chapel goes along so slowly," he told Wright. "I have never seen, in all my life, a building go along so slowly. It really makes me sick."[53]

Such remarks reveal the extent of Spivey's personal investment in the project. Ludd Spivey was a dynamic man whose tireless energy enabled the college to survive and thrive. A faculty member once said Spivey had a "gift for thinking in large dimensions and getting big results," an opinion confirmed by Spivey's many fundraising successes.[54] And a school historian wrote of accounts of Spivey's "intelligent aggressiveness," "optimistic spirit," and "persuasive manner."[55] By all accounts a workaholic, he kept a tight rein on the campus construction process. Spivey's autocratic manner became clear to Wright's staff within the first few months. "Dr. Spivey was most reluctant to place the operation in the hands of any one person and insisted on every smallest purchase, nails, wire, etc., for instance, being ordered through the college office, i.e. himself," wrote Peters to Wright.[56] Years later, and after much more experience, Peters would call Spivey "parsimonious in some matters to a degree bordering on real insanity."[57]

Although Spivey wielded almost unchecked power on the small campus, his personality seems to have been genial rather than overbearing. Most of the students and faculty seem to have liked Spivey. When the Halstead controversy broke out in 1939, publicizing charges that Spivey was a tyrannical dictator, he was generally supported by the students as well as the board of trustees. Likewise, a book of Florida Southern reminiscences published

Figure 3.11. Olgivanna Wright, Frank Lloyd Wright, and Ludd Spivey. Florida Southern College Archives.

in the late seventies is filled with favorable impressions of the man. He appears in these stories as gracious and helpful, but very busy. Spivey had suffered an epic tragedy in 1932, when his seven-year-old son Allan died of rabies from a dog bite. The loss devastated him; some have suggested that his workaholic ways and obsession with campus expansion were in some manner motivated by the pain of his son's untimely death.[58] And it may be true that Spivey's unquenchable drive manifested itself in brusqueness toward others at times. At least one former student hinted at a different side of Spivey's personality: "I remember the sarcasm of Dr. Spivey and how he would criticize folks for not supporting the college financially—and who never had a word of praise for any group or individual except Frank Lloyd Wright. However, I liked Dr. Spivey and he was, I might add, an individual not easy to like!"[59] Rumors of Spivey's womanizing and intemperate behavior continue to this day as part of the college folklore, but it is unclear whether the rumors are from actual misdeeds or are merely the lingering result of the charges leveled against him more than seventy years ago.

Esplanades

Two more elements of Wright's campus plan began to take shape in 1940: a group of seminar buildings and the esplanades that would eventually unite all of the Wright structures. Esplanade construction commenced early in the project, as pathways were laid through the orange groves, and construction foreman Robert Wehr started to make test columns. The esplanades may be the campus's most important architectural feature. In Wright's words, the esplanade "runs all over and finally gets together and makes a building."[60] By connecting the individual buildings—and often physically merging with them—the esplanades visually unified the campus and gave it a skeletal framework. They also played a key role in Wright's vision of a uniquely Floridian architecture, giving the campus "an outdoor garden character fit for Florida."[61] Covered walkways shaded students from the harsh tropical sun and frequent summer rains, while allowing natural breezes to help diminish the heat.

Although the esplanades were indeed a sensitive adaptation to local circumstances, their origins might actually lie in Wright's past work and his encounters with traditional collegiate architecture. As far back as 1904, Wright included long pergolas in the Darwin Martin and Burton Westcott houses; he also included pergolas of varying lengths in the Hollyhock House (1917) and his second home at Taliesin West (1937). The idea of covered walkways between buildings could have occurred to Wright for the first time in a proposed remodeling of the Hillside Home School for the Taliesin Fellowship (1932). Moreover, there is a definite concurrence between Florida Southern's esplanades and two of the premier works of American college design. As mentioned in chapter 2, Wright visited Stanford University in 1936 and 1938, the second visit only one week before his initial contact with Spivey, and though there is no record of his ever visiting the University of Virginia, Wright was a noted admirer of Thomas Jefferson. Both Stanford and Virginia feature extensive covered walks—arcades at Stanford and porticoes at Virginia (figs. 2.9 and 2.10). Historian Neil Levine characterized these Virginia walkways as "connective tissue" linking the campus buildings, a phrase that is an equally apt description of the Lakeland campus.[62]

In both of these earlier cases, however, the covered walkways, being attached to continuous buildings and facing rectangular or square open spaces, referred back to the tradition of the medieval cloister. In contrast,

Figure 3.12. Esplanade. Photograph by author.

Wright's plan altered the cloister by liberating the covered walk from the surrounding buildings, so that they not only stood alone but also acted as space-defining structures. At Florida Southern, moreover, the space defined by the esplanades was not orderly or regulated but natural, filled with trees and greenery.

More than one and a half miles of esplanades were originally planned for the campus, but less than that would eventually be constructed. The esplanades varied slightly in different parts of the campus, but all sections were formed from the same basic materials. Massive piers of plastered and painted concrete block, usually lining one side of the walk, supported a slender, cantilevered roof. An early, undated drawing of an esplanade pier, included on an elevation of the general plan, depicts V-shaped supports with their points touching the sidewalk and three concentric triangles stepping out from the piers' faces.[63] This version was rejected in favor of a design that more closely resembled a column, with "capitals" extending outward from the front and sides at sixty-degree angles from the "shafts," echoing the sixty-degree angles found in the campus plan. Each pier contained three distinct surfaces: a main column of striated block, smooth facets on the sides of the capital, and a geometric diamond pattern on the capital's front. Because of their shape, size, and patterning, the piers read

Figure 3.13. Wright entering Walbridge Seminar Building, 1949. Florida Southern College Archives.

as abstracted trees, perhaps in reference to the surrounding citrus groves; additionally, many were eighteen feet apart on center, a typical distance between trees in an orange grove. Wright might have used these structures as expressions of place to reinforce the connection between the natural site and the man-made structures.

In contrast to the thick piers, the esplanades' roof slabs were extremely thin. The roofs were made of concrete trimmed with sculptured copper fascias. Wright designed them with a human scale in mind, making them unusually low—in some places, a mere six and a half feet from the ground. In other areas the esplanades run down the hillside toward the lake, with changes in elevation solved by adding a Z shape to the roof. Although the materials used in the esplanades are constant throughout the campus, the esplanade's form varies in different places. The roofs are cantilevered from concrete piers in the areas between the buildings. At the science and industrial arts buildings the esplanades become extensions of the structural wall. Similarly, at the administration building the piers are embedded in the building walls and paired; in this area, which Wright called an "exedra," the esplanade was doubled and spliced open down the middle with planters and skylights. These variations in the esplanade forms contributed to the play of unity and individuality that was present in all levels of Wright's design.

The Carter, Hawkins, and Walbridge Seminar Buildings

The seminar buildings were slated for a spot to the east of the proposed Water Dome. The original program called for seven of these buildings, each holding about forty seats, with the structures separated by gardens and terraces "uniting them to the whole."[64] According to the "Programme for University" document, one seminar room was to be set aside as a "quiet place where a youth may retire to reflect and dedicate himself to the task of 'the Way' (Vespers appropriate here)," probably relating to Jones's suggestion of a room for "prayer and meditation." In May 1940 Spivey initiated the process of their construction by requesting "two little seminar rooms."[65] Wright sent the drawings down in August. Rather than creating a multistoried rectangular box full of identical classrooms, which was the contemporary practice in higher education, Wright made three smaller structures of a more intimate size.

All three buildings were identical, aligned in a row, and shared both simplicity and architectural formality, with major and minor axes and centrally located doors and corridors. Wright planned the seminars on a three-foot horizontal and vertical grid. They were the first of Wright's Florida Southern buildings to "hug the ground" with low, flat roofs and dominant horizontal lines, in Wright's familiar manner. Built entirely of concrete blocks, the seminars were attached to the esplanade that passed in front of them on the south side. Most of the blocks were patterned, but a few plain blocks without design were integrated into the corners. The seminar buildings' walls were used to test different colored concrete. The majority of these test blocks were used around the Charles W. Hawkins Building's entrance and corners, but a few were located at the corners and along the bottom row of the Isabel Walbridge Building. There were approximately eighteen different colored test blocks, ranging from tan, khaki, wine, and pink to gray and charcoal. The color ultimately chosen, and used in all of the other campus buildings, was a cream-colored tan.

Small courtyards with grass and trees sat between the seminar buildings. Upon entering one of the seminars, a visitor encountered a short

Figure 3.14. Isabel Walbridge Seminar Building, 1940. Florida Southern College Archives.

Figure 3.15. Concrete test blocks in the Charles W. Hawkins Seminar Building. Photograph by author.

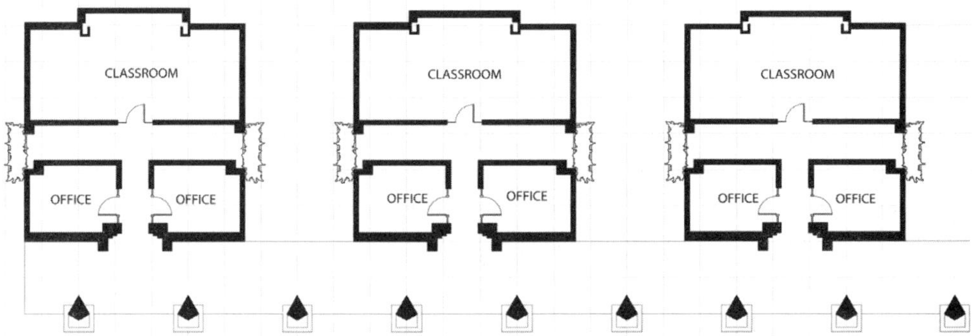

Figure 3.16. Seminar buildings plans, based on original drawings. Courtesy of Dan Price and Nathaniel J. Turner.

Figure 3.17. Spivey's office in the seminar buildings. Florida Southern College Archives.

hall flanked by faculty offices, ending in a cross-axial hall and a classroom stretching across the entire width of the building at the rear. All seminars were windowless; skylights, small sidelights, and colored-glass inserts in the concrete block provided natural illumination. Wright left the side walls at either end of the cross-axial hall open, terminating them with planters about two and a half feet tall. This design allowed fresh air to circulate through the building and gave occupants an opportunity to experience the courtyards intimately. The planters also helped bring nature into the structure, emphasizing the campus's "outdoor garden" character.[66]

Construction on the seminars commenced in September 1940; at that point, Spivey had enough money for only one of the three buildings but anticipated funding for another any day. Foundation pouring for the first seminar began in mid-December. By October 1941 all three buildings were completed and occupied, with Spivey moving his office into one of them—thus defeating the purpose of creating more classroom space. The seminar buildings were the first completed educational spaces of Wright's project. Though small, they brought some relief to a campus that desperately needed room to grow.

Curriculum

Because Florida Southern was sponsored by the Methodist Conference, its religious tendencies may have been more prominent than at private secular colleges, but that aspect did not define it. Instead, the Jones Foundation's intention of harmonizing science and religion was readily apparent, despite the foundation's impending decline. Spivey once defined "ideal education" as "an equal blending of religious, cultural, and scientific knowledge," and this view was reflected in the school's official statement of aims and purposes.[67] The main curricular goals in 1938 were:

1. A democratic, Christian philosophy.
2. Conservation and promotion of physical and mental health.
3. Straight, accurate thinking which develops intellectual skepticism, prevents credulity, and leads to a scientific outlook on life.[68]

The college contained six divisions at that time: Fine and Applied Arts, Education, English Composition and Literature, Foreign Languages, Physical Science, and Social Science. In 1940—after the arrival of Spivey's University of Chicago mentor, Shirley Jackson Case—a Religion division was added and a religious education department formed; the existing religion and philosophy departments then relocated from the Social Science division.

As the school's enrollment climbed during the late forties, the administrators changed its pedagogical intentions and curriculum offerings. The student population, just under 1,000 when Wright became associated with the college, doubled by 1950—increasing the urgent need for new classroom space. "In order to secure diversification of the work of the students and to eliminate specialization," the college added new divisions (Arts, Humanities, Science, and Social Studies) and departments (Fine Arts, Applied Music, Music Literature and History, Journalism, Speech and Drama, Italian, Russian, Citrus Science, Secretarial, and Geography).[69] A list of the college's goals in a course catalog from 1949 showed a slight shift in approach; the first religious reference was not found until the third objective, preceded by "1. A desire for scientific inquiry and investigation into all fields of knowledge, so that education will be one unified procedure, synthesized into a balanced whole," and "2. The maturing of the student as he gathers in a richness of culture and an appreciation for the social heritage in which he participates."[70] With this reprioritization, Spivey's mission to shape Florida Southern into a prototype for a new model of higher education based on the melding of religion and science was complete.

Financial and Labor Issues

Early in 1940, while the seminar buildings were being finalized, Wright embarked on a decades-long campaign to pressure Spivey into paying his debts. Wright began sending long letters filled with tallies of unpaid bills and subtle threats. He created the template in the first such letter, sent in January. Claiming that he began the project by taking a financial loss (agreeing to create a preliminary study for the college for a quarter of his normal fee), Wright reminded Spivey of their pact, whereby Wright would take a 10 percent commission on each building at completion, and Spivey would pay all traveling expenses for Wright and his assistants. Wright calculated that Spivey thus far owed almost $9,000 for the original scheme and drawings of the chapel, faculty homes, men's dormitory, and a private house for Spivey in Ft. Lauderdale. "I haven't pressed much knowing your condition, somewhat, and sincerely wishing to see you successful with your high minded, unusual enterprise," wrote Wright. "I pitched in and talked and did my best to help your propaganda—a thing I never did before and never expected to do." But now the time had come for action, as Wright claimed the lack of income was critical. "You will have to help me now . . . Dr.—what can you do *now*?"[71]

Uncharacteristically, Spivey did not respond for almost three weeks, and then largely sidestepped the issue. "This is the greatest financial tragedy that has happened to this state in thirty years," he wrote, referring to another disastrous freeze. "Everything is gone, all the vegetables, all the fruit and I am afraid the trees are in such a condition that they will not bear next year." He then challenged Wright with his own understanding of the agreement: "I want to remind you Mr. Wright that you promised that if I would put $10,000 into this project that you would finish the Chapel—and then, I would pay for the other buildings as we go along." But Spivey ended on a note of optimism, versions of which would be repeated many times in the future: "I am not discouraged at all for I am determined that we are going to finish this whole project."[72] He also enclosed a check for $500.

Meanwhile, the actual building of the campus barely progressed. The labor situation at Florida Southern would be an ongoing source of dissatisfaction to both Wright and Spivey, for a variety of reasons, and on a number of fronts. Much of the tension came from the school's utilization of student workers. They were inexperienced and worked only part-time. Wes Peters was critical of the system from the beginning. He arrived in Lakeland in October 1939 to organize the construction process and immediately characterized Florida as "the home of all sloppy sleepy labor."[73] "I don't know what to do about this job down here," he wrote to his wife. "They apparently don't have enough money to go ahead with the job in decent fashion:—that is with hiring capable workmen to do the thing right. They keep trying to run things with these damn college boys—and that's no way to either build a good building or get anything done at any rate of speed."[74]

Later that month Peters was shocked when the student laborers left campus "without warning" for Thanksgiving vacation, not to return for a week. "This is part of the ridiculous set-up that still exists here in spite of my most determined efforts to hammer some sense into the Doctor's head," he told Wright.[75] Spivey realized the situation was less than ideal and had his own criticisms. He complained to Wright, "The men spend about half their time over the blueprints trying to find out what to do" instead of working.[76] He refused, however to use union carpenters, and he even considered hiring migrant farm workers to build the buildings in an attempt to save money. Labor supervision was another problem. Numerous foremen and contractors involved with the project over the years either were fired by Spivey or quit because they found it "exasperating to work with the Doctor."[77] Those supervisors who remained on the job inevitably failed to meet Wright's standards or understand his instructions. In the spring of 1940, Robert Wehr, a Hungarian-born architect, builder, and Florida Southern faculty member who served as construction supervisor, incurred the wrath of Taliesin when he began to make esplanade piers and pour the mezzanine level of the chapel without sending photographs or progress reports; Peters eventually ordered a work stoppage until he could assess the situation. Wehr oversaw construction on the Wright buildings until mid-1945, when Wright fired him, complaining to Spivey that "he has proved inadequate, conceited and unreliable. His criminal negligence of explicit instructions in writing . . . justifies me in asking for someone down there who will follow instructions from this office no matter who says what (and that means you as well, my dear Dr.) or else we will just drop the whole thing."[78]

As the letter indicates, Wright and his associates often considered Spivey an impediment. The president intimately involved himself in the construction process, questioning workers and supervisors, watching the progress, even physically exerting himself at times.[79] Wright's staff, however, was often aggravated by Spivey's meddling and questioned his grasp of the big picture. Peters epitomized their exasperation in a letter to Wright: "Frankly, from many things I have seen here I don't believe that Dr. Spivey has the slightest understanding of what the buildings are all about . . . and I somewhat question whether he ever will." Peters criticized Spivey's "almost idiotic whims around the job" and his parsimoniousness "to a degree bordering on real insanity." "At the same time he will not hesitate to sink money stupidly in some gadget that will ruin the entire character of a building," Peters declared. "[I]t is characteristic that Dr. Spivey does not think of consulting the Architect concerning such an addition and furthermore is not offended by the monstrosity himself."[80]

The E.T. Roux Library

Slow progress on the chapel and seminars and a chronic lack of money failed to discourage Spivey from pursuing his vision of a grand new campus. In January 1941 he asked Wright to begin planning a library. Claiming, "There is nothing in this college that we need so badly as the library," Spivey promised to send $500 per month once Wright started working on the plans. His statement was no exaggeration; the college's existing library occupied two rooms in Edge Hall, with a remodeled hallway housing book stacks, and when the new seminar buildings were completed, they were pressed into service to hold books.

The E. T. Roux Library, named for the longtime treasurer of the Florida Southern College board of trustees and early savior of Southern College, would be the first of Wright's circular buildings to be constructed, and only his second library.[81] Wright's affinity for circles had been growing since the 1920s and would culminate with one of his most famous commissions, New York's Guggenheim Museum (1957).

The Florida Southern College library was not entirely circular—only the reading room had that form, and it was appended to a hexagon that contained book stacks and administrative spaces. The circular reading room was an unusual design decision. It is unclear why Wright chose the circle motif for this building. As historian Neil Levine has pointed out, Wright's initial foray into circular plan and form—the Strong Automobile Objective and Planetarium (1924–25)—associated the circle with a social and intellectual gathering place in his mind, while subsequent projects like the

Figure 3.18. Frank Lloyd Wright, E. T. Roux Library, preliminary drawing, 1941. Copyright © 2009 The Frank Lloyd Wright Foundation, Taliesin West, Scottsdale, Ariz. 4118.001.

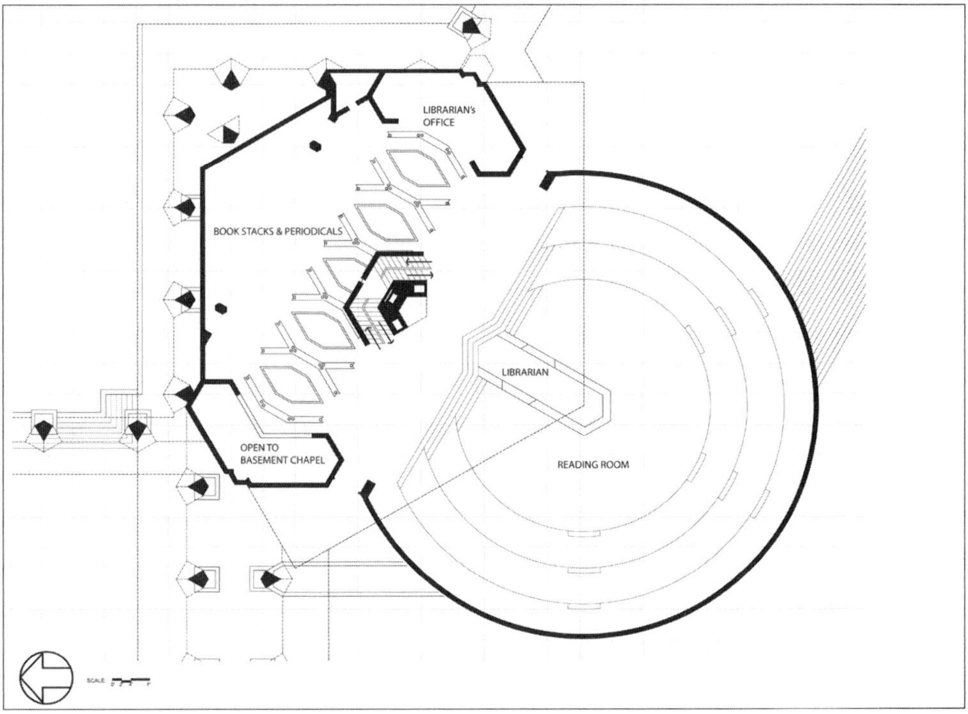

Figure 3.19. E. T. Roux Library, first-floor plan, based on original drawings. Courtesy of Dan Price and Nathaniel J. Turner.

Monona Terrace office complex (1938) connected circular geometries with the element of water; these correlations could help to explain the library and the campus plan.

Semicircular or apsidal reading rooms were not uncommon in the late nineteenth century, and familiarity with the published plans of such buildings in architectural journals might have reinforced Wright's interest in the possibilities of circular forms for library spaces.[82] His esoteric personal symbolism undoubtedly played a part in the design decision as well. However, there is not enough evidence, apart from his 1912 article that mentioned how "certain geometric forms have come to symbolize for us and patently suggest certain human ideas, moods, sentiments—as for instance: the circle, infinity," to determine exactly what circular forms really meant to Wright.[83]

Perhaps the best explanation is that circles and semicircles are a recurring motif throughout Wright's campus plan, and the library was one of the few buildings where he thought a circular form could be used without seriously interfering with the building's function. Wright's campus, in its original conception, was anchored on both ends by semicircles: the "arboreal hemisphere" around the Water Dome at the north end and the amphitheater at the south end along Lake Hollingsworth. The Water Dome was circular, along with two chambers of the unrealized music building project (1943, 1946). Later additions to the project added more circles (the little theater in the industrial arts building, a later version of the amphitheater/swimming pool complex) and semicircles (a proposed children's building attached to the unbuilt arts building, the domed planetarium on the science building) in both plan and elevation. Wright could have assumed, or known from early talks with Spivey, that a library would be one of the first new structures for the college, and so it may have seemed a likely candidate to introduce the circular form. At the same time, he must have recognized the difficulties inherent in trying to force the functions of either a chapel or classroom building—also among the most likely to be built first—into such a shape.

Wright's interest in interpenetrating forms of different shapes—like the library's hexagon and circle—dated back to the "Romeo and Juliet" Windmill (1896) he designed for his aunts in Wisconsin. The idea of specifically merging a circle and hexagon was actually recycled from Wright's unbuilt "Little Dipper" Kindergarten (1923) for Alice Barnsdall's Hollyhock estate in Los Angeles. The Little Dipper was supposed to be a kindergarten and playhouse for neighborhood children—much like Wright's Coonley Playhouse (1910) in Riverside, Illinois—and part of a large complex intended by Barnsdall as a residence, artists' colony, and retail center. For the children's building, Wright combined a schoolroom and stage in a distorted square structure (bisected by an elongated hexagon) with a circular outdoor seating "bowl" of terraced benches. He sited the building in dramatic fashion on the edge of a steep slope, which emphasized the main structure's verticality.

For Florida Southern, Wright adopted the Little Dipper's basic scheme but made significant adjustments, transforming the outdoor seating area to an indoor reading room and reshaping the square portion into a hexagon, while retaining the horizontal-vertical interplay in elevation between the two parts. This design allowed Wright to utilize the bifurcated plan characteristic of American libraries of the time. In most academic and public libraries around the country, reading and book storage functions were segregated into distinct spaces. Wright recognized that the Little Dipper's circle-hexagon combination could accommodate these uses in a way that was visually interesting and conveyed the library's different interior spaces through disparate exterior forms. The hexagon, approximately ninety feet long and fifty feet wide, would contain most of the library's spaces on three levels. A basement level included restrooms, shelving space, and a small chapel, which became a memorial chapel for the Roux family. The first and second floors housed book stacks and periodicals, with a librarian's office on the ground level just inside the main entrance. The second floor was a mezzanine that partially extended into the semicircular reading room above the circulation desk.

Wright sank the reading room floor six steps below the entry to emphasize its spatial separation. The room, ninety feet in diameter, was terraced into three levels, each with a continuous desk that almost reached around to a complete circle; this circular seating arrangement on terraces echoed the Little Dipper's outdoor seating bowl. The reading room desks contained bookshelves on one side and chairs for readers on the other. A circulation desk protruded into the center of the circle at floor level, flanked by card catalogs. Behind the desk and in the library's center, at the intersection between the semicircle and hexagon and serving as a visual and structural anchor as in his earlier Prairie-style houses, was a typical Wrightian

Figure 3.20. Frank Lloyd Wright, proposal for the unbuilt "Little Dipper" kindergarten, Los Angeles, California, 1923. Copyright © 2009 The Frank Lloyd Wright Foundation, Taliesin West, Scottsdale, Ariz. 2301.006.

touch—a fireplace, which introduced a domestic feature into the building and screened the stairs leading down to the basement and up to the second floor.

Wright employed a complex structural system to create the unique spatial effects of the two-part building and to introduce natural light into the interior. Poured concrete and structural steel carried the building's weight, with a concrete block shell for the walls. An absence of interior supports allowed the building's two distinct areas to flow gracefully into each other on two floors. Natural light entered these spaces through a variety of direct and indirect sources. The reading room, which was visually closed off from the outside like the chapel, was lit only from above. Wright created a roof of three concentric, cantilevered, reinforced-concrete circles, layered on top of each other with small windows in between. Sunlight filtered between the roof layers, then reflected off a series of concrete beams on the underside of the ceiling, radiating out from a concrete disk above the circulation desk. The reading room interior was painted white to increase the reflection. Operable clerestory windows ringed the room's walls beneath the lowest roof section to provide extra light and help circulate air.

The library's hexagonal section also received light from above via a row of triangular skylights running the length of the roof. Directly below the skylights, both the first and second floors were perforated with five lozenge-shaped light wells that let sunlight reach all the way down to the basement. A row of clerestories below the roof permitted light to enter the second floor spaces horizontally as well as vertically. Finally, Wright created another light well along the back (western) wall of the library by stopping the first and second floors short of the wall; again, this opening let natural light shine down to the basement level.

An early drawing of the proposed library envisioned more direct lighting for the reading room from a generous, clear-glass clerestory—much larger than that which was built—that capped the upper wall just below a wafer-thin roof.[84] The skylights over the hexagonal section in this proposal were also different from the constructed building; it seems Wright was attempting to harmonize the roof with the chapel tower through matching metal trellises and concrete panels with concentric squares.[85] The proposed concrete panels, and the two chimneys visible in the drawing, created a more vertical emphasis than would be present in the gable-roofed final structure; had this proposal been built, the library and chapel would have strongly resembled each other.

Color Plate 1. Annie M. Pfeiffer Chapel. Photograph by Larry Leshan.

Color Plate 2. Colored glass inserts in concrete blocks, Pfeiffer Chapel. Photograph by Larry Leshan.

Color Plate 3. Pfeiffer Chapel skylights. Photograph by Larry Leshan.

Color Plate 4. William H. Danforth Chapel. Photograph by Larry Leshan.

Color Plate 5. William H. Danforth Chapel interior. Photograph by Larry Leshan.

Color Plate 6. E. T. Roux Library (now the Thad Buckner Building). Photograph by author.

Color Plate 7. Esplanades. Photograph by Larry Leshan.

Color Plate 8. Cora Carter, Charles W. Hawkins, and Isabel Walbridge Seminar Buildings. Photograph by author.

Color Plate 9. Concrete test blocks in the Charles W. Hawkins Seminar Building. Photograph by author.

Color Plate 10. Watson Administration Building pool. Photograph by Larry Leshan.

Color Plate 11. Water Dome. Photograph by Larry Leshan.

Color Plate 12. Refectory, Lucius Pond Ordway Industrial Arts Building. Photograph by author.

Color Plate 13. Frank Lloyd Wright, second proposal for unbuilt music building, 1946. Copyright © 2009 The Frank Lloyd Wright Foundation, Taliesin West, Scottsdale, Ariz. 4611.001.

Color Plate 14. Frank Lloyd Wright, proposal for unbuilt swimming pool and outdoor theater, 1947. Copyright © 2009 The Frank Lloyd Wright Foundation, Taliesin West, Scottsdale, Ariz. 4732.002.

Figure 3.21. E. T. Roux Library reading room. Copyright © 2009 The Frank Lloyd Wright Foundation, Taliesin West, Scottsdale, Ariz. 4118.033.

While formally innovative, Wright's library suffered from functional problems. The building's ambitious natural lighting system was the main culprit. The skylights and light wells in the hexagonal stack section let in too much sunlight and, along with Wright's provision for natural ventilation rather than air-conditioning, endangered the books. On the other hand, the indirect overhead lighting of the reading room proved inadequate. "We used reading lamps, because we didn't get sufficient light," recounted Oween Sumner, the school's head librarian. "The light was up above and wasn't sufficient for students to read. We had desk lamps for reading or reading lamps." Sumner added, "I really didn't care for it. Not from the library angle at all."[86]

The building also bore an uneasy relationship to developments in contemporary library architecture. Although conceptually interesting, it was on the verge of being outdated. The bifurcated plan, separating the stacks and reading room, dated back to the days when librarians refused to let users have direct access to the book stacks. At about the same time Wright started to work on the E. T. Roux Library, however, a new approach to library design, called modular planning, was being developed. The modular planning movement—as advocated by an influential group of librarians, architects, and engineers called the Cooperative Committee on Library Building Plans—sought to utilize modern standardization techniques to develop flexible, expandable libraries with integrated book stacks and reading areas. Combining standard and easily constructed modules to create a library building would be cost effective and therefore practical, while spreading the stacks throughout the building eliminated the need for larger sections for book storage (called stack towers) and created new spaces for studying or interactions among patrons, books, and staff.

Modular planning would become the norm in the 1950s, when articles filled the library and architectural literature urging "Simplicity, efficiency, economy, [and] flexibility" in new library designs.[87] College and university administrators and librarians were resolute in their advice to architects to allow room for libraries to grow. "[T]he rapidity with which the library conditions change suggests that a permanent architectural memorial may not meet present library needs," wrote one administrator in *American School and University*. "Elasticity of plan which permits even major modifications of the original plan is of prime importance."[88]

None of these concepts truly described Wright's Florida Southern library. Insufficient space and inelasticity would prove to be serious problems in the new structure. Wright provided no way to easily enlarge the building to house an expanding collection or serve more students. Before Wright designed the library, Spivey apparently told him that the college possessed about 25,000 books, a figure Peters later described as "ridiculous."[89] The building Wright conceived could hold anywhere from 100,000 to 200,000 books.[90] But it was soon apparent that there were space shortages. Four years after opening, the library's collection had grown to approximately 60,000 volumes.[91] By 1957, with the library just over a decade old, new shelving was needed, and the building was "close to the limit" in terms of book capacity, according to Taliesin apprentice Nils Schweizer.[92] Wright's library would reach full capacity shortly thereafter, influencing the college to construct a new library in the late 1960s.

The library would be the Florida Southern building most affected by World War II. Wright made most of the drawings during the early summer of 1941, and construction began that fall; when the cornerstone was laid on March 6, 1942, the walls had been raised up to the level of the clerestory windows. But after that point, the war impacted manpower, money, and materials and significantly impeded the library's progress.

First Building Completed

In early 1941, as the chapel was nearing completion and set for dedication during the annual Founders Week ceremonies in early March, Spivey requested Wright's presence for that occasion. A month later, after numerous requests had been ignored, Spivey pleaded with Wright to either attend or send Peters. Wright responded that he could not attend but would send a letter to be read to the gathered crowd. That letter summarized much of what Wright sought in the campus design:

> I am sure [the chapel] does not lack charm or distinction. When the flowers are in the boxes and climbing up the metal trellises, and the round bronze bells are ringing above them Florida will have found an expression in building of her proper name. I hope and believe the chapel strikes, with new clarity, the chord between Florida character and beauty and the life of your many boys and girls—as they have it day by day with you down there . . . There will be many, still, who "disbelieve" and long for accustomed religious forms. But they, at least, will have a glimpse of the world to come in this little window we have set there on the campus of Florida Southern College to look out upon that world.[93]

The dedication was a gala affair, attended by representatives of more than sixty colleges and universities, four bishops from the Methodist church, and various other dignitaries. Reactions to the building were favorable. Dr. Yehi Hsieh, a visiting Chinese diplomat, said he thought the chapel was "like an ancient temple. When I first stepped in here I knew this was a place of worship. Clear cut simplicity done on so large a scale makes one feel humble and awed."[94] The chapel's main donor, Annie M. Pfeiffer, presented the keys to the building to the chairman of the college's board of trustees and complimented the school for its "spirit." E. Stanley Jones was noticeably absent from the festivities, and unlike Wright did not send a statement. The Jones Educational Foundation had disappeared from official college pronouncements by this time and was not a part of the ceremonies; in the press coverage of the week's events, the lone reference to the foundation came in a local newspaper story where the reporter claimed that

Figure 3.22. Florida Southern College, aerial view, late 1940s. Florida Southern College Archives.

Bishop Arthur J. Moore's dedicatory address "summarized the essential aim of the E. Stanley Jones foundation . . . that of harmoniously merging science and religion for the most effective training of youth."[95] That kind of language, so prominent a few years earlier, had not been heard in some time, as the building campaign shifted from an attempt to materialize the Jones Educational Foundation's goal to Ludd Spivey's dream of a "great education temple."

The balance of 1941 saw Wright and Spivey continuing to joust over money—although Spivey did manage to send at least seven $500 payments, more than any previous year—while the student workers put the finishing touches on the chapel and began the library. Spivey asked Wright at various times for sketches for a "minor chapel" and an industrial arts building, in both cases because he thought he had a potential donor; neither opportunity came to fruition. Those projects would soon be set aside as larger problems loomed on the horizon.

FOUR *The War Years, 1942–1945*

America's entry into World War II exacerbated an already poor situation at Florida Southern. Like colleges across the country, the school lost students and faculty to the armed forces, which in turn reduced income from student tuition. Additionally, wartime restrictions on materials and a diminished labor pool severely handicapped construction. By the end of 1941, only three weeks after Pearl Harbor, Spivey was already feeling the effects. "The war is closing in on us. I do not know how long we can carry on," he wrote to Wright. "It [sic] almost impossible to get either money or materials now. I wish I had better news for you."[1] Less than a month later things were even worse, as Spivey described to Wright: "I am sorry to tell you that it is not possible for this college to send you any more money at this time. I do not even have the money to pay my teachers. I don't have to tell you that it is most difficult to get money now. I hope that things will change for the better soon."[2]

Wartime Hardships

Despite the difficult circumstances, the construction work on campus did not stop. As the walls of the E. T. Roux Library rose slowly, substitutions were made to adjust to material shortages. Wood replaced steel in the window sashes, for example, and concrete took the place of steel in some structural supports. By the spring of 1942, Wright produced his first drawings for the music and industrial arts buildings, and the college's situation had improved. During Founders Week, Florida Southern dedicated the seminar buildings, naming them for Cora Carter, a retired schoolteacher and donor; Charles W. Hawkins, professor of ancient languages; and Isabel Walbridge, a dormitory hostess. That week the school also held a cornerstone ceremony for the library. Annie Pfeiffer returned to campus later in March to be honored for contributing a $20,000 organ to her namesake chapel.

These positive events provided good public relations for the college and Spivey's grand project. As Spivey told Wright numerous times, construction progress and finished buildings were the best possible advertisements to attract money to the campus. And for a brief time that seemed to be the case. "We are going ahead but very slowly, however, I am glad to tell you that things look better than ever before right now," said Spivey in a March 1942 letter to Wright. "It may be that we are going to carry on in a much larger way in the near future."[3] Spivey was optimistic because he thought he had again identified donors for the industrial arts, science, administration, and music buildings, as well as a small chapel. Never before had the outlook for realizing Wright's campus been so promising.

But the realities of the wartime economy soon stifled these opportunities as the project entered its most difficult phase. None of Spivey's prospective benefactors contributed to the campaign. In mid-May 1942 Wright visited Annie Pfeiffer in New York City to persuade her to fund a small chapel—"as a child of the larger one bearing her name"—as a memorial to her late husband. She evidently liked the idea but found it "an inopportune time . . . to give money."[4] Finances were on everyone's mind. In the same letter that reported the unsuccessful Pfeiffer meeting, Wright once more detailed his argument for financial justice, in many places echoing his similar statement of January 1940. He calculated that the college owed him $13,305 for work already produced and another $3,150 for the small chapel and music building plans he was about to undertake. "No one can be more eager to help you get Florida Southern realized that [sic] I am. I have raised my voice in your behalf whenever occasion offered—as well as my talents," he wrote. "But now we have run into dry times where I can no longer divert money received from other work into the work on Florida Southern. We must have money to carry on the hand to mouth existence we have known for so many years. How can you provide it?"[5]

Five weeks later, Wright backed off and tried a softer approach: "I did not intend to thrust a heavy financial burden upon you at this time—but did intend to show you where our end of the stick was and ask an evening-up of the load that was reasonable. You will not find me uncooperative so long as I can go along. But I feel, now, that you should divert money in our direction. The slate shows why."[6] Spivey's response was typical. He sent a check for $250, taken out of the teachers' salaries, and claimed nothing more could be done until school resumed in the fall. Wright accepted the small sum, and another flare-up of a long-smoldering issue was extinguished.

The construction situation, however, was not as easily resolved. The combination of war and summer's slow season had wreaked havoc on the college's economy. Spivey had to borrow the next $250 he sent Wright in August. College enrollment dropped by almost 40 percent. But the decline ended when the navy opened a V-1 officer training school on the campus sometime during 1942.

At some point in October of that year, work on Wright's buildings essentially stopped. Activity resumed in early 1943, just about the time Spivey's request for permission to buy steel to finish the library was denied by the War Production Board. A despondent Spivey told Wright, "We are working a little on the library every day, but very little. The government is getting ready, I am afraid to close down on us permanently."[7]

By fall 1943, with little construction or fundraising to show for the past year, Spivey grew philosophical. In a remarkably personal letter to Wright, thanking him for the gift of *An Autobiography*, Spivey simultaneously revealed his optimism, skepticism, Deweyan outlook, and love of education:

> We must ever keep in mind that we live in a universe, as you are always saying, that is constantly changing. No one can predict exactly how the changes will be made, or in what direction. Our little plans and dreams, set in a vast, changeable, fluid world like our own, are in danger of going to pieces, at any time. All that we can do is to have our little "ends in view." Try these "ends in view" out and see what happens, look for tendencies and everlastingly keep in mind that man is the measure of all things. I'm not sure that in the beginning man was intended, but now that he is here his welfare is the goal.
>
> One of the things that always puzzles and frustrates us is that while we struggle and fight for great masses of men, we sometimes have to doubt whether they are worth fighting for or not. I mean by this just exactly how

> much can we lift this common lot? I still think that education is the cure, but what kind of education? And when we decide on the kind of education, there looms up before us how you are going to get the people educated.[8]

Spivey proceeded to mention that construction of the library was "still struggling along" with a severely reduced work crew of only five students per day. But lacking more than fifteen tons of steel, the project was not going to get very far until the government eased its material restrictions or the war ended.

The Music Building Project

During this period when Wright's and Spivey's dream reached its nadir, Eleanor Searle Whitney appeared and promised to save the entire venture. Whitney had spent her freshman year at Southern College in 1926–27, before quitting school and moving to New York City to study voice. In the early forties she became the third wife of Cornelius "Sonny" Vanderbilt Whitney, who had inherited tremendous wealth from both of his parents' families. Thereafter Eleanor continued her singing career while becoming a great patron of the arts. Despite leaving Florida Southern after only a year, Eleanor established long-lasting ties, later serving on the board of trustees, decorating and equipping the Eleanor Searle Whitney Drawing Room in Joseph-Reynolds Hall, and receiving a citation (and her husband an honorary degree) from the school she once called her alma mater. This relationship began in earnest with a proposal for a new music building.

Ludd Spivey came into contact with Eleanor Whitney sometime in early 1942 and piqued her interest in making a donation to the college.[9] By late May, Wright had made some sketches and attempted, unsuccessfully, to meet her during a trip to New York City. The historical record is mute for the next year and a half, with the exception of an undated telegram from Wright asking Spivey whether he "should see Mrs. Whitney to save Music Building from destruction her demands have entirely disposed of what unity the building possessed"; this language indicates that Whitney had her own ideas about the project rather early on, which would prove to be a major source of conflict in the coming years.[10]

Wright had included both a "Music Study and Performance" building and a "Model Theatre" in his original master plan for Florida Southern. The music building, which was never developed in any further drawings,

Figure 4.1. Eleanor Searle Whitney and Ludd Spivey. Courtesy of Special Collections, Lakeland Public Library, Lakeland, Florida.

appears on the aerial plan southeast of the Water Dome, next to the chapel and science building (figs. 2.2 and 2.3). The one-story structure formed an elongated hexagon with a large enclosed courtyard. In the "Programme" document, the features for the music building included a "Small recital hall" with 150 seats, ten soundproof practice rooms, a library for sheet music, and spaces for band practice and instrument storage.

Wright placed a proposed theater immediately west of the library along the edge of campus. The "Little Theatre" in the university program document, which corresponds to the "Model Theatre" in Wright's earliest drawings, was intended to seat 400 and to be "Adapted to new sense of the play as a circumstance instead of a picture."[11] Wright made at least five drawings for this project. Like the chapel, his proposed theater's form incorporated obliquely angled walls that mirrored the diagonals of the esplanades in plan. The building's outer shape was rectangular, but the stage and seating areas were enclosed in a hexagon clearly visible from the exterior; this design linked the building to the similarly hexagonal chapel. Inside, Wright used a unique combination of a circular, revolving stage and an apron extended

Figure 4.2. Frank Lloyd Wright, proposal for unbuilt Model Theatre, 1938. Copyright © 2009 The Frank Lloyd Wright Foundation, Taliesin West, Scottsdale, Ariz. 3817.001.

to either side, angled in the form of an arrow and curved at the ends. The aprons contained underground lifts for scenery changes. The interior was virtually identical to Wright's unbuilt New Theatre project (1931), where he had attempted to revolutionize stage design and "Free the legitimate stage from its present peep-show character and scenery loft, establishing a simple, workable basis for presenting plays in the round, performers and audience together in one room, allowing staging more like sculpture than like painting."[12]

Perhaps the most interesting aspect of the planned theater, however, was its exterior. Perspective drawings—and even a drawing of the proposed library with the theater in the background—depict a building with completely smooth surfaces and no traces of the textile blocks so prominent in other campus designs. Clerestory windows ran along three sides of the building just below a flat overhanging roof. Overall, the design resembled a slightly altered version of the earlier New Theatre project.[13]

In November 1943 Spivey urged Wright to prepare sketches and a proposed budget for a music building, disclosing that "Mrs. Whitney is ready to put some money into this project now" and "seems to be in a great hurry about the matter."[14] Wright responded within weeks with a new plan and elevation that he deemed "a good scheme—(a remarkable one really)," but he prodded Spivey, asking how much Whitney was willing to pay for the building.[15] By the end of December, more drawings were prepared, and Wright sent them to Spivey and Whitney.

Even before Eleanor Whitney's involvement as a potential donor, Wright had reimagined the music building as an experiment in circular forms. In his new conception, which he described as "a musical instrument itself," he envisioned a long, low, two-story structure with a small half-globe at one end and a larger one at the opposite end.[16] Such circular performance spaces were, as Wright admitted, "unique" at the time. The smaller globe, labeled "Star Chamber," was designed for recitals, student performances, and band practice. The larger globe, entitled "Symphony," would be the main auditorium on campus and contained 350 seats on the main floor and another 150 in the balcony. Both hemispheres were dug down so that the seats were actually below ground level. Wright used tympanum screens hung from the ceiling to control sound. "There can be no reverberations or echoes anywhere with this scheme of overhead," Wright boasted. "Both Auditoriums should be better than good acoustically."[17] The smaller Star Chamber screen was convex, while the Symphony had a flat screen, and groups of small glass tubes, beads, and circles were to be hung from it as a type of chandelier to provide light. Notations on one of the drawings hinted at the fantastic interior Wright imagined for this structure: "Thin Tympanum of fabric hanging free in a brilliantly lighted dome, patterned with planetary bodies and stars, perforations through which the light of the dome falls on the audience." In a letter to Spivey and Whitney, Wright explained that the fabric would be gold, suspended but not touching the walls.

Figure 4.3. Frank Lloyd Wright, first proposal for unbuilt music building, 1942. Copyright © 2009 The Frank Lloyd Wright Foundation, Taliesin West, Scottsdale, Ariz. 4211.010.

In plan, Wright merged the Symphony's circular form with an oval containing the foyer, balcony stairs, and backstage area; a smaller circle for the music library; and another oval for the entrance lobby (changed to a circle in subsequent drawings). The result of the intersecting shapes was a symphony of interpenetrating curved spaces—perhaps intended to echo the simultaneous layers of sound from the different instruments in a musical performance. Wright related the building to the larger campus plan by angling the main axes of the performance spaces at the structure's ends forty-five degrees off the central portion to form reflex angles, which he reinforced with an esplanade alongside the building in the initial drawing. Between the two performance globes Wright created a long, low connecting loggia with classrooms and soundproof practice rooms on two levels. Like other buildings on campus, these spaces would receive light through a combination of clerestory windows and a curved skylight over the hallway.

The building's exterior profile was low and horizontal. Esplanades on both ends connected it with the rest of the campus and reinforced this horizontality. One esplanade became a semicircular roof around the smaller hemisphere, while another turned into a square-shaped "perforated trellis" that bisected the larger globe at its midpoint. A garden in front of the music building introduced a natural component. The building's dominant horizontality was balanced by the domes of the two performance spaces and a tall flagpole—seen in all drawings—arising from the roof above the lobby.

"Withal it is extremely simple, easy to build and adequate so far as I can see—appropriate both to purpose and to Florida Southern," Wright claimed in his correspondence. He was proud of the building, calling it "a gem—a famous building in its way and not only a new thing but a better thing in a building for music-culture than exists anywhere at this time."[18] Little did he know that this would be only the opening salvo in a battle that would last more than four years with no resolution. It would begin a pattern whereby Whitney, often after consulting friends and experts from the New York theater world, would offer detailed critiques of Wright's designs, causing Wright, while polite and responsive to alterations for the most part, to become increasingly embittered as the project lagged. Spivey played the role of mediator, desperately seeking to appease both parties and find a mutually acceptable solution. He knew Eleanor Whitney was probably the biggest potential donor he would ever attract to his campus project, and in many letters to Wright over the course of almost four years, he repeatedly attempted to convince Wright of her significance to the future of their mutual endeavor.

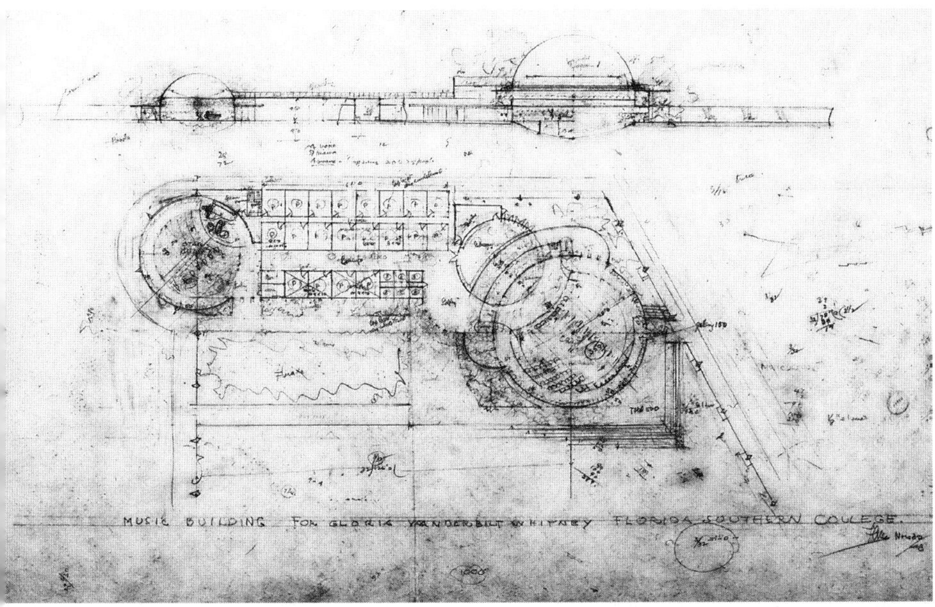

Figure 4.4. Frank Lloyd Wright, music building plan. Copyright © 2009 The Frank Lloyd Wright Foundation, Taliesin West, Scottsdale, Ariz. 4211.001.

The first sign of a problem came in a letter from Whitney to Spivey in late January 1944. As she was reviewing Wright's drawings, she suggested Spivey use an upcoming trip to visit other colleges and perform "research work" "on requirements, best layouts and most beneficial ideas" for a music building, implying some dissatisfaction with Wright's work.[19] Her official response to Wright's proposal followed shortly thereafter, and after a meeting with Whitney, Spivey relayed her proposed alterations to Wright. Whitney was interested in bringing symphonies, operas, and large-scale music productions to Florida Southern, and Wright's Symphony space simply did not appear to be large enough. Wright, on the other hand, had purposely kept the building small and intimate to match the scale of the rest of the campus; he viewed the space as more of a companion to the chapel for lesser college activities. Spivey reminded Wright of the magnitude of this commission, and suggested a course of action that would be repeated over the next few years. "I would like for you to sit down and draw with a pencil the exact floor plan for the practice rooms and class rooms, then let me take it up with Mrs. Whitney, criticize it, and return it to you," he wrote. "I want you to keep in mind this is one thing we must do in order to keep harmony. This is a wonderful opportunity for us but we must handle it with a little care or else it can be spoiled."[20]

Wright was compliant for the most part but was ruffled by Whitney's request for a larger space. "Mrs. Whitney's desire for a big auditorium is ruinous and so is the excessive number of practice rooms but we will see what can be done," he wrote to Spivey. "Quantity instead of quality gets to be the obsession that stands in our way. However we will observe what you say always and do our best."[21] He set about making small changes in the plans in the spring of 1944. While he was working, Spivey continued to remind him how profitable it would be to satisfy Whitney, viewing her as the savior of his dream of a "great education temple." Urging Wright to "let her criticize" his ideas, Spivey claimed, "All that Mrs. Whitney wants, is to have a little share in the matter."[22] "I feel that we have the answer to all of our problems if we can manage to please the Whitneys," he confided a few days later.[23] Wright sent Whitney the revisions, and once more received a detailed list of changes in response.

Spivey viewed Whitney's reply with optimism and must have felt excited to be close to securing an agreement from a member of one of America's wealthiest families and the largest donor in Florida Southern's history.

Wright, however, did not share Spivey's enthusiasm. His response lagged, causing Spivey much anxiety, and leading Whitney to grow "very very [sic] restless" about the project.[24] But he did revise the plans. When Wright finally contacted Whitney about his modifications, he suggested "that the present solution is even better than the original."[25] The most significant changes involved turning an interior hallway into an outdoor loggia and increasing the seating of the main auditorium, although Wright seems to have failed again to design the space for as many seats as Mrs. Whitney wanted. The amended plans held fewer than 800 seats for this room, but Wright assured her it could be enlarged if necessary. But instead of doing so, Wright attempted to persuade Whitney: "My feeling is always to keep on the inside as to numbers—preferring pressure to empty seats. It's hard to get the feeling of a successful occasion with empty rows of seats—you know. So let's stay small and coveted rather than big and covetous."[26]

In the following weeks Whitney must have raised new objections to the auditorium's seating capacity because of its circular form and the lack of traditional footlights on the stage, among other things. At the end of July, Wright sent another explanatory letter. "I am so convinced that a round building is the building of the future I want you to allow me to at least present a sketch for it," he told Whitney. "As you know, my whole life has been spent in creating what I call functional architecture. More and more I am convinced that it is to be the architecture of the future."[27] He defended the circular building, which had now grown to a capacity of 1,500 seats. In a short passage Wright tried to explain his working method so that Whitney would not think the drawings she had seen thus far were definitive. "I believe you have misunderstood my sketches. It just so happens that the only way I can create is to do my work in this way. These sketches are really not plans," wrote Wright. "I want you to remember that every building with me is a new creation and therefore requires a great deal of detail work on my part. Don't be afraid to scribble or to suggest any changes on these sketches. I usually re-make them several times."[28] Wright concluded the letter by affirming his commitment to Florida Southern College, which he felt "is to be one of the outstanding institutions of learning in this country," and restating his willingness to do whatever was necessary to see the music building become a reality.

But again, in what was becoming for Wright and Spivey a frustrating pattern, Eleanor Whitney was unsatisfied with the revisions. While awaiting the latest critique, Spivey once more suggested Wright make simple sketches to help punctuate his ideas, and he evaluated their status frankly: "If you will lead her along, we are elected. Otherwise, 'our goose is cooked.'"[29] When Whitney's letter arrived, it demonstrated that she viewed the design of the music building as a collaborative, ongoing procedure, in contrast to Wright, who would have preferred that his potential client agree to his ideas and step out of the way. Whitney had been discussing the project with Robert Gayler, a musician and Florida Southern faculty member. She now accepted the round auditorium but had doubts about Wright's ability to put a proper stage in it. She also was skeptical of his stage lighting system. Whitney argued that future enrollment growth required a larger auditorium; she now wished it to seat up to 1,700, with the possibility of expanding to 2,200. The negotiations were clearly far from over.

Spivey perceived Whitney's letter as good news and prompted Wright to continue contacting her. "You are the key to the whole matter. See what miracles your letter accomplished. Write to her frequently; send her some little pencil sketches. She is a detailed woman, as you see," he wrote.[30] For the next few months the back and forth continued, with Whitney suggesting changes and enlisting the opinions of others, including Robert Gayler and Gail Potter, Florida Southern's drama director. The circumstances induced Wright to exclaim at one point, "I've got a job on my hands, I see. But I'll do my best. What they want, apparently, is an Opera-house. A little absurd."[31] As winter approached with the project making no headway, Spivey grew despondent. "I tell you the truth—unless we do something right away the Whitney's [sic] are going to throw the whole thing up. It is too bad this is true, but it is true," he lamented. "She has just sent a representative to see me from New York who tells me unless I do something right away the whole thing is going to come to an end. This is what I want to tell you that if we can keep the Whitney's [sic], we can have the money to do the whole thing here, but if we lose them, we will have a hard time."[32]

Wright sent Whitney a revised campus plan in mid-November 1944 to show her how the music building (and a proposed art building, also supported by Whitney and discussed below) would mesh with the existing campus fabric, but this time he received no response. The Whitneys' only child was born that month, and Eleanor's attentions turned elsewhere. After numerous drawings, revisions, and disputes, the music building was no closer to reality than it had been eight months earlier.

The Whitney Memorial Project

During the development of the music building, Spivey and Whitney formulated an idea for another campus building, an art school and museum dedicated to Eleanor's recently deceased mother-in-law, the sculptor Gertrude Vanderbilt Whitney. Developing the "Mrs. Harry Payne Whitney Memorial Building" proved to be a slightly less aggravating process for Wright, but since its fortunes were tied to the music building, his efforts were in vain.

From the earliest campus plans Wright intended a nearly continuous line of buildings and esplanades to define the western boundary of the Florida Southern property along Johnson Avenue from the Water Dome to Lake Hollingsworth (figs. 2.2 and 2.3). Along with the first version of the theater (which later developed into the music building), most of this space was to be occupied by an art complex. Wright titled the building "Art Museum" in the "Programme for University" and "Studios Art Exhibition and Exposition" on the initial master plans and imagined a combination of uses for it, including serving as a small lecture hall. Standing in line with this complex at the southwest corner of the campus would be a child study center, described as an "Experimental Child-garden for 99 children," ages three to nine; the building would contain a small cinema and artworks loaned from the art museum and would be surrounded by playgrounds and working gardens.[33]

Wright's first opportunity to develop these ideas beyond the master plan drawings came in the spring of 1944. His perspective, plan, section, and elevation drawings of the Whitney Memorial depict a row of buildings from north to south, just south of the proposed theater. Included were two studio-residences for artists, studios for art students, a combination museum and "Nature Study Library," and a children's building. The artist residences were two-story structures, with studio space, a living room, and a kitchen on the first floor and multiple bedrooms above. Their blocky forms rose above the esplanade and the attached student studios, anchoring one end of the complex in much the same manner as did the two-story museum at the other end; in this way Wright duplicated the basic format of the music building (and later the science building) with two vertical forms connected by a small, horizontal loggia. The studio space featured a slanted roof that opened to the west, allowing a wall of windows in that direction to receive natural light; the eastern, or "garden," façade included clerestory windows above the esplanade that ran the length of the building.

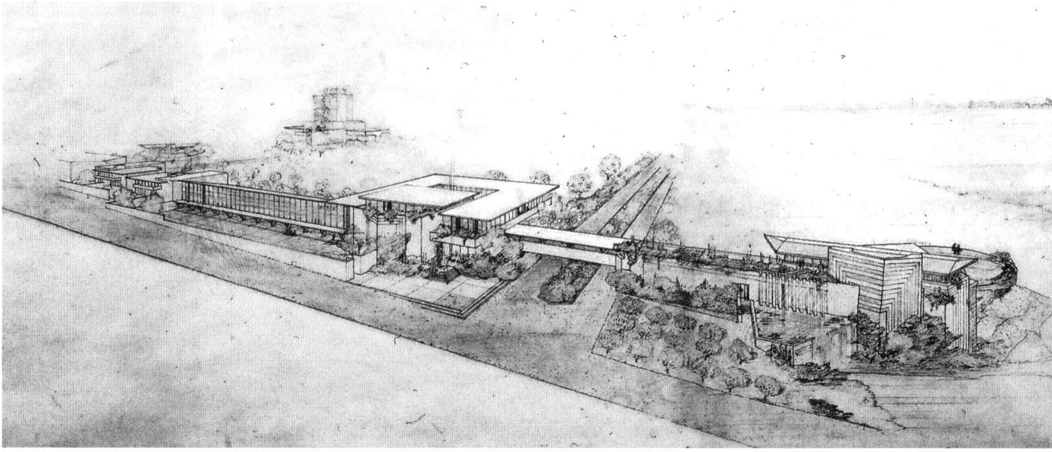

Figure 4.5. Frank Lloyd Wright, proposal for unbuilt Whitney Memorial Building, 1944. Copyright © 2009 The Frank Lloyd Wright Foundation, Taliesin West, Scottsdale, Ariz. 4405.003.

The art museum was clearly the complex's highlight. From the outside a viewer would see a series of layered horizontal planes of varying thickness—thin concrete roofs overhanging glass walls, concrete parapets, and a second-floor cantilevered balcony recalling Wright's famous Fallingwater. An enclosed courtyard, open to the north at ground level and bisected by a long, thin "Mirror Pool," allowed Wright to bring nature close to the building and to fulfill an objective stated in the "Programme for University": "Exhibits in wide corridors open to gardens."[34] Inside the museum a series of galleries and exhibition spaces encircled the court, and on the east side a block rose slightly higher than the rest of the structure, containing a lecture hall on the first floor and opening to a mezzanine-level library.

Wright's proposed art complex demonstrated his ability to vary the basic grammar of his campus buildings. It utilized the constituent materials and design motifs of the rest of the campus but in new ways. The children's building, however, was something entirely different. Connected to the museum by an elevated esplanade over a rerouted Lake Hollingsworth Drive (now straightened to a strict east-west course and renamed "Whitney Drive" in Wright's drawings) and occupying a lakeshore site, the children's building appeared heavy, massive, and out of place compared to its light and elegant neighbor. For this building, Wright resurrected, with minimal changes, the Little Dipper Kindergarten of two decades earlier. As a result, while the building's plan—with its intersecting circle, square, and elongated hexagon—related to the E. T. Roux Library, its elevations showed a different block pattern than other campus buildings, and its gabled roof with upraised ends evoked Japanese and Prairie-style structures instead of the library, chapel, or seminars.

For an architect who prized unity of design in an ensemble of buildings, reviving a twenty-year-old proposal in a different style seems an odd choice. Wright addressed this anomaly obliquely, calling the children's building the "terminal or bud" of the main esplanade—"the sensitive blossom on this stalk that is Florida Southern College."[35] He later downplayed the building's origins, refusing to admit that the children's building was actually a minor reworking of the Little Dipper.

Wright's art complex drawings also revealed more detail about the proposed campus landscapes. The perspectives showed the buildings surrounded by trees, as might be expected, with a stream and series of pools and statues winding past. The east, or garden, side of the complex opened to a strange checkerboard-like landscape of orderly rows of citrus trees in what appeared to be sunken terraces that Wright referred to as the "orange-tree-garden" (fig. 4.6). In one of the plans, garden plots were interspersed with these trees. The scene's rectilinear formality clashed with Wright's idea of a campus arising naturally out of an existing citrus grove; perhaps he intentionally devised this formal section to offset the small stream that meandered through it, or else he felt that more orderly surroundings might be more likely to meet the Whitneys' approval.

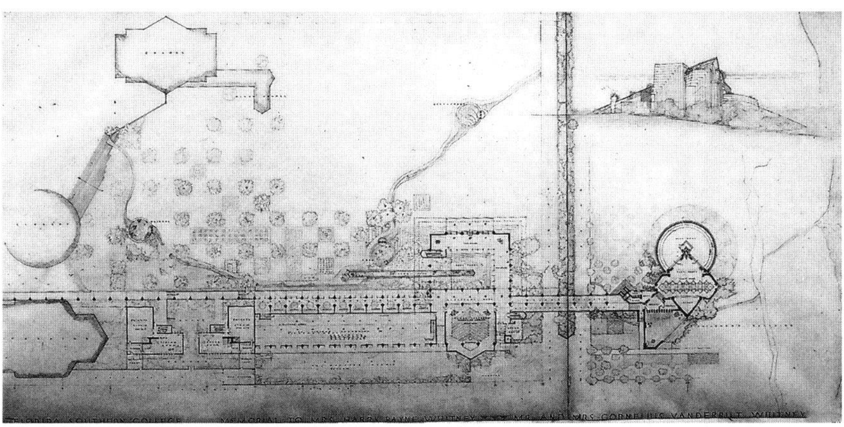

Figure 4.6. Frank Lloyd Wright, Whitney Memorial Building plan. Copyright © 2009 The Frank Lloyd Wright Foundation, Taliesin West, Scottsdale, Ariz. 4405.004.

Hints were provided in Wright's only extended description of the project, a letter to Spivey in March 1944 that focused on the landscaping as much as the buildings. "The scheme in toto represents the whole spirit of the architecture of Florida Southern College and has quietly woven into it the character which is Florida and the repose that should be the characteristic of good memorial architecture," wrote Wright. "I've tried to keep the whole scheme as free with spacious vistas to emphasize freedom and unity, and that rhythmic movement that makes everyone feel a part of a great living organism."[36] This quest to evoke "rhythmic movement" might have been the source for the formal landscape. Practical reasons could have played a part as well; Wright described how "each member of the school, young and old," would be given his or her own garden plot (depicted in the drawings by the squares) to cultivate.

In general Wright seemed quite proud of the Whitney Memorial proposal, and Eleanor Whitney must have been either satisfied with it or preoccupied with the music building project, for the existing record of correspondence contains none of the detailed lists of revisions found in the music building letters. She did request some minor changes, and Wright reoriented a portion of the complex in October by angling the studios and artists' residences thirty degrees off-axis (presumably to make more room for the ever-expanding music building), but there is nothing to suggest any major disagreements between client and architect over the basic idea of the proposal. In the fall of 1944, however, the project died a quiet death.

The Sculpture Project

The Whitney Memorial building would have been intricately related to one of the more intriguing aspects of Wright's Florida Southern plan—an unrealized proposal for an integrated water and sculpture program that would have further reinforced the campus's connection to nature. Following E. Stanley Jones's suggestions for a set of symbolic sculptures depicting an anxious student entering college and a confident graduate flanked by figures of Science and Religion, the original "Programme for University" document included two separate mentions of such a project. On the first page, Wright wrote notes about "Important features" at the entrance, "to be a heroic size figure of Youth—entering as novitiate—alone. Subject to the cultivations of Art, Science and Religion." Then on a later page describing the gardens and terraces, Wright hastily scribbled notes about a second set of figures at "the lake end" of campus, depicting an heroic-size statue of the former novitiate standing between representations of "Art, Science and Religions."

Only a month after receiving the commission, Wright contacted Carl Milles, a Swedish sculptor living at the Cranbrook educational community in Bloomfield Hills, Michigan.[37] Milles was known for his fountains, which often featured sinuous bronze depictions of mythological beings. Wright admired Milles, calling him "probably the greatest" contemporary sculptor and "the power behind the throne at Cranbrook."[38] The two men exchanged a series of messages between May and October 1938, containing tantalizing hints of the proposed sculptural scheme for Florida Southern.

Early in the design process Wright apparently decided—or was persuaded by Spivey—to include Jones's sculptural groups. This decision raised an immediate problem. Since Jones imagined the statues in front of and behind a single building, but Wright was thinking in terms of a multibuilding complex, where should the statues be located? While Wright pondered that question, he left Milles to work out the details of the individual figures. In June, responding to Milles's request for blueprints, Wright briefly described his point of view: "The figures for Florida Southern may be fountains I guess or whatever you elect. I have no drawings for them. They are free standing features probably heroic size. Youth entering his university and youth leaving it. Could be done in semi precious stone."[39]

Milles suggested a fountain—his specialty—in his first response. In his most elaborate description, Milles chafed at the restrictions of the Jones proposal. "Youth could always be represented in a young man or woman," he wrote, "but religion—how will you symbol [sic] that without a literary—terrible—composition. The same as with science." Instead, Milles described a fountain with a "wild, powerful, dark bronze" Triton, "surrounded by a ring of fishes" and water jets.[40]

The Milles sculptures never materialized, but the idea of a sculptural program was still alive as late as the 1940s, as the Whitney Memorial drawings demonstrate.[41] Instead of Jones's entering and graduating student, or Milles's fountain, Wright conceived of a series of streams, pools, and sculptures flowing through the campus. He intended the Water Dome at the north end of campus to be the source for a stream that would connect a series of smaller pools throughout the grounds in a symbolic gesture representing the flow of student life.

A statue of a male student entering college—a holdover from Jones's proposal—would be placed in the center of the Water Dome. Several smaller pools at various points throughout the orange grove, connected by the small stream, would contain similar statues. Wright described them in a letter to Spivey: "A characteristic group of several figures is placed on a globe on the rim of each pool, reflected in the water. Each group represents the allegory—'the stages of development in the culture of a true democratic citizen' such as we hope sure ours will become when our country emerges from the rule of the business man into the light of rule by the bravest and the best."[42] A statue depicting the graduating student flanked by a man representing religion and a woman representing science would stand in a final pool near the Whitney Memorial building. From there, the stream would flow into Lake Hollingsworth, symbolizing the student's entry into adult life. A 1944 plan for the Whitney Memorial specifically labeled these pools: in front of the library was a pool called "Sciences"; in front of the arts building was an "Arts" pool; and to the east of the proposed arts building was a pool entitled "Statecraft." A branch of the stream would flow past the children's building, down a waterfall on its west side, and into the lake.

Such a large-scale combination of water and statuary was unique in Wright's vast oeuvre, and it was particularly interesting coming from an architect who often recycled design ideas in projects that might be decades apart. Although elements of water and sculpture had previously appeared in some of Wright's work, figural sculpture was rare; some of the few examples include his own studio (1897) in Oak Park, Illinois, with two human figures by Richard Bock; the Larkin Company Administration Building (1903) with more Bock creations; and the Midway Gardens, with abstracted "Sprites" by Wright and Alfonso Iannelli.[43]

Water was much more common. Wright was particularly fond of water, including natural features like lakes, streams, and ponds whenever possible, and creating water forms when plausible.[44] An important precursor to the Florida Southern program can be found in the Johnson Desert Compound (1924), where Wright envisioned a large circular fountain anchoring one end of the property, spawning a channel of water that changed into cascading pools before taking shape as a series of irrigation canals in the valley below the house. In the San Marcos in the Desert project of the same year, water actively flowed through the heart of the building complex. Wright's Barnsdall House complex on Olive Hill in Los Angeles (1917) contained, on a smaller scale, a water path similar to that of the Johnson Compound. A formal, square pool and fountain in front of the house at one end of the main axis fed water into an underground stream that surfaced inside the house in a small pool around the main fireplace; the water then went underground again before reappearing in a circular pond surrounded by a semicircle of tiered seat-like steps at the other end of the axis.

In all of these designs, Wright used water to introduce a natural element to the site and to create a sense of journey or motion. But perhaps the Florida Southern proposal's closest relative was a set of statues Wright envisioned for the Nakoma Country Club in Madison, Wisconsin (1924). At the entry to the country club property, Wright intended a pair of large sculptures flanking the road and introducing Native American themes. On one side an eighteen-foot-tall depiction of "Nakomis," an Indian warrior, would stand in a circular pool seventy-five feet in diameter. Across the road, a figure of "Nakoma," a woman, with a child by her side and another in a papoose, would stand in a pool of equal size and shape.[45] While Wright inherited the sculpture's thematic content at Florida Southern from the Jones Foundation initiative, it seems evident that he appropriated the circular pools and the duality of sculpture and water from the unbuilt Nakoma proposal when dealing with a client interested in "heroic figures" more than a decade later. None of the ambitious water and sculpture plans, however, were carried out, leaving Wright's West Campus without a fundamental aesthetic and interpretive component.

A Setback and a Move Forward

In October 1944, as construction on the library was moving slowly forward, music building negotiations were about to reach a standstill, and Spivey was preparing to launch a $1 million campaign for additional endowment, disaster struck Florida Southern when a deadly hurricane toppled the Pfeiffer Chapel's tower. One-hundred-mile-an-hour winds swept through Lakeland, pushing down the towers' walls and cracking the skylights. Admitting, "This is embarrassing to us all," Wright responded by blaming the construction superintendent for not following his instructions properly—and, amazingly, by pleading ignorance of Florida's weather. "There was no precaution taken against Hurricanes in the tower as I never realized we were down in the terrific Hurricane belt," Wright wrote to Spivey. "But a one-hundred-mile wind should not have damaged the tower. We will rebuild it now to stand anything Florida has ever had."[46]

Spivey used the opportunity to gently suggest that Wright make some alterations when rebuilding the chapel tower to reduce the amount of sunlight that entered the building. "I want you to keep in mind that actually there is a little too much sun in the building," he offered. "When the sun passes across the building during midday, it is almost impossible to sit in it for even 20 minutes."[47] He also recommended a revised skylight design and a moveable rather than a stationary pulpit to accommodate the various types of gatherings that occurred in the building. Wright modified the tower but fixed his attention on Spivey's last request, trying to dissuade him from altering the original chapel by reminding him that once the proposed music building was completed, there would no longer be any need to have anything but religious services in the chapel, and thus no need ever to move the pulpit.

The year 1944 thus ended with a stalemate between Wright and Whitney on the music building, the Whitney Memorial in limbo, a damaged chapel, and sluggish progress on the library. Not much changed in regard to the first three projects through early 1945, but during Founders Week in March, celebrating the school's sixtieth anniversary, the E. T. Roux Library was dedicated. It was the fifth Wright building to be finished on the Florida Southern campus.

That summer, Wright fired Robert Wehr, longtime construction superintendent, blaming him for causing the chapel tower's collapse and castigating him for not following instructions. Harold Turner, a builder and designer Wright admired who had supervised construction on the Hanna house, was his replacement. Then Spivey told Wright he had located another potential donor and asked Wright to make plans for an administration building to house the president, deans, registrar, bursar, and publicity office. Uncharacteristically, Wright sent a set of drawings within three weeks, which suggests that he had previously formulated his ideas and perhaps even some preliminary sketches.

The Watson and Fine Administration Buildings

For the administration building, to be sited immediately west of and only a few feet from the large circular pool and Water Dome, Wright proposed two structures joined by a double esplanade: a U-shaped building with a garden in the center and a smaller square structure, slightly less than half the size of its neighbor and closer to the Water Dome.[48] The impression one gets from the plan is that the smaller building has been pulled out of a larger rectangle and then shifted slightly off its center axis. In what appears to be the earliest drawing of the project, Wright experimented with triangles as an addition to his typical vocabulary of flat overhanging roofs and cantilevered balconies. At this stage Wright envisioned triangular windows in the side walls and triangular skylights, similar to those in the library roof. Repeating the triangular motif in the administration building would relate it to the chapel and library, as well as echo the triangles of the master plan.

Wright created a more extensive set of drawings in July 1945. The portion of the administration complex closest to the Water Dome, which would become known as the Benjamin Fine Building, housed the bursar's and registrar's offices. The Fine Building featured a two-story lobby with a mezzanine that cut diagonally across the square space; this motif of a double-height room with mezzanine also existed in the chapel and library

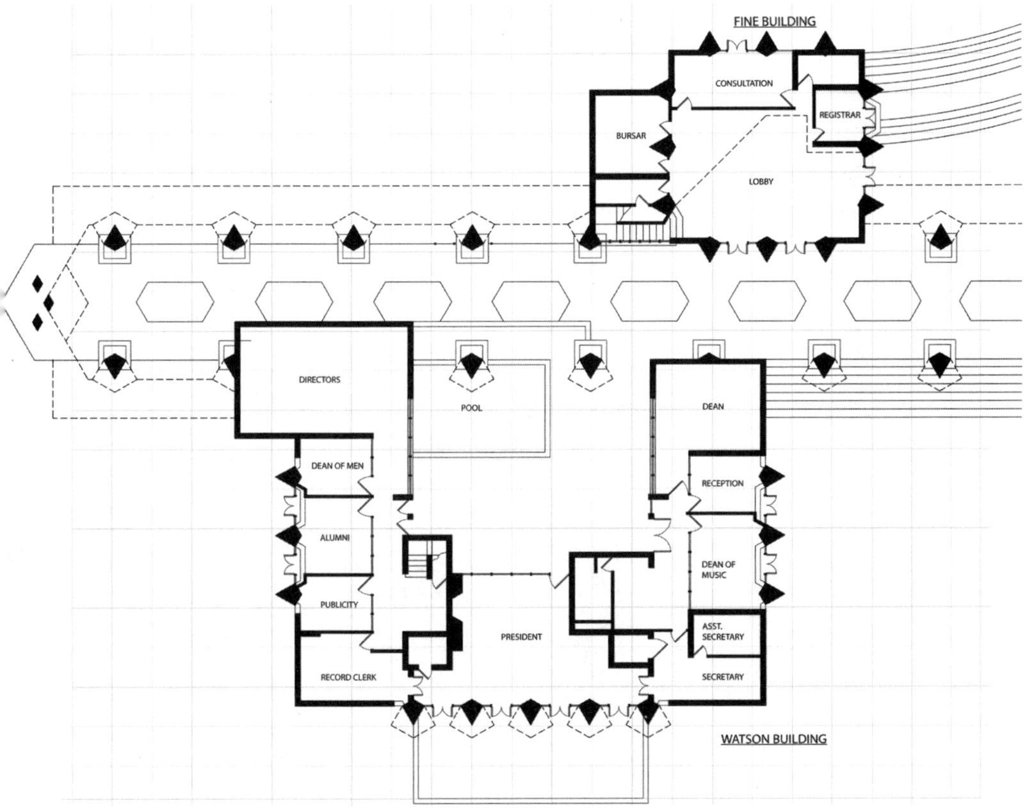

Figure 4.7. Benjamin Fine and Emile Watson Administration Buildings plans, based on original drawings. Courtesy of Dan Price and Nathaniel J. Turner.

and would reappear in the Whitney Memorial project and the minor chapel. The larger administration structure, later to be named the Emile E. Watson Building, had a small pool and fountain and much vegetation in the center of its horseshoe, adding to the "outdoor garden" experience. The Watson Building contained offices for the dean of music, dean of men, dean of the college, and the president, in addition to a meeting room for the board of directors. Spivey's new office was the complex's interior highlight. His space ran along the Watson Building's western wall and was lined with French doors opening to a terrace that overlooked the parking lot along Johnson Avenue. Wright included a built-in desk and fireplace for the president.

Both sections of the administration building were two stories, and they shared the now-standard materials (concrete blocks, Red Tidewater Cypress trim, copper fascias) with the other campus structures. Wright used the fascias extensively throughout the interiors as a way to unify them with the exteriors and the esplanade that divided the two structures. That esplanade expanded to eighteen feet wide between the two administration buildings, providing space for an "exedra"—a double-esplanade passage with diamond-shaped patches of greenery inserted along the center of the walk beneath similarly shaped skylights in the esplanade roof.

Figure 4.8. Fine Administration Building, 1945. Florida Southern College Archives.

Figure 4.9. Watson Administration Building, 1945. Florida Southern College Archives.

Figure 4.10. Exedra between Fine and Watson Administration Buildings. Photograph by author.

Figure 4.11. Florida Southern College, West Campus, aerial view, early 1950s. Florida Southern College Archives.

Spivey was more involved with the design of the administration building than any of the other Wright structures, sending extensive lists of suggestions and requirements during the summer of 1945. He also proposed a new entry. Uncomfortable with the way the building turned its back on the public, with the entrance inside the horseshoe court, Spivey recommended opening a door in the west façade onto the parking lot so that visitors

could enter into his secretary's office without having to circumambulate the building. Spivey failed to understand that the indirect, often circuitous entry sequence was one of Wright's most cherished design elements. Not surprisingly, Wright does not seem to have reacted to the suggestion, and Spivey did not press the matter.

Wright's rapidly produced drawings for the administration building would contrast with the slow pace of their actual construction. After work began with a groundbreaking ceremony in December 1946, the project dragged. Ten months later Spivey complained to Wright. "The Administration Building is moving along just as slowly as it could move. Personally, I am unable to find out why it cannot make any progress, but I suppose there is a real reason," he wrote. "As far as I can see, I think it will take another year to finish it, and instead of costing $60,000 or $70,000, as we originally thought, this little building, unless something is done about it, will cost at least $250,000 or $300,000."[49] Kenn Lockhart, a Taliesin apprentice sent to Lakeland to supervise construction, cited material shortages and increased costs for the delay, while Spivey blamed the contractor, Ben Fulghum, whom he labeled "a piddler."[50] The college nonetheless dedicated the unfinished building during Founders Week in March 1948, naming the larger structure for trustee Emile E. Watson and the smaller one for Benjamin Fine, the education editor for the *New York Times*. They appear finally to have been completed that fall.

Spivey was pleased with the building and proudly reported, "The administration building is beautiful, and we are having thousands of visitors to see it."[51] It was prominently featured in an eight-page *Architectural Forum* article.[52] But just a few years later, the complex, despite Spivey's initial enthusiasm, was the first of Wright's creations to require significant alteration. In 1955 Taliesin apprentice Nils Schweizer, who had replaced Lockhart as Wright's on-site representative, enclosed an outdoor balcony on the Fine Building and expanded the bursar's and registrar's offices underneath the esplanade to fulfill the need for more administrative space. Only three years later Schweizer relayed a similar request from the college to create more room by enclosing the esplanade between the two administration buildings with glass to address a "critical" need for more space.[53] There is no record of Wright responding to such a request and, fortunately, it was never executed.

As 1945 drew to a close, Florida Southern College's future looked brighter than ever. With five Wright buildings constructed, the administration complex on the drafting board, the war finally over, wartime restrictions lifted, and students poised to return, the school looked forward to an unprecedented period of growth.

FIVE *A "Florida Form"* Postwar Development, 1946–1957

After the end of World War II, things continued to improve for Florida Southern College, Ludd Spivey, and the Frank Lloyd Wright project. The lean years had passed, and over the next fourteen years enrollments and income would increase, more donors would be found, and much of Wright's proposed campus would be constructed. When Wright died in 1959, marking the end of the Spivey-Wright era, the small college in Lakeland, Florida, could boast the largest unified collection of Frank Lloyd Wright architecture in the world.

The Music Building Project Redux

The late forties marked the rebirth of Wright's ill-fated music building project after more than a year in limbo. During that time Eleanor Searle Whitney donated funds to create a College of Music at Florida Southern with Robert Gayler as the dean. She renewed her efforts to erect a music building in early 1946 after setting it aside following the birth of her son. The time away had not changed her approach, however, and she still required approval of Wright's plans from some outside expert before agreeing to fund the building. This stipulation angered Wes Peters, and he complained to Wright about Whitney's approach. "Dr. Spivey says that Eleanor 'Surly' Whitney is ready to come across with the money as a deduction from here [sic] 1946 income tax if made before 1947 (Jan 1) if she receives a statement from a stage authority, or equal, as to the workability of the scheme," he wrote. "Dr. Spivey is honestly troubled about this. I told him I thought it was a disgrace that any person of her ilk should even ask for such a thing. The Doctor admitted it, but says he doesn't know any other way to get the money."[1] Spivey suggested sending the drawings to Michael Todd, Broadway (and later Hollywood) producer, to satisfy Whitney. Peters felt this was "an insult," but informed Wright about the offer. Wright must have agreed because in April 1946 Spivey mailed the most recent version of the music building drawings to Todd in California.

For the second incarnation of the music building, Wright synthesized his first design with the Model Theatre project of 1938. He retained the basic motif of two auditoriums at opposite ends of a central loggia section, but reversed their original placement so that the Symphony was now at the north end, closest to the library. Wright reworked the Symphony into a hexagonal shape, like Pfeiffer Chapel, with the same revolving stage design as the earlier theater project. He also enlarged it to hold up to 1,550 seats and included an orchestra pit, which had been one of the major omissions, according to Whitney and her advisors. The smaller Star Chamber retained its spherical shape and function as a practice and recital space. The loggia still held practice rooms and offices, but it was expanded into two rows of rooms separated by an enclosed central gallery.

This new iteration of the music building failed to satisfy Whitney. Similarly, Mike Todd must not have fulfilled Whitney's expectations; in late 1946 Spivey contacted noted Broadway set designer Lee Simonson to review the drawings.[2] Simonson, who described Wright as "a great functional architect" and said, "He could do a fine functioning theatre, if he could be gotten to understand how flexible a modern theatre must be in order to function," agreed to become involved with the project, and by late February 1947 Wright had received a list of seven "desirable changes" to the building.[3]

Wright's measured response focused on how the Whitney team was missing the point in their desire to place a large auditorium on campus for traditional entertainment. "It would appear to me that the college needs more the building that will enable new life to come to the theater (as well

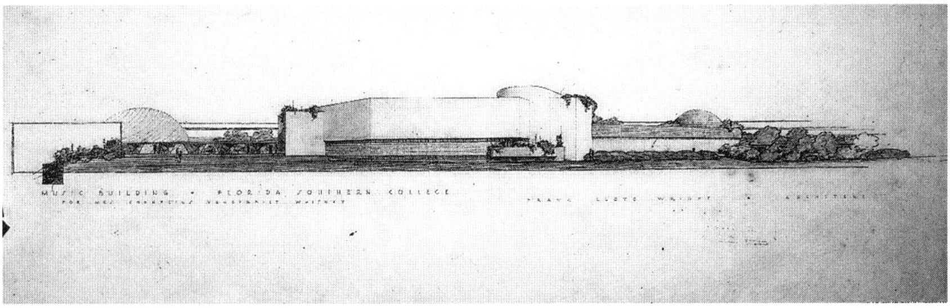

Figure 5.1. Frank Lloyd Wright, second proposal for unbuilt music building, 1946. Copyright © 2009 The Frank Lloyd Wright Foundation, Taliesin West, Scottsdale, Ariz. 4611.001.

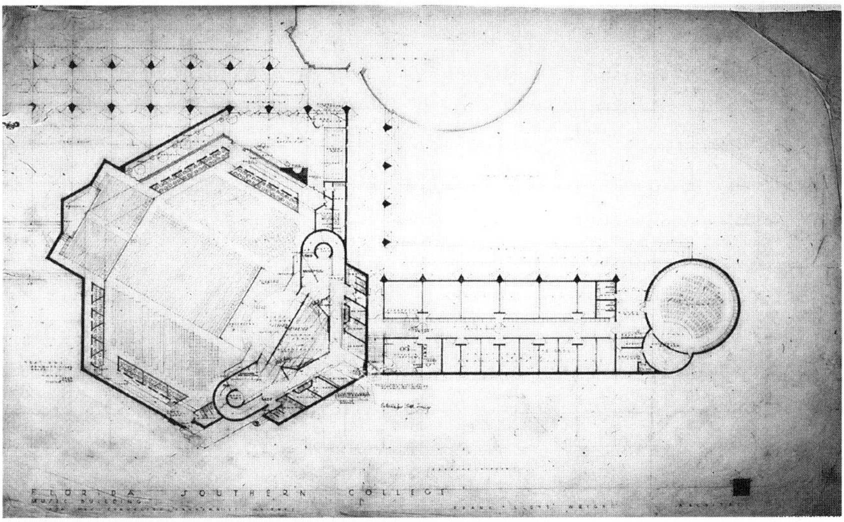

Figure 5.2. Frank Lloyd Wright, music building plan, 1946. Copyright © 2009 The Frank Lloyd Wright Foundation, Taliesin West, Scottsdale, Ariz. 4611.003.

as the opera) than it should need to continue and perpetuate the ponderous anachronisms of the past. Now just what are, not only the possibilities but probabilities, of that future which is really our present duty when we build?" he wrote. "Is it not the elimination of the insignificance we call 'ham'—and the opportunity for fuller expression of human qualities in more human scale? Simple accessories and a technique that misses no significance and ensure [sic] that no subtlety be lost?"[4] He rebutted each of the proposed changes and acerbically referred to Whitney's desire for a "grand opera" before suggesting that the project be terminated. "So—why not buy an adjoining lot and let the Vanderbilt interests build their own building there," Wright asked Spivey. "Let us build a more modest educational one on our campus to let the growth take place that could not possibly occur in the old cliché."

Of course this put Spivey, as the middleman, in a precarious position. He had been promised between $300,000 and $500,000 by Whitney, a sum that would pay for a music building and much more. She represented the attainment of Spivey's dreams, but he could never seem to finalize the deal. He pleaded with Wright once more to draw a simple sketch that would satisfy Whitney and her reviewers. In the meantime he contacted Philip Johnson of the Museum of Modern Art in New York for his opinion of Wright's latest edition of the music building. Johnson sent his few questions directly to Wright and gave every indication of a favorable response. "Mrs. Whitney apparently does not even wish to look at [the drawings], but requests a letter from an authoritative source," wrote Johnson. "I believe that our Department of Theatre Design could write such a letter, signed by both myself and Mr. Amberg, who is Curator of Theatre Design. He is very familiar, of course, with all kinds of stage mechanics."[5] A few weeks later Johnson told Wright, "All of us here at the Museum are more than anxious to have buildings like your theater erected, and as soon as possible."[6]

Although this was the type of authoritative review Whitney had been seeking for years, the Museum of Modern Art's favorable verdict was not enough to save the music building. Sometime in the summer of 1947—more than five years after the first contacts between the college and Whitney—the project came to a bitter end, as Whitney elected to solicit other architects. Wright documented his feelings in a "To whom it may concern" letter: "So far as I am concerned I could not forgive myself were I to allow the unity and distinction of what has already been done to be destroyed by accepting conventional ideas and building-standards and allow them to enter in unsympathetic minds," he wrote.[7] Wright magnanimously gave his consent for Whitney to build her auditorium—as long as it was on the opposite side of the Florida Southern campus and in no way resembled his own structures there.

Despite the death of the music building, Eleanor Whitney continued to have a relationship with Florida Southern College. No building was ever erected with Whitney's money, however. Years later her explanation for the Wright proposal's demise was skewed by her own disappointment; she claimed Wright "was not willing to modify his unworkable interior," which included an orchestra located "in the right hand balcony."[8] The available evidence disproves both assertions. In the end, the project died because two strong personalities clashed over whether the structure should be a large-scale auditorium for Broadway-type shows and operas or a small-scale, intimate building for college productions. But the idea of a performance space on campus survived this dispute and would be resurrected in the late 1950s.

Florida Southern's dramatic enrollment increase after World War II accentuated the need for such a performance space. Like schools across the country, the war's end and the G.I. Bill resulted in more college students than ever before. Florida Southern's student body in September 1946 numbered almost 1,500 students—nearly twice the size of the school in 1940. These new students were a combination of returning veterans and the first wave of a general population increase that had reached college age. Florida Southern was forced to expand its campus beyond the Wright project. In the late 1940s the school constructed a $1.5-million, eighteen-building complex of dormitories, apartments, sorority houses, and a student commons building; all of these structures, designed by Robert Law Weed of Miami, were on the east side of campus away from the Wright buildings.[9]

The Water Dome

The late forties also marked the debut of the Water Dome, one of Wright's most unique projects for Florida Southern. From the beginning of his involvement, he imagined an impressive natural display at the northern end of his West Campus between the administration building and seminar buildings. A circular water basin 160 feet in diameter would be ringed by a copper pipe with a series of regularly spaced holes. In theory, when pressurized water was run through the pipe, streams would shoot out of the holes approximately 50 feet into the air toward the circle's center, creating a sensational dome-like effect. The water would be pumped from an artesian well dug behind the seminars. Behind the dome, Wright arranged an "Arboreal Hemicycle"—a four-level exedra of bushes and Australian pine trees encircling the northern end of the pool, providing a stunning natural background for the water while also screening the campus from the adjacent residential neighborhood.

Early aerial renderings of the campus depict the Water Dome as an impossibly perfect hemisphere of water, rising high above the neighboring buildings, dwarfing onlookers, and falling neatly to the ground. These im-

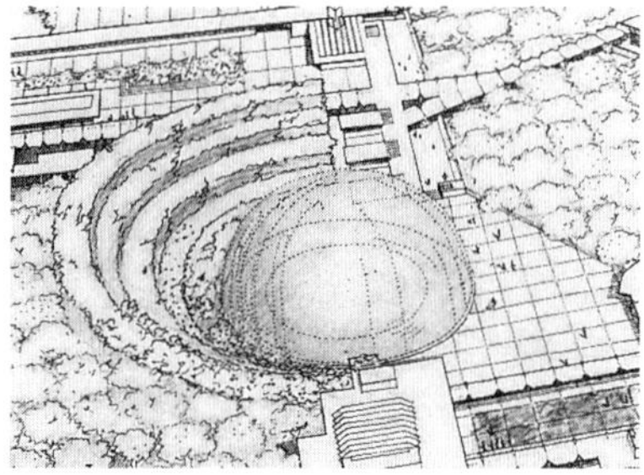

Figure 5.3. Frank Lloyd Wright, Water Dome. Copyright © 2009 The Frank Lloyd Wright Foundation, Taliesin West, Scottsdale, Ariz. 3816.003.

ages presented the Water Dome as the symbolic centerpiece of Wright's campus plan and the sensorial focal point, one that would involve sight, sound, and touch. As intended, the dome of water would have been visible from most of the upper end of the campus, and the Australian pine trees behind it would have grown to become the tallest objects at Florida Southern, reaching eighty feet or more upon maturity. Additionally, the sound of shooting water would suffuse the surrounding area, while the wet spray would be felt many feet away, depending on the wind. Beyond engaging viewers' senses of sight, sound, and touch, the dome would also provide a unique marker to reference both the history of American college architecture and Wright's architectural theory.

Wright's Water Dome can be read as both a specific and a general critique of monumental educational and civic architecture. Undoubtedly he was familiar with F. H. Trimble's proposed Southern College campus design from the 1920s, with its dominant central building topped by a grand dome to be located on or near the spot where the Water Dome was erected. It is possible to imagine Wright's Water Dome as a reinterpretation, rendered in a natural material, of not only Trimble's domed building, but also those existing at historic campuses like the University of Virginia and the Massachusetts Institute of Technology.[10]

The traditional dome was one of Wright's favorite critical targets; he vehemently denounced domed buildings whenever possible. In a series of lectures in London, given less than a year after conceiving the Florida Southern campus, Wright decried the famous dome of St. Peter's Cathedral in Rome, a "singularly bastardized expression of architecture, be-corniced and be-plastered, false, untrue to itself," and he bemoaned how it "became the symbol of official authority the world over."[11] He later called the dome a "ponderous anachronism" in his autobiography.[12] Given this disdain, the Florida Southern Water Dome may be interpreted as a critique of this historical component. Wright's Water Dome is a negative dome that subverts the traditional image by borrowing its form but employing water instead of stone or metal, thus symbolizing nature rather than human authority, in keeping with Wright's organic approach to architecture. The Water Dome would be light and transparent compared to the heavy, opaque masonry dome; it would be at ground level, able to be touched by visitors, whereas the majestic domes of authority rose hundreds of feet off the ground. And it would be kinetic—the constantly moving streams of water would counteract the typical dome's static mass.

At almost the same time that he was designing Florida Southern, Wright was working on another version of the negative dome. In the unbuilt project for the Monona Terrace office complex (1938) for Madison, Wisconsin, he envisioned three glass hemispheres—labeled "Water Domes"—rising over an underground structure, with fountains cascading water over the domes. In that project, the small, transparent domes directly challenged the massive granite dome of the Wisconsin state capital three blocks away.[13]

The Water Dome allowed Wright to continue his exploration of circular forms in the Florida Southern plan. In what appears to be Wright's earliest campus plan (fig. 2.1), the Water Dome is the only circular shape, contrasting with the rigid orthogonals of the other structures. In subsequent plans it is the largest circle in a group that initially included the library reading room and the science building's planetarium, but that later expanded to include the various versions of the music building auditoriums, the terrace of the proposed children's building, the little theater of the industrial arts building, the swimming pool, and the small pools that were to be scattered across the campus. The circular fountain also anchored the north end of campus, while echoing the semicircular amphitheater of early plan variations that terminated the site's southern end, and balancing the water and circular shape of Lake Hollingsworth.

The structure's moving water conceptually linked the fountain to the larger campus plan. As described in chapter 4, the Water Dome was part of a larger design scheme using water to symbolize a student's journey through life. The dome's circular pool served as the source for the stream that would wind its way around the buildings and down the hill to Lake Hollingsworth. The continually flowing water would further express the idea of activity that formed the foundation of Spivey's progressive educational outlook. Just as the campus plan's "reflex" angles invited movement through the landscape, serving as a metaphor for active learning, the Water

Dome fountains, together with the stream and secondary pools, reinforced the notion of activity as education's foundation and its natural form.

Wright may not have been thinking strictly about subverting authority symbols or materializing educational concepts when he conceived the Water Dome. A more immediate inspiration may have come from the 1933–34 "Century of Progress" World's Fair in Chicago. That event featured a prominent water fountain in the shape of a flattened dome 150 feet in diameter, with jets arranged in a circle and projecting water toward the center. Centrally located and illuminated with multiple colored lights at night, it would have been quite impressive and difficult for visitors to miss. Whether or not Wright saw the fountain is uncertain—he submitted some designs for the fair, but it is not known whether he ever attended it. His encounter with Japanese architecture at the 1893 World's Colombian Exposition, also in Chicago, and its influence on his architecture has been documented; it could be that a similar episode forty years later inspired Wright's Florida Southern College Water Dome.[14]

Although it was a crucial symbolic element in Wright's vision, the Water Dome was less practical and consequently less necessary than some of the other proposed structures, so it was not until the mid-1940s that Spivey asked Wright to make drawings for the project. Construction was far enough along by the summer of 1946 that the basin pool could hold water. It was completely filled in 1948. However, the Water Dome was never finished. There is no record of it ever being turned on in its original form. A small fountain was placed in the basin's center in the 1950s, and the pool was largely paved over to create a series of smaller pools in the late 1960s.

Figure 5.4. World's Fair fountain, Century of Progress International Exposition, Chicago, Illinois, 1933–34. Postcard, author's collection.

Figure 5.5. Water Dome basin and Fine Administration Building. Florida Southern College Archives.

According to a member of the design team that created a new Water Dome for Florida Southern in 2007 based on Wright's plans (see chapter 6), the original fountain could not possibly have worked because the necessary plumbing was never installed.[15]

The Swimming Pool and Outdoor Theater Project

Wright intended for another water feature to occupy the opposite end of the campus—an outdoor swimming pool complex, appropriate to the Florida climate. Spivey and Wright's original program for Florida Southern included a $20,000 structure described as "Outdoor Theatre and Games in large Hemi-cycle," with seats for 500 spectators along one side of the hemi-cycle and a swimming pool extending into Lake Hollingsworth.[16] The structure also had meaning as the last building in a line leading down the hillside from the Water Dome; Wright wrote of it as "a Garden Feature—terminating the series of units."[17] In the earliest drawings the pool lay on the campus's main axis, emerging from the esplanade that ran straight south from the chapel into the lake (figs. 2.1 and 2.2). Wright depicted an elongated oval pool, shaped like a Roman circus, built into the lake, using earth to create a barrier from the water; on the other side of the esplanade was a semicircular amphitheater. He revised the location and form of the swimming pool over the years, but no progress was made on actually building it until the mid-forties. Spivey asked Wright to draw plans for the structure in 1946. "Since we do not play football, we are in great need of some aquatic sports. Our GI's must have something to do," he wrote.[18]

As Wright focused his attention on the swimming pool, its shape changed from oval to circular, and the entire complex was moved farther out into the lake, possibly on Spivey's suggestion. "Instead of creating a regular swimming pool, why not build a retaining wall, either circular or square out in the lake?" asked Spivey. "And, that we pump all the lake water out of the place and fill it full of nice sand and make a sand beach and use the water from our artesian well to fill it from time to time."[19] His main concern was water quality, but a problematic aspect of Wright's master plan also troubled him: Wright disregarded the existing road that ran along the lakeshore (Lake Hollingsworth Drive), placing his amphitheater and pool complex directly in its path. Spivey's suggestion was therefore more practical, avoiding the costs—and bureaucratic irritation—of trying to reroute a much-used thoroughfare.

The proposed design featured a circular pool separated from the lake by earthen banks sixteen feet wide across the top and rising three feet above the water level. Drawings depict the pool's depth ranging from six to twenty feet. The swimming pool and amphitheater complex engaged Wright's penchant for including water in designs and linking the campus to its most prominent natural feature. In the Monona Terrace project he also extended a structure into a lake, and his rationale was "to recover the waterfront for urban use" and make the lake part of "the life of the entire city."[20] A similar thought process probably informed his design for the Florida Southern swimming pool.

Spivey enlisted the alumni association to sponsor the swimming pool project. Ground was broken in March 1947. The alumni created a sub-

Figure 5.6. Frank Lloyd Wright, proposal for unbuilt swimming pool and outdoor theater, 1947. Copyright © 2009 The Frank Lloyd Wright Foundation, Taliesin West, Scottsdale, Ariz. 4732.002.

scription plan to raise funds whereby donors could purchase seats in the outdoor amphitheater connected to the pool for thirty dollars per seat. This drive was moderately successful; a photograph in the *Southern* in early May 1947 shows students in front of a bulletin board tallying 958 subscribers to the seat selection campaign. But the swimming pool would eventually rival the Whitney Music Building in terms of the amount of effort put into an ill-fated project never to be completed. In the case of the swimming pool, however, there was no dispute over design. Beginning in the fall of 1947, much work was actually carried out to create the structure, including dredging tons of sand at the lakeshore to form the earthen barrier needed to create the pool's walls. The spot chosen was slightly west of the original site indicated in earlier versions of the campus plan, in order to provide some distance between the complex and Spivey's house.

Spivey wanted to have the complex ready by fall semester, 1948, but as usual he was overly ambitious. Dredging continued though much of the year, but there is no record of specific work being done the following year except for a contract in the Florida Southern College Archives to move 100,000 tons of sand from the site.

The project was briefly resurrected in 1950. The *Southern* reported that the finished structure would be a 300-foot ring extending into the lake, enclosing an 80-by-176-foot swimming pool and supporting a 5,000-seat amphitheater. "Work started on this project three years ago but progress has been slow up to this point. Now it can safely be said that completion is in sight," claimed the reporter optimistically. "Sand is already being dredged up."[21] By 1953, however, the sporadic work on the swimming pool and amphitheater appears to have ceased for good. In 1954 the college opened a conventional swimming pool in a different location on campus.

Historicism

The swimming pool and outdoor theater complex hinted at the lingering historicism that lay beneath some of the aspects of Wright's Florida Southern design. In the final decades of his life, Wright's work shifted toward a slightly more obvious—though still subtle—use of historical elements. In this sense Wright was not alone, as other high-profile American architects like Minoru Yamasaki, Edward Durrell Stone, and Philip Johnson revived traditional architectural elements in their work in an attempt to enrich modernist architecture.

In addition to the correspondences between Wright's campus plan and the University of Virginia and Hadrian's Villa described in chapter 2, there were historical echoes in some of the individual buildings. The historicism emerged not so much in the details of the buildings as in their shapes, and possibly their relations to one another. The swimming pool and outdoor theater were the most overtly historical components. In the earliest plan drawings the pool took the elongated oval form of a Roman circus, while the theater's stepped half-circle and flat circular stage area mimicked the Greek theater. Although neither ancient building type had anything to do with water, Wright must have liked the interplay of their shapes, and he was determined to site these two structures on the shoreline. When he reconceived the pool as a large circle sometime in the 1940s, the theater retained its Greek form and continued to do so throughout all of the various design iterations.

Perhaps more evident is Wright's debt to Mayan architecture, first revealed in his use of textile blocks beginning in the 1920s. Wright was openly fond of Meso-American architecture. He wrote lovingly about how "primitive American architecture—Toltec, Aztec, Mayan, Inca—stirred my wonder, excited my wishful admiration" as a boy.[22] This architecture of mountain-like block forms and broad plateaus featured a "grand simplicity of concept and form," a monumental quality where "Architectural grandeur was thus made one with the surrounding features of mountainous land"—both concepts Wright strove to emulate in his own work.[23] When an article appeared in an art journal interpreting the Mayan influence on Wright's work, he wrote a letter to the author in response: "Had I not loved and comprehended preColumbian [sic] architecture as the primitive basis of world-architecture, I could not now build as I build with understanding of all architecture."[24]

The patterned blocks used at Florida Southern are a direct legacy of that influence. This type of block construction was rather archaic by the late 1930s. Wright's deliberate choice of a method for building that was essentially premodern seems to further indicate his desire to impart an aged feel to the campus. And the associations with Mayan architecture may extend beyond construction materials. Spivey's request for a "great education temple" might have prompted Wright to recall his affinity for Mayan forms and monumentality, which is intimated in the campus's rather small-scale buildings by the use of repetitive masonry blocks. The plazas depicted in the original plans could also owe something to the Meso-American building complexes that Wright admired, as well as the overall concept of a group of imposing buildings surrounded by lush forests. It is possible that Wright related Florida's semitropical location to the jungles on the other side of the Caribbean, where the great Mayan monuments rose; Mayan architecture may have helped provide a historical foundation for a region with no discernible architectural heritage, but with a similar history of pre-Columbian settlement.[25]

Administration Building Completed

After the library was completed in 1945, the next building on the Wright campus to be finished was the administration building, which was notable for its far greater cost and length of construction in spite of its seemingly uncomplicated design.[26] The pace of progress and significant expense perplexed Spivey. At one point in October 1947, he predicted construction would take another year; only a week later he doubted that it would be finished by the start of 1950.[27] "I agree with you that for the life of me I cannot understand why the administration building is costing so much," he complained to Wright. "Already we have spent about $100,000, and I want to tell you it isn't even out of the ground."[28] Spivey believed the main problem was that Ben Fulghum, the supervisor, was "a piddler," but Peters, who was visiting again to evaluate progress, attributed these delays and excesses to the entire work organization and predicted more of the same for future buildings. "We have been desperately busy trying to get this most unorganizable place organized," he told Wright. "In spite of appearance of greater prosperity and the fact that the place is crowded to the guards with G.I. Bill-of-Rightzers, the place is the same old shiftless outfit with little recognizable direction."[29]

The dedication of the administration building and the Water Dome in March 1948 brought the number of Wright structures on the Florida Southern campus to seven. Spivey showed no signs of slowing the pace of construction, continually prompting Wright to begin making drawings for new projects. In a May 1949 letter to a Mrs. George Grimes, Spivey included an ambitious list of buildings yet to be erected on campus: "Science, Home Economics, Industrial Art, Small Chapel, Art, Music, Little Theatre, Out Door Theatre, Swimming Pool, Three Seminars."[30] At the time, dredging operations were being carried out in Lake Hollingsworth to create the swimming pool and amphitheater complex, and preliminary work was under way on what would be the largest Wright building to that point, the industrial arts building.

The Ordway Industrial Arts Building

The early "Programme for University" document noted separate buildings for manual training and home economics. The manual training structure was to emphasize "applications," according to Wright's handwritten notes, and to include spaces for agricultural, dairy, and horticultural experiments, while the home economics unit would house tea rooms and areas for flower arrangement, food preparation, "Dietetics," and the "Chemistry of Foods." In Wright's first campus drawings the two proposed structures had been merged into one manual arts and domesticity building. The building formed a U facing the north-south esplanade just east of the seminar buildings, surrounding on three sides an open courtyard with a rectangular reflecting pool. There is evidence that Spivey had intended this structure to be among the initial group of new campus buildings; as early as May 1940 he expressed his desire to build an "Industrial Arts & Home Economics building" that summer.[31] Spivey began to ask for drawings of an industrial arts building in December 1941, claiming as usual to have someone interested in funding its construction, but the first drawings did not arrive until early April 1942. Prior to their arrival Peters promoted the project: "I think that you will be overjoyed by this building—both because of its great beauty and practicality and its economy of construction."[32]

Wright's scheme pleased Spivey, but the school lacked funds to begin its construction. Thereafter the plans sat for almost seven years awaiting a benefactor. Spivey finally was able to gather enough money to reactivate the project in 1949; in June he told Wright they were ready to begin, having found "a man who is interested in putting $100,000 in this building." Spivey also suggested some changes to the existing scheme. The most important of these involved reducing the building to one story to save money and inserting a recreation space to accommodate student dances and other gatherings. He added a caveat based on his personal experience with the previous Wright structures: "Let's not have any more buildings like the Seminars. The three we have are fine but I think the new buildings should have some windows or at least glass in the sides. It is very difficult in Florida to keep openings in the top from leaking."[33]

In Wright's drawings the industrial arts building evolved. In all versions the structure was low and horizontal, hugging the ground. The zoning of interior space by intended use—with arts and crafts and drafting areas along the building's northern arm, woodworking and metalworking shops housed in the eastern section, and domestic and dining spaces in the southern arm—was another constant. But the central courtyard underwent many changes. At one point Wright envisioned a sunken rectangular area, below grade, housing a greenhouse surrounded by "al fresco dining"; this was later removed as the courtyard transformed into a garden. Then Wright embarked on a major reworking of the building, adding a central recreation pavilion that split the courtyard into two smaller courts of unequal size, extending the southern portion almost to the esplanade to form a "refectory" (dining room), and creating a circular "lecture amphitheater" at the north end of the new central pavilion. These changes, which Wright probably made in response to Spivey's suggestions, almost doubled the building's size.

Wright attended the official groundbreaking ceremony for the industrial

Figure 5.7. Frank Lloyd Wright, Lucius Pond Ordway Building, preliminary drawing, 1942. Copyright © 2009 The Frank Lloyd Wright Foundation, Taliesin West, Scottsdale, Ariz. 4212.013.

Figure 5.8. Ordway Building, first-floor plan, based on original drawings. Courtesy of Dan Price and Nathaniel J. Turner.

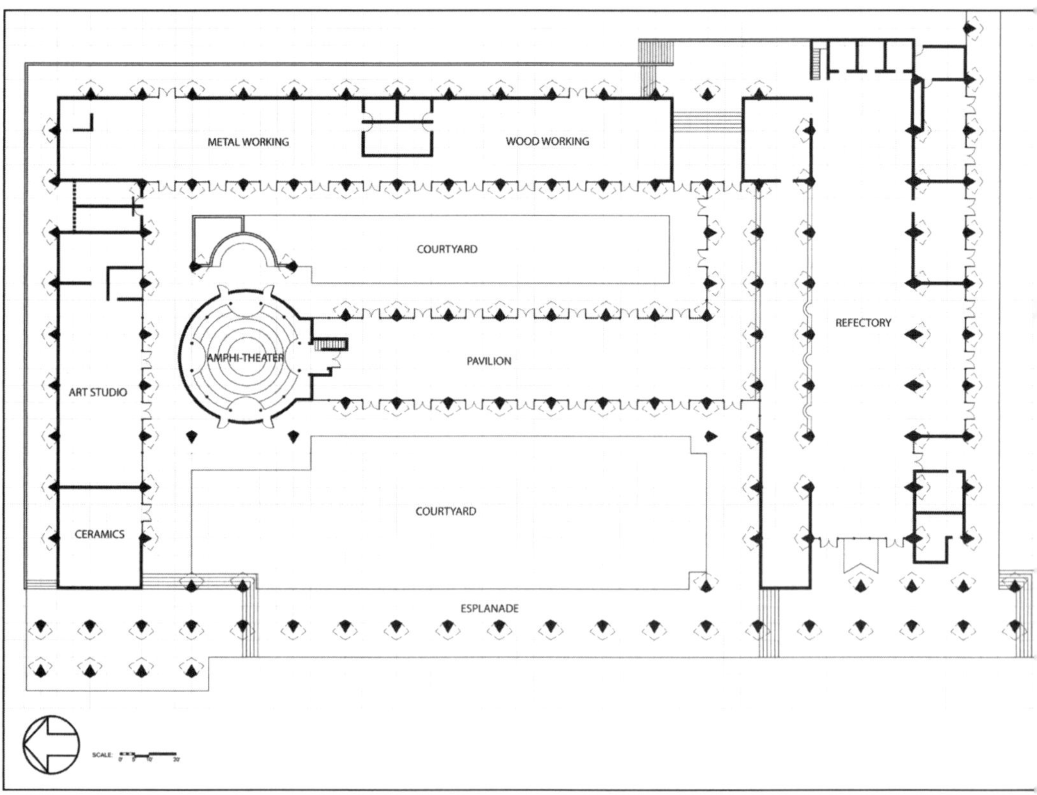

arts building in March 1950 and gave one of his most inspired speeches on Florida Southern to the assembled crowd. He spoke not of the new building but of the campus as a whole and the way it represented true organic architecture:

> In all America today, especially in our educational institutions, you won't find that architecture coming from within the soul of man. You won't find an architecture with a soul, not one with a heart! In other words, you won't find a genuine expression of that thing we talk about so glibly and think that we love to think that we have—which is democracy . . . How can you have a culture living in squalid, untrue, blind conditions? You can't. So here, on this little campus, your Dr. Spivey has planted a little green shoot in the realm of the spirit; something that is *true* to mankind, something that insists upon integrity throughout. It's not sufficient that it should stand up. Anybody can put two sticks together and make a pile of building material that will stand up. But that which will stand there in accord with the *nature* of the circumstances which put it there and with all a grace of rhythm, a *truth* such as you see in your trees, fruits, and flowers—that is *organic* architecture![34]

Wright concluded the speech with a call for the students to appreciate their surroundings. "Now, look upon these buildings and look upon this little college and look upon the wise doctor here as engaging in an adventure," he said. "The greatest, most important of all adventures—*an adventure in the realm of the human spirit,* searching for a greater harmony, a greater *truth* of being, and with it comes, God knows, a more blessed richer life."[35]

Wright's lofty rhetoric contrasted with the realities of construction. At the time of the groundbreaking, workers had begun the industrial arts building's foundation, and many of the building's more than 100 columns were erected, but the project still faced a serious lack of funding. Estimated costs ranged from $150,000 to $500,000, making the building the most expensive at Florida Southern College to date. But Spivey had a potential source of money—perhaps the "man" he had mentioned the previous year. As he reported to the board of trustees in June, J. William Horsey, a Canadian businessman with interests in the citrus industry, told Spivey he would either give or raise $178,000 for the college if it named the new building after him.[36] Spivey traveled to Canada to meet Horsey that fall, as work progressed on the industrial arts building; upon his return he reported that Horsey promised to hand over the money in New York the following month. The exchange, however, did not occur, leaving Spivey in a precarious situation. As he often told Wright, he needed to have nearly continual construction on the campus to convince potential donors of the project's ongoing viability, but the chronic lack of money made construction difficult if not impossible.

The college held a dedication ceremony for the unfinished Horsey Building in March 1952, while Spivey pressed forward with funding from smaller donors and hoped he could convince Horsey to honor his agreement. His periodic reports to Wright on the situation reflected diminishing hope. Throughout 1952 Spivey continually complained that Horsey "had not done his part yet," even though the building that bore his name was occupied (though unfinished).[37] By spring of the following year, Spivey recognized that Horsey's money would never appear. "Mr. Horsey, who promised to erect the building, went back on his promises, leaving me with a debt of nearly $500,000," he wrote to Wright. "For these two years I have been working like a mad man trying to [illegible] the money for this debt. Now I have it about paid."[38] Horsey's name was removed from the building.

Although it took a few years, Spivey eventually found a replacement for Horsey. During Founders Week in 1954, Spivey introduced the industrial arts building's new benefactor, Lucius Pond Ordway, who had actually donated to the project back in 1952, when Horsey was still involved. A businessman from St. Paul, Minnesota, who was the first large investor in the Minnesota Mining and Manufacturing Company (3M), and one of its first presidents, Ordway also had Florida ties as the owner of the West Palm Beach Indians minor league baseball team. Ordway's money helped recoup some, but not all, of the school's losses on the building. The structure was renamed in his honor in 1956.

In many respects the finished Ordway Building came the closest to Wright's ideal for the Florida Southern campus. It matched the early Jones Foundation press accounts—written before Wright's initial drawings—that predicted courts and gardens throughout the future campus, and it best demonstrated Wright's description in the *Architectural Forum* of an esplanade that "runs all around and finally gets together and makes a building."[39] The building emerged naturally from the esplanade that connected it with the rest of Wright's campus, due in part to the integration of the esplanade to form one side of the structure and the many columns throughout the building. As a writer for the *Architectural Forum* later described it: "The building does remain in character essentially a widened and heightened version of the esplanade, with walls added . . . With its beams growing from

Figure 5.9. Ordway Building, aerial view. Florida Southern College Archives.

Figure 5.10. Ordway Building, south side. Photograph by author.

sculptural buttresses and angled in an emphatic riblike row, it is very direct structurally."[40]

These myriad supports, both columns and esplanade, combined with expansive glass surfaces to create a building very open to the outdoors. Many parts of the building, particularly the original recreation pavilion and refectory, were little more than glassed-in esplanades with higher roofs.

Figure 5.11. Ordway Building, Refectory. Library of Congress, Prints and Photographs Division, HABS, FLA, 53-Lake, 1G-6.

Wright also adopted angled roofs, slanting toward the building's center at thirty degrees, for the three main sections of the building to allow larger clerestory windows and thus provide more light for studios and workshops. The roofs are similar to those he had recently constructed for the drafting room at Taliesin West. As with the Water Dome, they reinforced motifs found in the campus plan; here, they mirrored the thirty-degree angles found in the plans of the campus and other buildings.

During Wright's penultimate visit to Florida Southern in November 1955, he toured the campus and, according to an article in the *Southern*, "made not only constructive suggestions for general improvements, but he also was critical of several discrepancies in his own buildings." Wright felt "color, 'life,' and warmth were lacking in many of Southern's buildings," particularly the industrial arts building. "Mr. Wright suggested that a carpet and new, homey furniture be added to the I.A. Building's lounge," the student reporter claimed, "to provide a warmer, more home-like atmosphere to the lounge." The architect's comments were not all disparaging, however; the article further quoted Wright as saying, "I don't think I've ever done any building (that is) so completely strong and adapted to its purpose," leaving no doubt that his criticisms were directed toward the building's furnishings, not its design.[41] In the early sixties, on a Tampa television show about the college, both Spivey and sculptor Boris Blai related that Wright had told them he considered the industrial arts building "the finest building that he ever created."[42]

Publicity

As the industrial arts building neared completion, the *New York Times* noted its progress.[43] And shortly after it was finished, the *Architectural Forum*, the nation's leading architectural journal at the time, featured the structure in a six-page illustrated spread that described it as "long, low and muscular."[44] The construction of Florida Southern College had attracted a steady amount of attention in the architectural world as Wright's star shone brighter than ever. While not as heavily publicized as Wright's other high-profile projects of the period, like the Guggenheim Museum or the Johnson Wax Company headquarters, the campus did appear in more than a dozen journal articles between Spivey's initial contact and Wright's death.[45] The periodicals that carried these articles tended to be lower-circulation professional journals like *Architect & Engineer, Architectural Concrete,* and *National Architect*—with the exception of *Architectural Forum*, which presented Wright's Florida Southern work four times from the late forties to the mid-fifties.[46]

The *Forum* had become Wright's main organ of publicity in 1938, when it devoted the entire January issue entirely to Wright's work—an unprecedented move in the architectural publishing world.[47] That month he also was on the cover of *Time,* with Fallingwater prominently displayed behind him. The special *Forum* issue, with its emphasis on Fallingwater, catapulted Wright back into the limelight at age seventy, after a nearly three-decade decline brought on by personal scandal, economic depression, and changing architectural tastes. During those lean years, however, Wright had not faded into obscurity. He was one of the most publicity-conscious architects of all time, with an intuitive genius for self-promotion. From his clothing to his lifestyle to his public statements, Wright proved a master at attracting attention and stirring up controversy. He kept his name in the spotlight during the Depression through a continuous campaign of writing and public speeches.

Because of Wright's friendly relationship with *Architectural Forum* owner Henry R. Luce—who also owned *Time, Life,* and *Fortune*—it is not surprising that the *Forum* provided the most widespread coverage of the emerging campus. The initial item was in the January 1948 issue, which, like its January 1938 predecessor, was devoted solely to Wright. Florida Southern's "organic campus group" garnered five pages of text, photographs, and plans; much of the text explained the various building materials before turning specifically to the "Floral-Chapel" and its "Flower-tower." Wright's own description emphasized the chapel's "Floridian" character, which linked it to the larger ensemble. "The entire scheme is given an outdoor garden character fit for Florida by the continuous esplanades which connect all the buildings," wrote Wright. "When the building is completed, the U.S. will have at least one example of the cultural value of organic buildings well-suited to time, purpose and place."[48]

Three years later the *Forum* returned to Lakeland to view the campus's progress. The January 1951 issue included two pages with three color photos, while the September 1952 edition gave Florida Southern eight pages with nine photographs and a campus plan. This issue highlighted the administration building, but like its predecessors centered on the "outdoor-garden" character of the plan and buildings that perfectly revealed their Floridian character. The article on the industrial arts building was the final *Architectural Forum* piece on Florida Southern to appear during Wright's lifetime.

Other artistic and technical journals, like *Architect & Engineer* and *Design* offered less extensive coverage.[49] Aside from a few in-depth stories on the Pfeiffer Chapel, these articles contained no critical analysis and much mere description. None of them was more than three pages in length, and most existed merely to showcase photographs of the Wright buildings. The most elaborate account of the project came from Donna Stoddard, an art professor at Florida Southern, who described the campus as an "unparalleled campus grouping" and a "work of art"; her examination, however, read as if it could have been written by Wright himself.[50] The *Architectural Record*'s only report on the campus was a two-page presentation of drawings for the third version of the proposed music building, included in a larger overview of Wright's contemporary work in 1958. As a whole, the impression one receives from reviewing the published literature on Florida Southern during Wright's lifetime is that its sole purpose was to keep architects, designers, and the interested public abreast of a minor project Wright was involved with beyond the limelight of more attractive endeavors like the Guggenheim Museum, the Johnson Wax Company complex, and the Usonian houses.

Campus progress was also casually updated in the *New York Times*, which printed a half-dozen notices of varying length between 1938 and 1953. The initial article included a lengthy description of the Jones Foundation endeavor, written by Florida Southern journalism professor Harris Sims. Sims also contributed a story on the Pfeiffer Chapel after it opened. Later accounts, however, were limited to brief notes about non-Wright dormitories and the completion of the industrial arts building.[51]

The Danforth Chapel

Wright's initial drawings of the Florida Southern College campus plan included a "minor" chapel to the side of (and sometimes attached to) the larger chapel (figs. 2.2 and 2.3). This building was not described in the "Programme for University," however, and the first mention of it was not until autumn 1941. Spivey pursued it nonetheless, trying as always to lure donors; at one point he even sent Wright on an unsuccessful visit to Annie Pfeiffer in New York to see if she would invest money in a companion chapel next to the larger one bearing her name. Other potential benefactors came and went. Meanwhile Wright created some sketches for the building in 1942 without prompting from Spivey. "I am sending on the sketches for the minor chapel just the same," Wright wrote, "hoping that when donations are made for the building the plans will be considered as part of the legitimate cost of the building and be covered as well."[52] After that the project's momentum stalled for more than a decade.

This sluggishness was not for lack of funds, however. The *Southern* announced as early as March 1947 that an unnamed donor had given $45,000 for a small chapel "in memory of her deceased husband."[53] But the record is mute for the next six years, except for a single letter from Peters to Spivey, acknowledging the latter's request for working drawings. Not until 1954 did the project come to life, when William H. Danforth agreed to give money for the chapel. Danforth was a St. Louis businessman, founder of the Ralston Purina Company and the Danforth Foundation, an organization dedicated to educational philanthropy. Like Lucius Ordway and William Horsey, Danforth also had a Florida connection—Ralston Purina had mills in Tampa and Miami at the time. Spivey's letter to Wright introducing Danforth was frank. "This letter is an emergency one," he wrote. "Mr. Danforth is very old, and is liable to die at any time. Unless we can do something right away, I feel it will be too late."[54] Danforth was eighty-four years old at the time; Wright was almost eighty-seven.

Wright always conceived of the minor chapel in tandem with its larger neighbor, emphasizing contrasts between the two structures. It was originally aligned on a strict east-west orthogonal like the main chapel, but at some point in the early fifties, Wright rotated it thirty degrees to the southwest to match the alignment of a proposed science building. The small chapel's ground-hugging horizontality was a counterpart to the larger chapel's soaring tower. What appear to be the earliest drawings depict the minor chapel with a gabled roof in which triangular skylights are prominent, linking it to the Pfeiffer Chapel's triangular bow-tie bracing, the library's triangular skylights, and the early versions of the administration building, as well as the triangles of the campus plan. These drawings also show a flat-roofed, triangular-shaped seminar room with floor-to-ceiling windows extending off the chapel's side. Later drawings document the building's evolution into something resembling Wright's famous Unitarian Meeting House (1947) of Shorewood, Wisconsin; both buildings shared a broadly overhanging gable roof and a prow-like glass wall behind the pulpit.

The finished chapel used the same materials as the other Wright buildings at Florida Southern but differed from its predecessors in some significant ways. It was smaller; it was the only Wright building not attached to an esplanade; it was the only building with stained glass; and its gable roof gave it a slightly domestic appearance not unlike Wright's Prairie-style houses. Wright had experimented with gabled roofs in many of his initial drawings for campus buildings, but with the exception of the book stack section of the library, the roofs were always flattened before execution. The minor chapel's roof seemed a compromise. It was gabled, but only slightly, its peak barely rising above the side walls. Wright might have chosen such a roof design specifically for its ability to humanize the small chapel with a domestic reference, since it was intended to be a personal building for private services or personal reflection (Wright labeled the main space "meditation" in a number of early drawings).

The roof's pointed peak extended past the end wall at the "ship's prow" by more than fifteen feet. Beneath it was the building's highlight—the red, amber, and clear leaded-glass wall behind the pulpit that opened the structure to the campus, providing most of the interior illumination, framing the setting sun, and making the simple building more exciting. The prow was

Figure 5.12. Frank Lloyd Wright, William H. Danforth Chapel, 1953. Florida Southern College Archives.

an understated gem; its expansiveness belied its humble size and dramatically contrasted with the concrete block side walls whose only apertures were clerestory windows tucked beneath the roofline high above eye level. The glass wall gently bent around the chapel's main axis at 120 degrees, while above it the roof energetically thrust forward at a sharper eighty-degree angle to create a point. The combination of the jutting prow and the chapel's placement on a slope enlivened the structure, giving the impression that it might launch into flight at any time. Such implied motion conceptually tied the building to the themes of activity and movement found in the overall campus plan.

Inside, the small chapel was simple and modest. None of the spaces was a traditional square or rectangle—instead, the walls met at various angles. After approaching the building from the rear and entering through a secluded door in the side wall, visitors moved from a small foyer into the main space to view the pulpit and its dramatic glass background. The meeting area contained movable plywood benches, made by Florida Southern students, which seated approximately fifty people. Projecting into the space

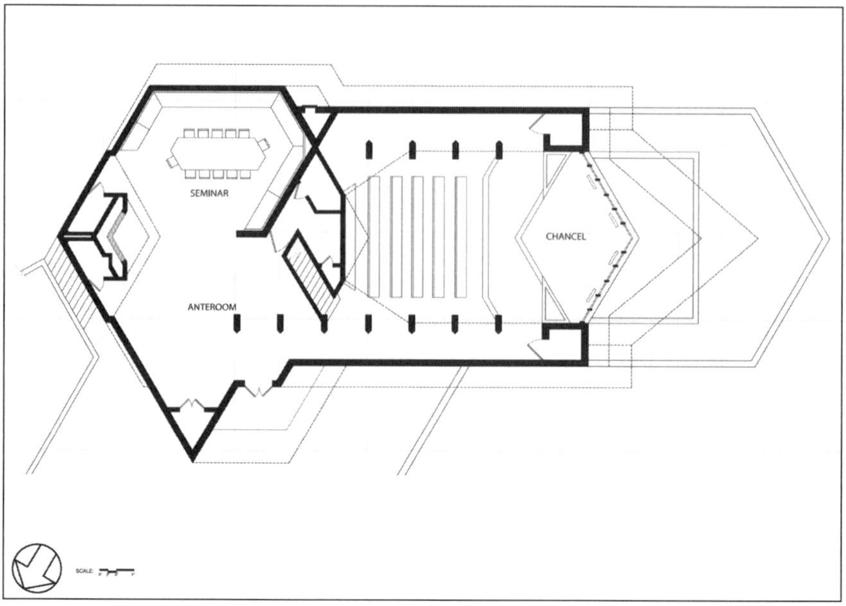

Figure 5.13. Danforth Chapel plan, based on original drawings. Courtesy of Dan Price and Nathaniel J. Turner.

Figure 5.14. Danforth Chapel interior. Library of Congress, Prints and Photographs Division, HABS, FLA, 53-Lake, 1B-3.

above the worship area was a second-floor mezzanine. It did not sit back around the perimeter but entered the space in the same manner as the balcony in the library. The mezzanine's projecting angle also echoed the west wall of the neighboring Pfeiffer Chapel. At the rear of the building, the second floor held two spaces originally intended for the religion department: a rather awkward lozenge-shaped classroom and an undifferentiated area for the department office. This area opened to a small outdoor balcony above the entrance, further emphasizing the building's connection with nature and its relationship with the larger chapel, of which this balcony provided an excellent view.

The groundbreaking ceremony for the minor chapel occurred in May 1954, and because of the building's small size, it was completed and dedicated during Founders Week only ten months later. The finished chapel pleased Wright; during a campus visit in late 1955 he said, "it is charming in the little what the Industrial Arts Building is in the large."[55]

The Polk County Science Building

The final Wright building constructed on the Florida Southern College campus would also be the largest and most expensive. The Polk County Science Building would be more than 300 feet from end-to-end and cost more than $1 million. It was still under construction and only partially occupied when Spivey retired and still unfinished during Wright's last campus visit in 1957.

The "Programme for University" outlined a nature study building containing departments of ecology, biology, ethnology, and horticulture, as well as a planetarium and small zoo. Wright's earliest campus plans depict the nature study unit as a one-story, linear structure forming one leg of a triangular, terraced court east of the main chapel. These initial drawings show the southern end of the building anchored by a square form topped by a dome—a planetarium that would carry through to the building's final execution. But the completed structure would be much larger than Wright's original conception.

As with the small chapel, the first mention of the science building in the correspondence predates the onset of its construction by more than a decade. In the spring of 1942, Spivey directed Wright to "think about the Science Buildings for I have someone who is vitally interested in them."[56] Eight years later, with no drawings made and no donor for a building expected to cost $350,000 (later adjusted to $500,000 before the onset of construction), Spivey decided to focus his fundraising efforts on Polk County, where Lakeland is located. The college had recently added a department of citrus culture and the Southern Bio-Research Laboratory and desperately needed to expand its science facilities.

Spivey launched a campaign in October 1950, enlisting the services of a New York public relations firm and advising Wright that he wanted the project under construction within two years. Things looked bright in the beginning: within four months, the *Southern* related that Polk County residents had pledged $350,000 for the science building.[57] But just two months later the same publication reported that Spivey had asked Florida Southern students and faculty for assistance in reviving the fundraising effort. Only half of the required amount had been collected, and according to the student reporter, "In the past few weeks the drive has been marked with a general apathy."[58] Undaunted, Spivey continued his commitment to getting the project under way. A groundbreaking ceremony held during Founders Week in March 1952 showed how speculative the scheme was, since actual construction did not begin for almost a year.

When construction on the science building finally commenced sometime in early 1953, Wright had not finished all of the necessary drawings. Spivey begged, but Wright did not work quickly enough. By fall an exasperated Spivey wrote to Wright: "For more than a year now, we've been trying to get the Polk County Science Building started. I am discouraged; my faculty, students and friends are beginning to make great sport of the fact that the building will never be erected. We are ready to go ahead, but we can't do one thing. I am keeping about twenty-five boys here in College with nothing for them to do. All this is because we can't get the footings I asked you about up in New York. For the life of me, I can't understand why someone can't give us this information."[59] His plea must have worked—a set of working drawings is dated eight days later.

A perspective drawing of the Polk County Science Building published in the *Southern* in March 1951 depicts a five-part building dominated by large gabled roofs reminiscent of Wright's Prairie-style houses.[60] The L-shaped building resembled the science building drawn in some of the earliest aerial views of the campus made more than a decade before. On the southwest side a section of esplanades attached to the building's wall opened onto a small rectangular terrace. The structure contained three separate gabled roofs, corresponding to a rectangular central section and square end pavilions, although all were connected into a unified whole. The square section nearest the lake housed a planetarium. In general, the building's massing suggested a modification of the unbuilt Whitney Memorial.

An undated sheet in the Frank Lloyd Wright Archives, contained with documents from 1951, includes Wright's notes on the "Nature Study" building and a sketch plan of a possible location.[61] The quick sketch shows the building occupying the spot Wright reserved for it in the early campus plans, but the triangular courtyard scheme had been abandoned and the building aligned along a strict north-south axis, with its west edge bounded by an esplanade running from the main chapel to the swimming pool and amphitheater; between the science building and this esplanade was an open courtyard. While lacking detail, the drawing reveals Wright was imagining the science building as something closer to the industrial arts building.

Wright's final version, created in 1953, kept many of these features. The structure remained L-shaped, but the short leg was moved from the southern to the northern end of the building. Wright retained the five units, divided into a citrus department, a physics and mathematics section, a biology and chemistry section, an earth and life sciences unit, and a "cosmography" unit. The citrus wing formed the short leg of the L by extending 100 feet from the main body at a right angle. It contained spaces devoted to the Florida Citrus Institute, including classrooms, laboratories, offices, and a small greenhouse. Wright buried this one-story wing four feet below grade so that its clerestory windows and flat roof barely peeked out over the ground.

The physics and mathematics section, which formed the pivot of the L, was a two-story building, roughly square in shape, housing physics laboratories on the first floor and mathematics classrooms above. Next to it was the long, rectangular section for biology and chemistry, almost 200 feet in length, with biology laboratories and offices topped by chemistry labs. A two-story open gallery ran through the middle of the building like an elongated atrium. Wright used unique aluminum columns, stepped in three parts to be wider at the top than the bottom, to support the esplanade along the unit's east side. The inner row of these columns was interspersed with floor-to-ceiling glass walls to achieve an openness that rivaled the industrial arts building. Behind the glass Wright left room for permanent science exhibits.

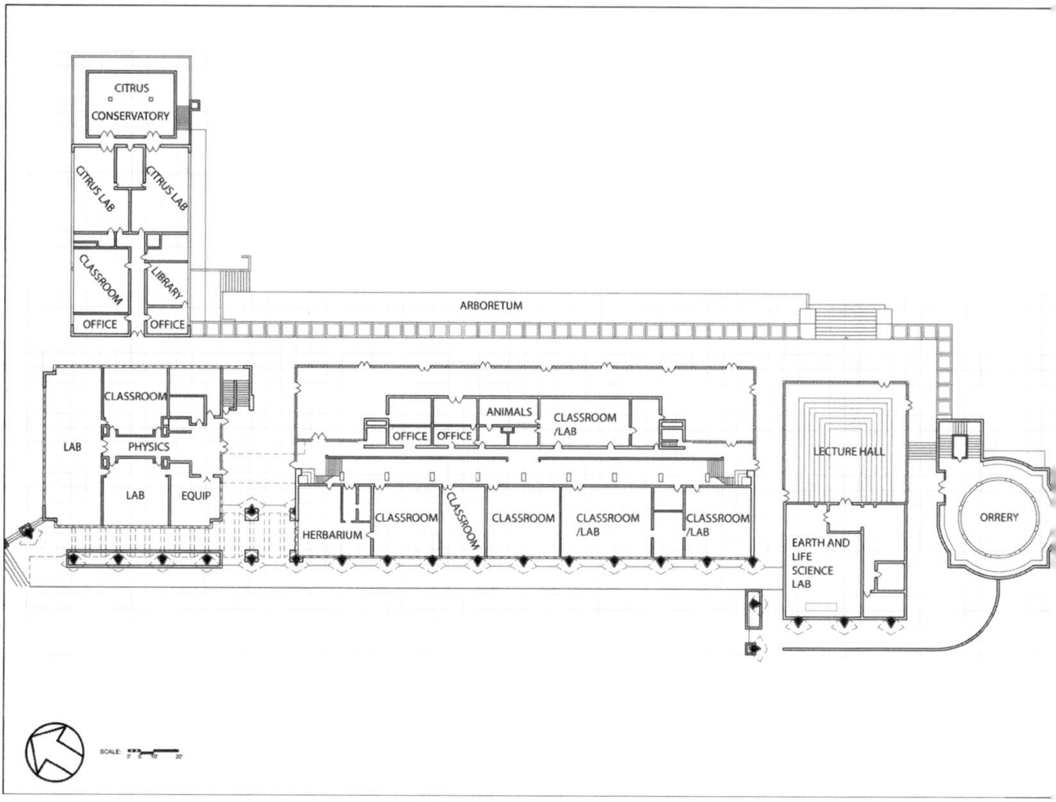

Figure 5.15. Polk County Science Building, first-floor plan, based on original drawings. Courtesy of Dan Price and Nathaniel J. Turner.

Next in line was the earth and life sciences unit, divided equally into two squares in plan, one a two-story portion containing laboratories and storage areas and the other a one-story lecture hall. Across a short breezeway, and terminating the science building's south end, was the last unit, which incorporated an orrery (a machine that illustrates the positions of the planets and moons in the solar system) on the first floor with an observatory above.

In elevation, the science building's multilayered horizontal planes stood out, but the separate structures did not read as individual entities. Wright unified the building's individual parts through the use of shared materials and their similar relationship to the esplanade. They featured concrete block construction—stuccoed on the upper level of the physics and math-

Figure 5.16. Polk County Science Building, Mathematics and Physics unit, 1953. Florida Southern College Archives.

Figure 5.17. Polk County Science Building, northeast side with aluminum columns. Florida Southern College Archives.

Figure 5.18. Polk County Science Building, southwest side. Florida Southern College Archives.

ematics section—clerestory windows, and flat roofs. Like the industrial arts building, the science building incorporated the esplanade on almost every side. The sloping site caused problems that were easily solved by dividing the building into freestanding units, but a similar solution for the esplanade along the east side produced an awkward section of five different esplanade levels. The incline also produced an ungainly connection where the esplanade roof for the walkway from the Pfeiffer Chapel disappeared into the flat stuccoed wall of the physics and mathematics section.

One significant change Wright made from his earlier sketches was to skew the science building off the north-south axis, aligning it along an esplanade that created another thirty-degree diagonal in the campus plan. Wright vacillated over the years about whether this building should emphasize the strict axis or break from it. His final decision heightened the plan's inherent dynamism.

The Polk County Science Building was not Wright's best design at Florida Southern College. The building was somewhat formal and straightforward, lacking the inspiration that made works like the Pfeiffer Chapel special. Apart from the east side wall of glass and aluminum columns, the vertical atrium slicing through the biology and chemistry unit, and the decision to separate the structure into distinct sections, there was little that revealed Wright's genius. Several factors might have combined to affect the building's uninspiring nature. Wright was extremely busy at this point in his career—in 1949–50 alone his office was working on more than seventy new commissions.[62] It may be that after spending fifteen years battling with Spivey for payment, his heart simply was no longer in the campus project. And he might not have found the rather pedestrian needs of a classroom building to be the most challenging opportunity, particularly when the campus structures with the greatest potential for spatial innovation or dramatic form, like the chapel and library, had already been built or remained on the drafting board. Overall, Wright's classroom buildings (seminars, industrial arts, and science) were not as visually interesting or spatially complex as his designs for the chapel, library, music, and arts buildings.

Figure 5.19. Polk County Science Building, interior hallway. Photograph by author.

The Polk County Science Building was the final Wright structure at Florida Southern and the only one he never saw in its completed state. Because of the building's size, the school decided to construct it in sections, beginning with the citrus wing, followed by the physics and mathematics unit, then the biology and chemistry unit along with the earth and life sciences unit, and finally the planetarium. Grading of the site was under way by summer 1954, and the first portion, the citrus wing, was completed during autumn 1955. The college dedicated the unfinished building in March 1958, but it was not fully occupied until later that year.

The Museum of Non-objective Painting

In the mid-fifties Spivey and Wright launched their final attempts to build the art and music buildings. The last effort to realize an art building was initiated by an unexpected source when, in the spring of 1955, Hilla Rebay decided to fund an art museum at Florida Southern.

Baroness Hilla Rebay von Ehrenwiesen was a German-born painter, collector, and tireless champion of abstract art. She helped Solomon R. Guggenheim establish his collection and served as the first director and curator of Guggenheim's Museum of Non-Objective Painting (now the Solomon R. Guggenheim Museum). In that capacity she first contacted Wright in 1943 to determine his interest in designing a museum building in New York and persuaded Guggenheim to hire him for what Wright would consider one of his most important commissions. In her initial letter, Rebay had effusively praised Wright and asked him to create "a temple of spirit" for Guggenheim's far-reaching collection of abstract art—a request strangely similar to Spivey's proposal for a "great education temple" in his first message to Wright.[63] Over the ensuing years Rebay and Wright developed a close relationship through meetings and extensive correspondence; Rebay's contributions during the inaugural stages of the Guggenheim Museum's design process could almost lead one to consider her a co-designer of the early schemes.[64] In early 1944, in a letter describing the museum's preliminary plans, Wright told Rebay about his work on the Whitney Memorial at Florida Southern; she hinted, "I would not mind having such a memorial myself."[65]

In the spring of 1952, the Guggenheim Foundation forced Rebay to resign her positions with the museum following Solomon Guggenheim's death. This expulsion did not temper her desire to create an ideal museum of non-objective art, and at some point she began to consider Florida Southern as the possible home for such an institution, probably because of her good relationship with Wright and the knowledge that the college had once attempted to establish an art museum without success. Rebay arranged to have a traveling show she curated, entitled "Art of Tomorrow—Bauer, Kandinsky, Rebay: Exhibition of Non-Objective Painting," exhibited at Florida Southern in February 1955. Shortly thereafter Rebay wrote a flattering letter to Wright, announcing her intention to begin work on an art museum at Florida Southern after a rigorous traveling schedule concluded in early summer. Her vision for the plan disclosed her bitterness over the Guggenheim situation (and quite possibly her dissatisfaction with Wright's misfortunes with Eleanor Whitney); Rebay imagined the building as "very *not* New York—one cannot do great things with a lousy lot of bourgois [sic] and selfish brutes."[66] Two weeks later Spivey reported on a successful meeting with Rebay in New York, in which she had agreed to donate $100,000 toward the museum, and her lawyer confided to Spivey that everything "would be in good shape" if Wright could make a sketch of his proposal.[67]

A draft agreement was drawn up for the "Hilla Rebay Museum Temple of Non-objective Painting," with Rebay as curator and director. Whether Wright made the drawing is unknown; the same can be said for the extent of Rebay's real commitment to the project. By fall the relationship had soured over Rebay's and Wright's dispute about his fee and the college's ongoing financial difficulties. By winter the negotiations broke down, erasing Spivey's and Wright's last real chance of funding any kind of art building. "I have decided not to go ahead with the Baroness," Spivey wrote. "She put down too many restrictions for me. I have too many worries now to take on more."[68]

The Music Building Project, Version 3

As he realized the final chance for the art building was probably passing away, Spivey determined not to let the cherished music building meet a similar fate. "What do you think of redesigning the music building, and let us start it?" he asked Wright in October 1955. "I want to start it to guarantee that it will be placed there whether I live or die."[69] Spivey doubtless felt the press of time more acutely than ever. He had suffered a heart attack two years earlier, and his health was declining, exacerbated by the pressure of constant fundraising. He was sixty-eight years old, had been at Florida

Southern for thirty years, and knew retirement was near. Spivey also knew that Wright was now eighty-eight. The music building, into which the two men had invested so much time and energy, would have to happen soon if it was to be realized at all.

The project had not been completely dormant since the breakdown of the Whitney negotiations; every few years it was resurrected for a brief but doomed appearance. In 1950 the Florida Methodist Conference, which met annually in Lakeland and used Florida Southern's facilities for lodging and meals, had accepted Spivey's offer to construct a permanent meeting facility—to be named the Florida Conference Auditorium—at the college. As the conference's flagship school, Florida Southern was an appropriate location for these meetings, but the campus desperately lacked suitable accommodations. Pfeiffer Chapel was too small, and its absence of air-conditioning made summer activities nearly unbearable. Spivey obviously intended to use Wright's existing music building plans for the Methodist auditorium. In an article in the *Southern,* he wrote that the new building "will also be used as the Music Building and Little Theatre" for the school.[70] Strangely, however, when the *Southern* published a sketch of the proposed auditorium "to be constructed in early 1951," it was a drawing of Wright's 1938 Model Theatre proposal for the college.[71] Since that unbuilt project had been intended for only 400 seats, and all accounts of the Methodist Conference auditorium noted its 1,500-seat capacity, it is unknown whether Wright intended to enlarge his theater building or whether a mistake occurred in the school's publicity department.

Spivey commenced another fundraising drive, this time to raise $250,000. As he traveled the state to encourage donations, the Methodist Conference called on its local churches to help by contributing at least one-fifth of the total they collected each year. Plans were made to begin construction in early 1951. But funds must have been difficult to find, and the campaign halted with no results.

Spivey tried again in 1953. That summer he informed Wright that he was starting a nationwide effort to find money for both the music and science buildings. Spivey wanted both structures to be completed by 1956 to celebrate his thirtieth year at Florida Southern. An article in the *Southern* detailed the new project, which was now estimated to cost $350,000. The facility, which could serve both the college and the Florida Methodist Conference, would include a "small hall" for chamber music, practice rooms, offices, and "a huge auditorium" seating 1,500–2,000 patrons—a description of Wright's existing music building proposal. Yet the drawing accompanying this account inexplicably depicted Wright's 1938 theater project again, which did not contain such accommodations.[72] Once more, the campaign lost momentum and failed.

So when Spivey raised the music building with Wright in late 1955, the architect probably was not surprised. This time, however, Spivey asked Wright to redesign the structure, which would mean a third version—not counting the Model Theatre. And this time Spivey seemed to be more determined than in the past: he stayed with the project after the initial wave of enthusiasm faded. A year after his suggestion to Wright, the *Southern* reported that ground would be broken in March 1957 for the now $500,000 music building (and, as usual, the newspaper included a sketch of Wright's Model Theatre project, then almost twenty years old).[73] Two weeks later Nils Schweizer sent Wright a list of music department requirements, which included more practice rooms and studios than in similar requests from the previous decade. By winter Spivey was prodding Wright for the new plans and the *Southern* announced a Founders Week 1957 groundbreaking ceremony—a mere seven weeks away.[74]

In Wright's drawings for the third music building, dated early 1957, he kept the two performance chambers at opposite ends of a one-story connecting loggia containing practice spaces, offices, listening rooms, and so forth. The functions of those performance areas remained the same as before: the larger node for larger audiences up to 2,500, the smaller for practices and recitals. But Wright altered their forms in this new edition. The Symphony space changed from the hexagon of his second version to the circular form that it originally had in the early 1940s. Instead of a hemispherical dome over the space, Wright now placed a slightly raised roof with a small spire. In elevation, the Symphony harmonized with Wright's other campus buildings, particularly the E. T. Roux Library, its closest neighbor. Both structures shared circular plans, textile block walls, clerestory windows, and overhanging roofs. The Symphony end of the music building borrowed from the library the motif of the upper wall slightly overhanging the lower portion, but now Wright distended it to form a more pronounced overhang that indicated the balcony inside. He also appended a triangular block to the circular auditorium's rear to allow for an elongated rear stage area, more backstage space, and room for the air-conditioning cooling towers.

Figure 5.20. Frank Lloyd Wright, third proposal for unbuilt music building, 1957. Copyright © 2009 The Frank Lloyd Wright Foundation, Taliesin West, Scottsdale, Ariz. 5320.003.

Wright also revised the smaller auditorium, previously named "Star Chamber" and now labeled "Band and Choir Practice Room," both inside and out. While keeping the circular plan, he removed the hemispherical dome that had marked the building in both previous incarnations, leaving the roof almost flat and the structure with a minimalist quality not found in any other campus building. The only interruption in its vertical block walls was a horizontal band of small windows that deftly connected to the row of windows that carried along the loggia. On the interior of this small circular space, Wright substituted benches for individual seating, a change that highlighted the informal nature of its function.

The central loggia now housed twenty-five practice, studio, and classrooms, a listening room, and a rectangular garden court in front of the small auditorium lit by square openings in the esplanade roof. This portion of the structure was marked by the incorporation of the esplanade with its inverted triangular piers and flat roof. An esplanade running diagonally from the plaza between the library and chapel intersected the music building off the east edge of the auditorium and then seamlessly merged with the central section; a similar synthesis of esplanade and building was also to be on the west side facing a parking lot. Wright emphasized the horizontal by incorporating these esplanade roofs and by raising the roof over the loggia's hallway with a clerestory window and another flat roof.

The End of a Long Relationship

Although the project was included in a twenty-four-page update of Wright's contemporary work in the *Architectural Record,* it once again stalled, most likely because of Spivey's retirement.[75] In September 1956 Ludd Myrl Spivey had begun his thirty-first and final school year at Florida Southern College. He had overseen a remarkable transformation at the school, which grew from barely 100 students and a handful of buildings to a record enrollment of 2,300 and more than forty structures. During many long, difficult years, faced with a chronic shortage of funds, Spivey never lost his determination, and he was ready to carry through until the very end. "You must keep in mind that I do not have long to stay here," he had warned Wright back in January. "You must know that I am extremely interested in completing this project in my day. Help me!"[76] The personal tone of Spivey's request reflected the two men's friendship. Spivey had been a frequent Taliesin visitor over the years, and he made two trips to see Wright in 1956, one to Arizona and one to Wisconsin. And in October, Spivey was asked by administrators of the Frank Lloyd Wright Endowment Fund to introduce the architect at a banquet celebrating Frank Lloyd Wright Day in Chicago, as proclaimed by Mayor Richard J. Daley. Spivey was an appropriate choice given the men's close relationship and the fact that Spivey was the most enduring client of Wright's career, spanning eighteen years at that point.

Wright returned the favor in March 1957, attending Florida Southern's Frank Lloyd Wright Day during Founders Week. Spivey had tried unsuccessfully to get Wright to appear during past Founders Weeks for fundraising purposes. This visit, Spivey hoped, would help raise interest in the ongoing science building and the music building project. It would be Wright's final trip to the campus he created and would mark the last time he would see his client and friend in person. Wright viewed the construction on the science building and saw the finished Ordway Industrial Arts Building and Danforth Chapel. Speaking to a crowd in the Pfeiffer Chapel, Wright prophesized, "Someday Florida Southern College is going to be notable, cherished in history, because it . . . has showed the way in denoting poetic principle . . . an architectural culture of its own."[77]

Two months later, at the college's commencement ceremony, Spivey announced his retirement. Ever since a heart attack temporarily felled him a few years before, Spivey had found his many commitments taxing and his energy diminished. By 1957 he reached the end of the line. "The reason that I am retiring is because of my health," he told the audience. "I don't mind saying that I am tired."[78] But Spivey doggedly pursued his dream until the very end—just before vacating office, he sought and obtained board of trustee approval for Wright's 2,500-seat music building, to be located on its originally intended site south of the library along Johnson Avenue.

SIX *A New Era*

When Frank Lloyd Wright died in April 1959 at the age of ninety-one, drawings existed for a number of unexecuted structures intended for the West Campus. The most pressing need, from the point of view of Florida Southern, was an auditorium for the Methodist Conference. The third version of the music building could have been used for such a space. But this building, which Spivey and Wright struggled for so long to realize, did not survive long after the death of its creator.

Initially the project looked to be in good shape even with Spivey's retirement. He had gained board of trustees approval for it before leaving office, and in July 1957 Taliesin apprentice Nils Schweizer, the last of Wright's apprentices sent to Lakeland to supervise the job, confided in Wright that construction might begin in six months.[1] At the beginning of the fall semester, Spivey's successor as president, Charles T. Thrift, Jr., met with Hans Schweizer (Nils's brother and design partner) and faculty from the music department to review Wright's plans and suggest adjustments. However, Schweizer's report of that meeting offered the first hint of future problems. "The college situation is that for the first time in it [sic] history it is diverting most of its funds to the maintenance of existing buildings; therefore its capacity for construction is shrinking and we are beginning to feel it in many small ways," he wrote.[2] A new era was dawning at Florida Southern, one that would mark the end of Spivey's and Wright's dream.

The music building situation began to look bleaker when bureaucratic bodies with influence over Florida Southern pressed the new administration to rearrange its priorities. First the National Association of Colleges and Universities persuaded the school to refrain from any new construction, according to Schweizer, without collecting at least 50 percent of the probable cost beforehand. By July 1958 Schweizer estimated that under this constraint work on the music building would not begin for another three years.[3] A few months later, Thrift asked Schweizer to tell Wright to cease activity on the music building, partly in response to a recommendation by the Methodist Conference that the school halt all new construction to concentrate on restoring the existing buildings and paying off the Polk County Science Building's $500,000 debt.

Accounting

While Wright had been aware of the college's financial problems for decades, the matter of his own compensation dominated his final years on the Florida Southern project. One of his last acts concerning Florida Southern was to prepare another detailed grievance about his lack of adequate remuneration. Six months before he died, Wright drafted a letter to Spivey—most likely out of habit, since Spivey was no longer the college's president—that once again raised the thorny issue of payment. The letter went through two versions, so it is not clear which, if any, was actually sent; a third version by Wright's widow, Olgivanna, was mailed to the college a month after her husband's death.[4] The letters all claimed an outstanding balance in excess of $100,000 for services rendered.

Olgivanna's letter was only one part of the process of handling Wright's legacy; another important matter for his successors was to determine Florida Southern's future plans. When Wright died, his architectural practice, with approximately $30 million in outstanding commissions, passed to a group of apprentices and Taliesin fellows that would become known as the Taliesin Associated Architects (TAA).[5] Wes Peters assumed the position of president and chief architect. The firm would complete many of the works in progress at Wright's death, including the Gammage Memorial Auditorium (1959) at Arizona State University, as well as begin to receive numerous new commissions from clients desiring something as close to Wright's designs as possible.[6]

Although TAA viewed continuing the work on Florida Southern as a pressing issue, the college's attitude was less certain. When Spivey had received word of Wright's demand, he wrote a revealing letter to Thrift. "If I were you I would pay no attention to this," Spivey suggested. "My advice is for you to send him a check for one thousand dollars now and then and let it go at that. I am sure that he dies [sic] not keep books. He has no idea how much the college has paid out for his helpers. Nor do I think he knows how much the college has paid him."[7] Such a callous response is surprising, given the close relationship that he and Wright developed over the years. Spivey's attitude, however, was partially influenced by his own ignorance about the accounting situation. He had an opinion about the cost of certain buildings, but no evidence to support it, since the college's bookkeeping was as inadequate as Taliesin's.

While the dispute between Wright and Spivey over money began early in their relationship and continued for two decades, the disagreement had become more serious in 1949, when Wright asked the college for an accounting. Spivey responded with figures showing Florida Southern had paid more than $48,000, which he claimed was actually an overpayment given the standard 10 percent architect's contract.[8] Wright's caustic seven-page reply accused Spivey of having "very little realization of the cost of architect's services" and of the sacrifices Wright had made for the project—including the "absurdly low price (amounting to a generous gift)" he charged for the original drawings and the free promotional services. "If we went along with others as we have with you, my dear Doctor, we would have to give up Taliesin," he wrote. Wright maintained the college owed him $116,500 at that time.[9] Spivey countered by steering the argument away from numbers with a sentimental plea to consider all that they had accomplished together: "As I see it, we are working together to build a great institution which will, after all, be a great monument to your labors. We must continue it to show our enemies that we can win."[10]

Spivey's strategy must have worked, because there is no evidence of Wright complaining about payment again for four years. The two men clashed one final time in the spring of 1956 over Spivey's promise to send $1,000 checks every month, although Spivey admitted that he was in arrears. In the final year of his life, Wright returned to the issue of just compensation, and Olgivanna carried on the fight after his death.

Upon receiving Olgivanna's request, Thrift stalled for time by pleading ignorance. Almost four months earlier, when Spivey had alerted him to Wright's allegation, he had concurred with Spivey that the best course of action was to "ignore [Wright], at least for the present."[11] But in his response to Olgivanna, Thrift claimed to be unaware of the facts.[12] The college then sent Business Manager Corning Tolle to Taliesin in July 1959 to discuss the money issue. By all accounts, the meeting was friendly and marked by mutual admissions of confusion over the amounts owed and paid over the years. Both parties agreed that something could be worked out.

Tolle's trip to Taliesin buoyed the hopes of both parties that the compensation issue could be resolved. The college recognized the Wright Foundation's entitlement to more money than had been paid, while the Taliesin group concurred they had actually received more than the college records indicated. Neither side was inclined to litigate. The meeting ended with mutual promises to provide further information. Two years later, however, nothing more had been accomplished; negotiations and activities apparently ceased after Tolle's visit.

TAA, through Peters, reopened the matter in August 1961 by complaining about the school's lack of progress and seeking at least $125,000 of outstanding compensation.[13] Spurred by Peters's letter, Thrift suggested another visit to Taliesin, but was apparently not too eager to actually follow through on the suggestion since it took almost two more years to schedule the trip, and then Thrift backed out, claiming the need to attend a Methodist Conference meeting. He sent Tolle and Ray Lott, a former president of the Florida Southern Alumni Association, in his place. Before Tolle embarked, Thrift wrote a remarkable letter to him, advising that Spivey never had the authority to enter into a contract with Wright, particularly for so much money, and thus any contract between Wright and the college was actually void.[14] The college realized that this was not a complete defense, however. So the second meeting between the parties produced a settlement with three conditions: the college recognized "the extent of the 'gift' nature of the donation of services" by Wright; the parties agreed to "in effect extend the continuity of the understanding and cooperation" between Florida Southern and TAA; and the college would make sixty monthly payments of $133.33 to TAA to settle its indebtedness.[15] Thrift confirmed the terms, and there is a record of his sending the first two payments on May 1, 1963.

A New Auditorium

In the meantime, the college was being pressed by the Methodist Conference on the auditorium issue. Almost a decade had passed since the conference accepted Spivey's offer to construct a permanent meeting facility on campus. The conference resurrected the project after the death of Methodist bishop and board of trustees member John Branscomb in January 1959. It swiftly formed a committee to honor Branscomb with a memorial, and its report, released in June 1959, recommended an auditorium be built in Branscomb's name on the Florida Southern campus. The conference then created a separate committee to choose an architect for the project.

What happened next is shrouded in mystery and not entirely clear from the documentary evidence, but the end result sealed the fate of Wright's music building and quashed any possibility of the school's continued association with TAA. It began when the Branscomb Memorial Auditorium building committee expressed mixed feelings about constructing any more Wright buildings. Although a photograph published in the *Southern* showed the members—including President Thrift—gazing at a drawing of Wright's third proposal for the music building, it seems to have been determined early in the process that a new design should be solicited.[16] Thrift later related that "there had been widespread objection throughout the Conference to our buildings designed by Mr. Wright. The objections, some reasonable and some baseless, were based on leaking, poor ventilation, lack of utility, high cost of erection and maintenance, etc. Some, even members of the Committee, did not want to even invite [TAA] to participate."[17]

After deliberating, the building committee decided to seek designs from at least eight architectural firms, including TAA. Since the project was totally under the Methodist Conference's control—as Thrift liked to point out in later years—this put the college in the awkward situation of watching as the successor firm of its longtime campus architect, to whom the college acknowledged it still owed money, was forced to compete for the right to design an auditorium on campus—while that firm already possessed three sets of detailed drawings for such a structure.

TAA was interested in the project but offended by the request to submit sketches for work they felt entitled to by nature of the school's relationship with Wright. The firm apparently replied that it would neither compete for the job nor consent to an interview or provide drawings until awarded the commission. This response prompted the building committee to eliminate

TAA from consideration. Peters later condemned the solicitation and subsequent decision as "rather inconsiderate, if not unethical," and lamented that "the organization which I represent and which Mr. Wright led so far in the great work for Florida Southern College has deserved better at the hands of the College."[18]

According to John Cook, a former professor at Florida Southern, after the remaining architects under consideration made their presentations, the building committee wanted to take two weeks to study their options before making a decision. During this period someone suggested Nils Schweizer's architectural firm to Thrift. Schweizer, now practicing in Orlando with his brother, had the advantage of being a known commodity, having spent almost six years on campus supervising construction of Wright's buildings. Although he was not one of the original invitees, the committee agreed to meet with him and liked his presentation.[19] A few weeks later he was hired. On June 27, 1961, Schweizer and Associates signed a contract to construct the Branscomb Memorial Auditorium, marking the official end of the Frank Lloyd Wright era at Florida Southern College.

Figure 6.1. Nils Schweizer, Ludd M. Spivey Humanities and Fine Arts Center (1970, foreground) and John Branscomb Auditorium (1964, middle), with Polk County Science Building (background). Florida Southern College Archives.

The West Campus Since Wright

With the construction of Branscomb Auditorium, Nils Schweizer became Frank Lloyd Wright's successor as Florida Southern's campus architect. He designed four of the five structures the college added to the West Campus since that time. In Schweizer's first three buildings he attempted to meld the new construction with Wright's existing work while maintaining his individuality; his last building made no concessions whatsoever to the Wright campus.

The Branscomb Memorial Auditorium, when finished in 1964, was a bulky 1,800-seat structure at the southern end of the West Campus. It rose in half-steps down the slope toward Lake Hollingsworth, terminating in a massive concrete wall facing the water, topped by a similarly blank rectangle. The auditorium thus occupied a commanding position on campus, dominating the view from the lake and blocking the Wright buildings. The sheer size of the auditorium violated Wright's desire for human-scaled architecture.

Schweizer followed with a new library in 1968, named in honor of former trustee E. T. Roux and his wife (confusingly creating another Roux Library). There was an unquestioned need for more library space by that time, as Wright had underestimated the rate of expansion of the school's collection. The new Roux Library was situated directly north of the Water Dome basin. Unlike the Branscomb Auditorium, it was clearly Wrightian in spirit, with design elements that referenced the decorative blocks used in the older buildings and clerestory windows under a broad, overhanging cornice. But once more the human scale was missing. Roux Library towered above the northern end of campus in the same manner that the Branscomb Auditorium loomed over the south.

In 1970 the college completed Schweizer's Ludd M. Spivey Humanities and Fine Arts Center. Placed next to the Branscomb Auditorium, the complex was slightly larger than its neighbor, though not as tall. The Spivey Center was created to house the school's art, music, and drama departments, along with an art gallery and theater. As with the auditorium, a Wright design existed that might have been adapted for such a complex—the Whitney Memorial project of 1944. But once more the school ignored Wright's unbuilt proposals, resulting in yet another large-scale building that failed to harmonize with the Wright structures.

Schweizer's final design for Florida Southern, the Carlisle Rogers Building (1984), with a somewhat severe rectilinear concrete wall facing Wright's work and a curving, glazed wall of glass block on the opposite side, made no effort to blend with the Wright campus; unlike Schweizer's previous buildings, it did not contain a single reference to its older neighbors. The Rogers Building may have been Schweizer's most interesting design at Florida Southern, and doubtless would not have caused raised eyebrows if constructed on the East Campus, but its location behind the seminar buildings was unfortunate.

The Rogers Building was Schweizer's last at Florida Southern. But it was not the last addition to the West Campus. In the summer of 2006, Florida Southern College decided to reconstruct Wright's Water Dome. After a donation from a trustee and a matching grant from the State of Florida, workers began removing the concrete plaza that had been created over the original basin. During this process it was discovered that adequate plumbing had never been installed beneath the basin, explaining why the fountain had never worked as intended.

The construction team consulted the Frank Lloyd Wright archives but found no final working or engineering drawings for the Water Dome, or any other documents containing explicit guidance for the project. They did determine, however, that enough information was available for the team to understand Wright's intentions. Thus, the re-created Water Dome is based on Wright's drawings, but compromises needed to be made. For example, the State of Florida building code requires that any water feature deeper than twenty-four inches must have a fence around its perimeter; the original basin held almost thirty inches of water. Rather than construct a fence, which was not in keeping with Wright's conception, the designers made the new basin pool slightly shallower than its predecessor. Also, engineers determined that the best way to achieve the illusion of a hemispherical shape with the water was to use individual jets angled toward the center. All agreed that Wright's idea of a single circular pipe with small holes would never work due to lack of adequate water pressure. And while Wright intended the water to shoot toward the center from the very edge of the basin, the design team realized that this would result in too much water spilling over the sides. So they moved the water jets in 10 feet from the perimeter, resulting in a circle 140 feet in diameter rather than 160 feet.[20]

The new Water Dome was inaugurated in October 2007 in an event that was prominently featured by local media sources, and that had been featured two weeks earlier in a story on National Public Radio's *All Things*

Considered. The fountain has since attracted many visitors and has become a favorite spot for local photographers.

In 2009 the school opened the Sarah D. and L. Kirk McKay, Jr., Archives Center adjacent to Schweizer's Roux Library and the new Water Dome. The archives center resembles a smaller version of Schweizer's structure from the north, but the southern side opens to a dramatic, largely glass curve that echoes the reading room of the old E. T. Roux Library, with concrete panel walls imprinted with patterns that mimic Wright's textile blocks. It is nicely done—and sorely needed—but also uncomfortably close to the administration building.

In addition to this new construction, many changes occurred to the Wright buildings at Florida Southern after Wright's death in 1959. Some of these were no doubt unnecessary and constituted change for its own sake, but a great deal of the alterations were necessitated by faulty construction, poor workmanship, improper planning, and student enrollment increases.

Almost all of the original furniture for the buildings disappeared. Wood trim around doors and windows was replaced by metal. All of the buildings were renovated to include air-conditioning. Unfortunately, the air-conditioning units required by this renovation are quite visible in places. Additionally, almost all of the foliage that surrounded the buildings back in the 1940s disappeared. There are a few citrus trees remaining, but the groves that once filled the empty spaces between buildings are gone. And the lush semicircle of greenery that ran along the northern edge of the Water Dome was removed to make way for the new Roux Library. While there are floral areas around the buildings, the "outdoor-garden" campus envisioned by Wright does not exist.

The decorative concrete blocks used to construct the buildings, which Wright said would "be standing a thousand years into the future," failed to live up to that prediction. Many of the blocks are cracking and disintegrating. The reasons are varied, but include the inexperience of the student workers who mixed the materials for the blocks, the blocks' composition, the stresses placed on them in some of the buildings, and the very design of Wright's "textile block" system. Over the years water has seeped into the wall cavities and caused the steel bars to rust, which in turn loosens the steel from the concrete block. As a result, the blocks have cracked. The same problem has beset owners of Wright's California textile block houses of the early 1920s.

The individual seminar buildings were combined into one (now called the L. A. Raulerson Building), eliminating the courtyards in between. A large addition, housing computing services, was attached to the north side of the complex next to the former Water Dome. The old E. T. Roux Library is now the Thad M. Buckner Building and is no longer used as a library. The service area, which contained the stacks and library offices, was redesigned and now contains offices. The circular reading room has been renamed the William M. Hollis Exhibition and Seminar Room and is used for meetings, conferences, and symposiums. The Hollis Room also contains the "Child of the Sun" Visitor Center and Esplanade Gift Shop. A low one-story wing was added to the north end of the Fine Administration Building. Overall, however, the two administration structures have fared well, with minimal alteration. The interiors remain devoted to administrative offices. In the Ordway Arts Building, both the striking refectory and the open pavilion running through the center of the building from the refectory to the theater were remodeled. The pavilion now contains offices. And the open breezeway that once ran through the center of the Polk County Science Building was enclosed with glass doors and windows at each end. The building has been sealed to allow for air-conditioning. For years, the building's east side, along the aluminum colonnade, was enclosed to form a greenhouse, but that unfortunate act has since been reversed.

Florida Southern College stands today as a testament to Ludd Spivey's determination and Frank Lloyd Wright's unique architectural vision. As the world's largest unified collection of Wright architecture, it provides an unmatched view of his creativity with an ensemble of buildings. But it is only a partial realization of Spivey's and Wright's shared dream. The campus that visitors experience today is not the one Wright imagined. It contains fewer than 75 percent of the educational structures Wright designed for it (not including the faculty houses and dormitories) and only a handful of the citrus trees that Wright considered so important. The West Campus lacks the sense of enclosure Wright sought because the buildings he intended for the site's western border were never erected. The music and arts buildings would have formed a nearly continuous wall along Johnson Avenue and would have created an area clearly segregated from the residential neighborhood around its edges.

Although the school's enrollment is not much larger than it was when Wright died, significant changes in higher education in terms of pedagogy, equipment, and faculty and student expectations have made it difficult to use some of his buildings. Wright's campus was constrained by one of its salient features—its wholeness. The idiosyncratic but united design and interconnected nature of the buildings guaranteed that any future structures located on or near the West Campus—something Wright may have consciously tried to prevent by spreading out the buildings as much as possible—would clash with his legacy. And his plan was inflexible, leaving no room for easy expansion in the event of enrollment increases or curriculum additions.

This design ran counter to the prevalent literature on college architecture and planning published in architectural journals from the 1930s on. For example, Kenneth Kingsley Stowell, editor of *Architectural Forum*, wrote in 1931, "It is well recognized now that the greatest need in buildings for colleges and universities is flexibility, so that the buildings may be changed to serve the purposes of changing educational methods with the least possible demolition and rebuilding."[21] Immediately after World War II, Joseph Hudnut, dean of the Harvard Graduate School of Design, offered a more pointed critique of unified campus plans like Wright's: "Every attempt to bind [new buildings] to a pattern laid out in advance has failed—and ought to have failed . . . Let no building depend for its character upon its relation to another, nor let any of the open spaces be of such absolute proportions that new constructions built into them will destroy them."[22] Commentators argued for buildings and plans that could be adapted to changing circumstances, which became particularly important during the postwar enrollment surge. Wright's plan, however, discouraged additions or alterations; instead it was adamantly authoritarian, perhaps reflecting the personalities of the two men most responsible for its existence.

But the school has persevered despite a small endowment. After decades of struggling to keep the Wright buildings viable, things are looking up at Florida Southern College. The school has been successfully raising both funds and public awareness through a series of high-profile aid programs. In 2006 the college received a grant from the Getty Center Campus Heritage program to continue ongoing preservation efforts; the following year the State of Florida gave $1.6 million to restore the esplanades. Florida Southern received money from the Save America's Treasures program for the Pfeiffer Chapel; the West Campus was part of a group of Wright structures named to the 2008 World Monuments Watch List of 100 Most Endangered Sites; and a National Historic Landmark nomination is planned.

In the final analysis, Florida Southern College is not the greatest work

Wright ever produced, nor is it the worst. Despite its flaws, the campus was a fascinating attempt to apply organic architecture on a broad scale. The Pfeiffer Chapel was a masterpiece, and the E. T. Roux Library and Ordway Industrial Arts Buildings were among Wright's most intriguing compositions. The college had the misfortune of being unable to construct two of Wright's best designs—the music building and the Whitney Memorial. Had they been erected, along with Wright's other proposals, Florida Southern would have been considered one of his most important commissions.

Florida Southern College deserves more attention if only for its size and the duration of the Wright-Spivey relationship. But beyond that, the campus is a singular achievement in American architecture as the first ensemble of modernist college buildings in the country. It reveals Wright operating at many different levels in a manner not found in his other projects. As Wright's West Campus attracts more attention in the architectural and popular press than ever before, and as more tourists curious about this underappreciated gem make the trek to Lakeland, this amazing collection of buildings might finally attain recognition as one of Wright's finest creations.

Notes

Introduction

1. Secondary sources on Wright's work at Florida Southern College include Siry, "Annie M. Pfeiffer Chapel"; Rogers, "Florida Southern College"; MacDonald et al., *The Buildings of Frank Lloyd Wright at Florida Southern College*; Kirwin, "Florida Southern College"; and Horwitz, "The West Campus at Florida Southern College." See also Doremus, *Frank Lloyd Wright and Le Corbusier*, 41–45; Futagawa, ed., *Frank Lloyd Wright Monograph 1937–1941*, 104–27; Futagawa, ed., *Frank Lloyd Wright Monograph 1942–1950*, 19–33; Futagawa, ed., *Frank Lloyd Wright Monograph 1951–1959*, 112–15; Gill, *Many Masks*, 396–402, 410, 463, 472; Hertz, *Frank Lloyd Wright*, 107–15; Joncas, "Pure Form," 325–32; Joncas, "Buildings for Learning," 120; Laseau and Tice, *Frank Lloyd Wright*, 19, 43, 134–35, 152, 160–61; Levine, *Architecture of Frank Lloyd Wright*, 308–10, 481–82; McCarter, *Frank Lloyd Wright*, 291–96; Secrest, *Frank Lloyd Wright*, 479–80; Storrer, *Frank Lloyd Wright Companion*, 260–66; Tafel, ed., *Frank Lloyd Wright*, 133–38; and Turner, *Campus*, 252–57.

2. Meehan, *Truth against the World*, 168.

Chapter 1. Florida Southern College, 1845–1938

1. That high school—founded in 1883 and known variously as the Southern Florida Institute, the Southern Florida Seminary, the Wesleyan Seminary, and the Wesleyan Institute—is the ancestor from which the present Florida Southern College traces its lineage. I am grateful to Mary Flekke of Florida Southern's Roux Library for information on the college's early years. On the early history of Florida Southern, see Haggard, *First 100 Years*, which unfortunately contains some inaccuracies regarding Wright's involvement with the college.

2. "Southern College to Open Sept. 22," *Lakeland Evening Telegram*, 13 July 1921.

3. Frederick H. Trimble (1878–1934) was born in Ontario, Canada, and attended Morningside College in Iowa. After graduation he traveled to China to serve as a missionary for the Methodist church, then moved to Florida in 1914. Working out of Fellsmere and later Orlando, Trimble designed a number of buildings in central Florida from the mid-1910s to the late 1920s, specializing in schools. His commissions included the Fellsmere High School, Orlando High School, Florida Theater (Vero Beach), and Orange General Hospital, in addition to the Women's Dormitory at Southern College. Around 1928 he moved to Brownsville, Texas. He

died in Canada in 1934 after an accident at a family reunion. This information was provided by Mary Flekke of Florida Southern College. Trimble's Southern College proposal survives only in a photograph of a long-lost model and a drawing of the administration building in Clark, *An Immortality of Remembrance*, 12.

4. F. T. Long, "Cornerstone of Southern College to Be Laid Today," *Lakeland Morning Star*, 25 May 1922.

5. Thrift, Jr., *Through Three Decades*, 7.

6. "Faculty Member Here Is Honored; Book Dedication," *Southern*, 30 September 1939.

7. *The Works and Aims of the Department of New Testament and Early Christian Literature of the University of Chicago*, 31.

8. On Case, see Hynes, *Shirley Jackson Case*. On the Chicago Divinity School, see Dorrien, *The Making of American Liberal Theology*, chapters 3–4.

9. In 1949 the student newspaper reported that Spivey was teaching a course entitled "Seminar of Educational Philosophy of John Dewey." "Dr. Spivey Visits Dr. John Dewey at Montego Bay," *Southern*, 25 March 1949. Copies of Spivey's lectures and sermons mentioning Dewey can be found in Spivey Collection Box 5–3, Folder 13-K-00: "Speeches by President Spivey, 1939–1943," parts I and II; and Folder 13-A-00: "Lectures & Speeches—Spivey Lectures and Speeches—Various 1 of 2," Florida Southern College Archives (hereafter FSCA).

10. See "Background Information of Dr. Ludd M. Spivey" in Spivey Collection Box 1–4, Folder 13-A-00: "Spivey, Ludd, M., Dr.—Biographical Bulletin—1949 and 1956."

11. "Some Interpretations of John Dewey's Educational Philosophy," *Bulletin of Florida Southern College, Lakeland, Florida* 67 (January 1951).

12. Spivey Collection Box MH 2–4, Folder F.0005.N: "Dewey, John. Information on and writings of; multiple dates. Spivey correspondence," FSCA. Many of the letters concern Spivey's failed attempt to create a Center for John Dewey Studies in Key West, Florida, after Dewey's death.

13. "Philosopher Dewey Here Tomorrow," *Southern*, 4 May 1944; "John Dewey Visits Southern," *Southern*, 25 April 1947; "Pres. Spivey Relates Talks with Dr. Dewey," *Southern*, 1 April 1949. For personal reminiscences regarding Spivey advocating Dewey's philosophy, see Thrift, Jr., ed., *Of Fact and Fancy*, 57, 100.

14. Throughout this book, all dates for Wright's non–Florida Southern buildings will come from Storrer, *Frank Lloyd Wright Companion*.

15. Spivey, untitled remarks to the Taliesin Fellowship (Spring Green, Wisc., 29 October 1950), Frank Lloyd Wright Foundation Archives (hereafter FLWFA).

16. Tebeau, *A History of Florida*, 386. See also Gannon, ed., *The New History of Florida*.

17. Thrift, Jr., *Through Three Decades*, 17; Haggard, *First 100 Years*, 52.

18. Spivey, television interview by Dr. Juliana Jordan, *Sags Auf Deutsch* (Tampa, Fla.: WEDU-TV, 1962), FSCA.

19. "Bond Issue to Aid Southern Gets Approval," *Lakeland Evening Ledger and*

Star-Telegram, 28 February 1928; Thrift, Jr., *Through Three Decades*, 19; Haggard, *First 100 Years*, 54.

20. Thrift, Jr., *Through Three Decades*, 20; Haggard, *First 100 Years*, 54.

21. Sledge, *Hands on the Ark*, 138.

22. Dorrien, *The Making of American Liberal Theology*, 3.

23. "Florida Methodists Exonerate Dr. Spivey of Charge of Heresy," *Tampa Morning Tribune*, 11 December 1931. One of Spivey's accusers, E. H. Crowson, documented the entire episode in a one-sided diatribe entitled "The Betrayal of Southern College. A Study in the Technique of Modern Infidelity" (1933). See also "Dr. Spivey Assails Hyman's Arguments in Religious Forum," *Tampa Morning Tribune*, 26 February 1931; "Religion and Science Not at War, Dr. Joseph Tells Large Audience," *Lakeland Ledger and Star-Telegram*, 2 March 1931; "Methodist Minister Says Dr. Spivey Is Traitor to Church," *Tampa Morning Tribune*, 2 March 1931; "An Open Letter to Dr. Ludd M. Spivey," *Lakeland Ledger and Star-Telegram*, 3 March 1931; "About Theology," *Lakeland Sunday Ledger and Star-Telegram*, 4 March 1931; "Methodists Consider Move to Oust Head of Southern College," *Tampa Morning Tribune*, 10 December 1931; "Dr. Spivey Describes Charges as 'Just Silly,'" *Tampa Morning Tribune*, 10 December 1931; and *Journal of the Florida Annual Conference of the Methodist Church, South* (Lakeland, Fla.: Southern Printing Co., 1931).

24. Sledge, *Hands on the Ark*, 242. See also Farish, *The Circuit Rider Dismounts*.

25. It is known that Spivey commissioned a house from Wright in 1939 for waterfront property he owned in Ft. Lauderdale, Florida. The house, with its circular forms and textile blocks, would have looked at home on the Florida Southern campus; it was never built. See Henning, "Frank Lloyd Wright's Other Florida Designs."

26. Eli Stanley Jones (1884–1973) grew up in Baltimore in a strict Methodist family. He briefly studied law before turning to the ministry at Asbury College (Kentucky). Following graduation, he briefly taught at the college and then traveled to India in 1907 as a missionary, where he would spend most of the rest of his life. Jones was particularly interested in promoting the common ground between Christianity and Hinduism and established a number of organizations devoted to mutual exploration and tolerance. He preached all over the world and drew extremely large crowds in India. Jones also authored twenty-nine books on various religious subjects, including *The Christ of the Indian Road* (1925), which sold more than one million copies and was translated into twenty languages, and *Abundant Living* (1942), which sold almost as many copies. Jones was nominated for the Nobel Peace Prize in 1961 and was awarded the Gandhi Peace Prize in 1963. See Ringenberg, "Eli Stanley Jones"; *The National Cyclopedia of American Biography*; "Jones Foundation Is Begun When Two Men Meet on Ocean Voyage," *Lakeland Ledger*, 9 March 1941; and Johnson, "The Christian Vision of E. Stanley Jones."

27. Corning Tolle recollection in Thrift, ed., *Of Fact and Fancy*, 58; *Sags Auf Deutsch*.

28. "Stanley Jones Guest of Dr. and Mrs. Spivey," *Southern*, 9 January 1937.

29. "Jones Foundation Is Begun When Two Men Meet on Ocean Voyage."

30. *Insuring Our Destiny* (New York: T. W. Willard Motion Picture Company, c. 1937).

31. Florida Southern College, *E. Stanley Jones for Christian Education.*

32. Harris G. Sims, "New Project Links Science, Religion," *New York Times*, 22 May 1938.

33. Jones, in *Insuring Our Destiny.*

34. Florida Southern College, *E. Stanley Jones for Christian Education*; Florida Southern College, *The E. Stanley Jones Educational Foundation*; Sims, "New Project Links Science, Religion."

35. Jones, in *Insuring Our Destiny.*

36. Florida Southern College, *E. Stanley Jones for Christian Education.*

37. Ibid.

38. Spivey, "The Authority of Social Intelligence," 10–13, in Spivey Collection Box 1–3, Folder 13-A-00: "Lectures & Speeches—Spivey Lectures and Speeches—Various, 1 of 2," FSCA. The article is not dated but must have been published in the early 1940s since it states, "But when the war is over and men can once again live peaceably."

39. See, e.g., "Jones Foundation Drive Ends with $63,415," *Lakeland Evening Ledger and Star-Telegram*, 21 February 1938; "College Drive in Two Cities," *Lakeland Evening Ledger and Star-Telegram*, 20 March 1938; "College Total Now $121,000," *Lakeland Evening Ledger and Star-Telegram*, 22 March 1938; and "College Drive Scores Again," *Lakeland Evening Ledger and Star-Telegram*, 13 April 1938.

40. None of these drawings has been found, but they can be seen in *Insuring Our Destiny* and *E. Stanley Jones for Christian Education.*

41. For example, there are strange intersections between the gabled roof and end pavilions, and the plan is centered on a "rotunda," which is intriguing since there is no dome overhead. L. Alex Hatton (1905–1975) was born in Las Cruces, New Mexico, grew up in Bartow, Florida, attended the University of Florida and Cornell University, and opened his own architectural firm in 1937, working in central Florida, particularly Orange and Polk counties. Like Frederick Trimble, he was also a Methodist. After Wright was hired to design the Florida Southern campus, Hatton engaged an attorney to seek reimbursement from the school for using his drawings in the Jones Foundation promotional campaign; Spivey paid him $100 in 1941, although he admitted no obligation was ever incurred. Hatton also made an unsuccessful attempt to get involved in Wright's project. See Frank Lloyd Wright to Charles Morgan, 27 June 1938, FLWFA; Wright to L. Alex Hatton, 13 June 1938, F013 E04, FLWFA; and E. A. Bosarge to Spivey, 14 December 1939, FSCA. I am grateful to Dorinda Morrison-Garrard of the Polk County Historical and Genealogical Library and the American Institute of Architects for biographical information on Hatton.

42. "Students Parade Will Open Lakeland Jones Foundation Fund Drive Monday," *Southern*, 12 February 1938.

43. "Alumni Council Votes to Build $50,000 Library as Part of Jones Foundation," *Southern*, 23 October 1937.

44. "Building May Begin within Three Months," *Southern*, 19 March 1938.

45. When Fisher died only a month later, he left his library and a replica of a Hindu temple to Florida Southern.

46. "Pres. Spivey Meets with Nat. Leaders," *Southern*, 9 October 1937.

47. "Launch Drive Monday Night for Southern," *Lakeland Sunday Ledger and Star-Telegram*, 13 February 1938; "Building May Begin within Three Months."

48. "Break Ground May 24th, for Jones Building," *Southern*, 2 April 1938.

49. E. Stanley Jones to Bishop Paul B. Kern, 17 December 1939, Jones Archives, Asbury Seminary. Jones repeated his claim of being exploited in a letter the same day to Gordon Halstead. E. Stanley Jones to Gordon Halstead, 17 December 1939, Jones Archives, Asbury Seminary.

50. R. E. Diffendorfer to E. Stanley Jones, 2 February 1940, Jones Archives, Asbury Seminary.

51. "Spivey Enthusiastic Over Prospects of Support for Rich Foundation," undated newspaper article, Spivey Collection Box MH4–2, Folder M-00-Jones, E. Stanley Educational Foundation, "Proposed E. Stanley Jones Educational Foundation, Late 1930s," FSCA.

52. "Dr. Jones Speaks on Religion," *Southern*, 14 March 1942.

53. Corning Tolle, recollection in Thrift, Jr., ed., *Of Fact and Fancy*, 58.

54. Ibid.

55. Roland D. Elderkin, "Your College: Past, Present and Future," *Southern*, 6 October 1961; Rogers, "The Academician and the Architect," FSCA; Hertz, *Wright in Word and Form*, 107; G. F. Zimmerman (former student) in "Through the Years," FSCA.

56. "Frank Lloyd Wright Speech to Fellowship, 10/29/50," FLWFA; repeated in "College Will Be Milestone of Culture, Wright Declares," *Lakeland Ledger*, 6 November 1955, and "At Florida Southern College," in Pfeiffer, ed., *Wright: His Living Voice*, 43.

57. *Sags Auf Deutsch.*

58. Spivey to Wright, 11 April 1938, F028 E03, FLWFA.

59. "It was easy . . . to see Wright chiefly as an old master, his life's work done, filling out his years by lecturing and writing his reminiscences; inveighing at the audacities of the young and bemusing himself and the world with occasional projects of an apparently quite fantastic character." Hitchcock, "Wright at the Museum of Modern Art," 73.

60. Wright, *Autobiography*. The quote is from Twombly, *Wright: His Life and His Architecture*, 200.

61. Wright, *The Disappearing City* (1932).

62. For a listing of the articles, see Sweeney, *Wright: An Annotated Bibliography*.

63. "Miami Goes over Top in Jones Drive," *Southern*, 23 April 1938. Also, the Florida Southern Alumni Council had voted the previous October to build a

$50,000 library building. "Alumni Council Votes to Build $50,000 Library as Part of Jones Foundation," *Southern*, 23 October 1937.

64. Wright to Spivey, 13 December 1938, F033 A05, FLWFA.

65. Lakeland Campaign on Behalf of E. Stanley Jones Educational Foundation, Florida Southern College, "Answers to Questions" (1938?), Spivey Collection Box MH4–2, Folder M-00-Jones, E. Stanley Educational Foundation, "Proposed E. Stanley Jones Educational Foundation, Late 1930s," FSCA.

66. Wright, *Autobiography*, 515.

67. A decade after Spivey contacted Wright, a similar scenario arose when Dr. Peyton Canary approached Wright to design the Southwest Christian Seminary in Arizona; Canary had even less money than Spivey, but somehow persuaded Wright to make drawings for a campus consisting of a chapel, administrative buildings, seminar rooms, a library, a Greek theater and faculty homes, none of which were ever paid for after the project fell through.

68. Rogers, "The Academician and the Architect," 6.

69. Pfeiffer, ed., *Wright: His Living Voice*, 43.

70. Harris G. Sims, "Frank Lloyd Wright to Plan Campus Buildings," *Lakeland Evening Ledger and Star-Telegram*, 10 May 1938.

71. Donna Stoddard, quoted in Thrift, Jr., ed., *Of Fact and Fancy*, 66.

72. Sims, "Frank Lloyd Wright to Plan Campus Buildings."

73. In June 1938, B. P. Reinsch, head of Florida Southern's mathematics department, sent Wright a topographic map with photographs of the site and noted, "there are 1000–1400 trees in all and quite irregularly located in parts." B. P. Reinsch to Wright, 6 June 1938, Florida Southern College, Rogers Files—"FSC Corr. Mentioning Campus."

74. The site's picturesque beauty makes historian Henry-Russell Hitchcock's description of the area in his 1942 book, *In the Nature of Materials*, suspect. Hitchcock erroneously sited the campus on a "flat lakeside, hardly above water level," and found the scenery as a whole to be "perhaps the most uninspiring with which Wright has ever had to deal." Hitchcock, *In the Nature of Materials*, 99–100. Hitchcock's inaccurate description was probably due to his never having visited the site, forcing him to rely on Wright, who was not above downplaying the landscape to make his own efforts seem more heroic.

75. The school's total enrollment, including part-time and summer-school students, was more than 1,300. Florida Southern College, *Florida Southern College Bulletin* (1938): 141. Interestingly, *The 1939 College Blue Book* lists only 376 students. Hurt and Hurt, *The 1939 College Blue Book*, 498.

76. For contemporary information on Lakeland, see Federal Writers' Project, *Florida: Empire of the Sun.*

77. Kjellmark, "Vegetation History of the Lake Hollingsworth Area," in Haldeman and Quetchenbach, eds., *Lake Hollingsworth*, 184.

78. Ibid.

79. *Sags Auf Deutsch.*

80. Thomas Mack, in Thrift, Jr., ed., *Of Fact and Fancy*, 69.

81. "Wright Drafts Be Ready Soon," *Lakeland Evening Ledger and Star-Telegram*, 16 May 1938. See also "Tampans Raise $10,000 to Open College Drive," *Tampa Morning Tribune*, 17 May 1938.

82. Interestingly, the article mentions Wright only once. Sims, "New Project Links Science, Religion."

83. Afterward he wrote to Spivey: "I am afraid I pulled a 'boner' at your last meeting in Tampa when I thought some explanation of the picture of the building shown them was needed, at the moment, and undertook to make it by saying that you and Dr. Jones, as things were in architecture in our country, were headed for some such tragic end to your ideals as that design for a building indicated—but thanks to your own acumen we had you both safe in port from anything like that now." Wright to Spivey, 16 May 1938, F030 C08, FLWFA.

84. Thrift, Jr., ed., *Of Fact and Fancy*, 37.

85. "Through the Years."

86. Spivey to Wright, 19 August 1938, F031 B03, FLWFA.

87. Spivey to Wright, 5 September 1938, F031 B07, FLWFA.

88. Spivey to Wright, 26 September 1938, F031 C06, FLWFA.

Chapter 2. Wright's Campus Plan

1. Wright to Spivey, 20 September 1938, F031 C04, FLWFA.

2. B. P. Reinsch to Wright, 6 June 1938, Florida Southern College, Rogers Files—"FSC Corr. Mentioning Campus."

3. Wright to Spivey, 13 June 1938, F030 E03, FLWFA.

4. To be fair, we do not know if this drawing was intended to represent Spivey's vision or Wright's, but it seems more likely than not based on his working methods that it reflects Wright's ideas.

5. "Programme for University," no date, 1502.279.019, FLWFA.

6. In 1941, however, Spivey asked Wright to design a gate for the campus at McDonald Street, claiming that the existing entrance there was a "disgrace"; this suggests that the north entry had become significant. But there is no record of any further action taken regarding that suggestion. Spivey to Wright, 1 October 1941, F048 B06, FLWFA. An administration building drawing from the mid-forties (4515.22) describes the structure as "to left of the college entrance." Over time the entry from the parking lot adjacent to the administration building has become something of a main entrance for visitors.

7. "Frank Lloyd Wright," *Architectural Forum* 68 (January 1938): 68.

8. Wright to Spivey, 20 September 1938, F031 C04, FLWFA.

9. Wright to Spivey, 13 December 1938, F033 A05, FLWFA.

10. Harris G. Sims, "Wright Views First Work on Large Program," *Lakeland Evening Ledger and Star-Telegram*, 20 December 1938.

11. Donna Stoddard, in Thrift, Jr., *Of Fact and Fancy*, 66.

12. Spivey, *Good News!* 4. Later that year, in a lecture in London, Wright would proclaim, "Out of the ground into the light—yes! Not only must the building so

proceed, but we cannot have an organic architecture unless we achieve an organic society!" Wright, "An Organic Architecture" (1939), 305.

13. Many modernist architects thought the expression of monumentality in a democratic society was especially inappropriate. For a discussion of this issue, see Collins and Collins, "Monumentality," and Summerson, "The Mischievous Analogy."

14. For a discussion of the Mayan aspects of Wright's architecture, see Tselos, "Exotic Influences on Frank Lloyd Wright," and Braun, *Pre-Columbian Art.*

15. "Noted Architect Foresees End of Big Cities," *Tampa Sunday Tribune*, 22 May 1938.

16. "An Organic Architecture" (1939), 302.

17. The following paragraphs are indebted to the work of David De Long and William Cronon. See Cronon, "Inconstant Unity," and De Long, ed., *Wright: Designs for an American Landscape.*

18. Wright, *Autobiography*, 16.

19. Emerson, "Art," 87.

20. Emerson, "Nature," 325.

21. Quoted in Olsberg, "Introduction," 11.

22. Emerson, "Art," 88.

23. Cronon, "Inconstant Unity," 13.

24. Emerson, "Nature," 315.

25. Ibid.

26. Wright and Brownell, *Architecture and Modern Life* (1937), 231.

27. Ibid., 219.

28. Ibid., 223.

29. Ibid.

30. Emerson, "Nature," 320.

31. Wright and Brownell, *Architecture and Modern Life* (1937), 240.

32. Ibid.

33. Wright, "Living in the Desert," 12.

34. Wright, *Autobiography*, 311.

35. Wright quoted in Green, with DeNevi, *An Architecture for Democracy*, front matter.

36. See, e.g., Harris G. Sims, "Frank Lloyd Wright to Plan Campus Buildings," *Lakeland Evening Ledger and Star-Telegram*, 10 May 1938; Wright to Spivey, 5 March 1941, F044 E09, FLWFA; "Frank Lloyd Wright," *Architectural Forum* 88 (January 1948): 129; "A Four-Color Portfolio of the Recent Work of the Dean of Contemporary Architects, with His Own Commentary on Each Building," 103; and "Florida Southern College Revisited for Glimpses of the Administration Group in Wright's Organic Campus," 125.

37. For another example of Wright's pursuit of regional modernism, see Siry, "Wright's Baghdad Opera House and Gammage Auditorium."

38. Gray, *Thomas Hastings: Architect* (1933), cited in Curl, *Mizner's Florida*, 59. Very little has been written on Florida's architectural history, and much of it has focused on Mizner or the state's resort architecture. For overviews, see Hatton,

Tropical Splendor, and *A Guide to Florida's Historic Architecture*. More specifically, see Curl, *Mizner's Florida*, and Braden, *Architecture of Leisure*.

39. "Florida," *Architectural Forum* 69 (December 1938): 449–64.

40. Sims, "Frank Lloyd Wright to Plan Campus Buildings."

41. Meehan, ed., *Frank Lloyd Wright Remembered*, 11.

42. "College Will Be Milestone of Culture, Wright Declares," *Lakeland Ledger*, 6 November 1955. The newspaper reported that Wright "heaped sulphuric scorn" on Miami's architecture after a recent visit there, declaring the city to be "just a little monkey-fied edition of New York City," and adding, "A Floridian is somebody from the North with a paralyzed imagination."

43. Wright, *Autobiography*, 9. In his recounting of the story of his decision to move to Chicago, young Wright defiantly exclaims, "all the Joneses, every one of them, is cracked about education. 'Education?' You sent me to the farm yourself for *experience*. Well, it's experience I want now." Ibid., 59.

44. Barney, *In the Valley of the God-Almighty Joneses*, 61.

45. Chase, *A Goodly Fellowship*.

46. Wright, *Autobiography*, 382.

47. Chase, *A Goodly Fellowship*, 94.

48. William E. Martin to Darwin D. Martin, 10 October 1910, Frank Lloyd Wright–Darwin D. Martin papers, University Archives, State University of New York at Buffalo.

49. Wright, *Autobiography*, 387. He had made a similar claim in the 1933 prospectus for the Taliesin Fellowship; see Wright, *The Taliesin Fellowship* (1933), 159. For an account that questions Wright's commitment to the Hillside Home School's resurrection, however, see Secrest, *Frank Lloyd Wright: A Biography*, 253.

50. During the course of Wright's involvement with Florida Southern College, for example, at least four Taliesin apprentices (Lee Kawahara, Kenn Lockhart, Robert Crosse, and Nils Schweizer) spent time on the campus supervising progress. On the fellowship's relationship to Wright's philosophy, see Twombly, "Organic Living." For an insider's account of the fellowship, see Marty and Marty, *Frank Lloyd Wright's Taliesin Fellowship*. Marty's *Communities of Frank Lloyd Wright* provides a more objective account, while an alternative, salacious history can be found in Friedman and Zellman, *The Fellowship*.

51. Emerson, "The Young American," 397.

52. Wright, *Autobiography*, 3–4.

53. This interpretation was first pointed out in Joncas, "Buildings for Learning."

54. Quoted in Meehan, ed., *Truth against the World*, 270.

55. Ibid., 326.

56. A child in these utopian schools would learn "not only to see clearly by learning to draw (define) what he sees but gradually taking other steps in practice to qualify himself to *build* organic structures." Ibid., 327.

57. Dewey, *School and Society*, 76.

58. Wright, *The Living City* (1958), 326.

59. Quoted in Westbrook, *John Dewey and American Democracy*, 102.

60. Wright, *The Living City*, 324.

61. Dewey, *School and Society*, 88.

62. Chase, *A Goodly Fellowship*, 117.

63. Wright, *My Father, Frank Lloyd Wright*, 60; Wright, *Autobiography*, 331.

64. Meehan, ed., *Truth against the World*, 269–70.

65. Ibid.

66. Wright, *The Disappearing City* (1932), 105.

67. Ibid.

68. "Quality, Not Quantity, Seen as Big Need by Mr. Wright," *Southern*, 23 November 1951.

69. "Frank Lloyd Wright," *Architectural Forum* 102 (April 1955): 116.

70. Whitman recurs throughout the *Autobiography* and other writings, and Wright mentions both Whitman and Emerson in a 1932 essay for *Scholastic* magazine, "Books That Have Meant Most to Me."

71. Whitman, "Democratic Vistas," 228.

72. Whitman, "By Blue Ontario's Shore," 323. Another of Wright's favorite authors, Henry David Thoreau, also was an outspoken advocate of individual freedom. Thoreau advised readers, "Keep on your own track," and in a famous passage from *Walden*, explained, "If a man does not keep pace with his companions, perhaps it is because one hears a different drummer. Let him step to the music which he hears, however unmeasured or far away." Thoreau, *Walden*, 156, 430.

73. Whitman, "Democratic Vistas," 205.

74. "Thus will you make of Democracy a religion—the only one the world will have developed—befitting freemen—free in the integrity of their bodies, free in the integrity of their thought. So doing, all aspects of your activities will change, because your thoughts will have changed . . . Naturally, then, as your thoughts thus change, your growing Architecture will change. Its falsity will depart; its reality will gradually appear." Sullivan, "What Is Architecture?" 240. For more on Sullivan and democracy, see Paul, *Sullivan: An Architect in American Thought*.

75. Wright, *Ausgefuhrte Bauten und Entwurfe* (1910), 106–7.

76. Wright, "Is It Good-By to Gothic?" (1958), 229.

77. Menocal, "Wright's Concept of Democracy," 154.

78. Wright, "The Language of an Organic Architecture," 345. For an interesting examination of the interconnections between organic architecture, democracy, and progressive education in Wright's thought, see Roche, "Building for Democracy."

79. Wright, "In the Cause of Architecture" (1908), 158.

80. Wright to Spivey, 20 September 1938, F031 C04, FLWFA.

81. Ibid.

82. Siry, "Annie M. Pfeiffer Chapel," 528.

83. Wright, "Sixty Years of Living Architecture" (1951), 34; Wright, "Frank Lloyd Wright Speaks Up" (1953), 67.

84. Wright, "Frank Lloyd Wright Speaks Up," 67.

85. For analyses of Wright's increasing use of the diagonal in the 1920s and 1930s, see Levine, "Wright's Diagonal Planning"; Joncas, "Pure Form"; Alofsin, *The Lost Years*; and Riley, "The Landscapes of Frank Lloyd Wright."

86. "This triangle is reflected in the general forms of all the cabins as well as the general plan." Wright, *Autobiography*, 311.

87. Wright, "The Japanese Print" (1912), 117–18.

88. Levine, *Architecture of Frank Lloyd Wright*, 301.

89. See Alofsin, *The Lost Years*, 120–26, for a further explanation of Wright's philosophy of forms.

90. The history of Jefferson's University of Virginia design is detailed in Sherwood and Michael Lasala, "Education and Architecture." For an analysis, see Wilson, "Jefferson's Lawn."

91. Wright, "Letter to the Editor," 368.

92. I have found no records, either in University of Virginia documents or local newspapers, of Wright ever visiting the campus. He was in Williamsburg, Virginia, in October 1938, for an exhibition of his work, but it does not appear that he made the trip to Charlottesville. The Florida Southern College plan had already been conceived by that time. On the Wright-Jefferson connections, see Doremus, *Wright and Le Corbusier*; Levine, *Architecture of Frank Lloyd Wright*; Biemiller, "Echoes of Jefferson"; and Hertz, *Wright in Word and Form*.

93. Jefferson was a political hero, not an architectural one. In *An Autobiography*, Wright invokes Jefferson while ranting against the government: "Thomas Jefferson. Where are you now? Is the muddy wave of an ism closing over your gracious head?" Wright, *Autobiography*, 414. Wright also said of Jefferson: "I never think of him in connection with classic architecture except as he happened to be wearing, also, silk knee breeches and lace at throat and wrists—a mere incident (or accident) of a temporal character. It was all he then knew." Wright, "Letter to the Editor," 368.

94. Hanna and Hanna, *Wright's Hanna House*, 39. A similar story is reported in Turner, "The Collaborative Design of Stanford University," 11. Stanford was actually designed by Henry Hobson Richardson's successor firm, Shepley, Rutan, and Coolidge (in conjunction with Frederick Law Olmsted), shortly after Richardson's death.

95. Scully, Jr., *Frank Lloyd Wright*, 29.

96. MacDonald and Pinto, *Hadrian's Villa and Its Legacy*, 322. James Marston Fitch challenged Scully's interpretation in a scathing review of Scully's book, *American Architecture*, calling the comparison "absurd" and based on similarities between drawings rather than actual built spaces. Fitch, "Facsimiles and Reality," 154. Scully defended himself against Fitch, saying, "among other things, the visual evidence is there." Ibid., 155. The exchange raises interesting questions about intention and interpretation in architectural history that are beyond the scope of this book.

97. The best overview of the history of American college architecture and planning is Turner, *Campus.*

98. Wright's Florida Southern College proposal was part of a remarkable series of events that occurred in 1938 and loosened the foundations of collegiate design. For the first time, modernism infiltrated American college architecture. Contests for a building for Wheaton College in Massachusetts, a new campus for Goucher College in Maryland, and a fine arts center for the American National Theatre and Academy to be located at the College of William and Mary in Virginia attracted an unprecedented number of modernist proposals (and resulted in competition winners in the case of Wheaton and the ANTA project). At roughly the same time, Black Mountain College in North Carolina commissioned Walter Gropius to create a new campus plan. Although the Wheaton and ANTA projects were never built, and the Black Mountain proposal produced only one building, the modernist movement had begun to gain a foothold in a long-established bastion of traditionalism, led by Wright's inspired work at Florida Southern. On these competitions see Kornwolf, *Modernism in America.* For Black Mountain, see Duberman, *Black Mountain.* It should be noted that 1938 was also the year Ludwig Mies van der Rohe arrived in Chicago to become head of the Department of Architecture at the Armour Institute (later to become the Illinois Institute of Technology, or I.I.T.) and began working on his own campus plan, which would be unveiled the following year.

99. Edgell, *American Architecture of To-Day.*

100. Larson and Palmer, *Architectural Planning of the American College,* 23–24.

101. Ibid., 25.

102. Klauder and Wise, *College Architecture,* foreword.

103. Ibid., 25.

104. Ibid., 44.

105. See, for example, Walker, "Expression—And the Collegiate Style"; Ackerman, "The Planning of Colleges and Universities"; and Hamlin, "The Educational Influence of Collegiate Architecture."

106. For examples of Jefferson-influenced campus planning, see Turner, *Campus,* 191–203.

107. "Into College Plants Has Poured $2,250,000,000," 52.

108. "Where is Modern Now?" 468.

109. Wright, "An Organic Architecture" (1939), 302; Wright to Spivey, 20 September 1938, F031 C04, FLWFA.

110. Klauder and Wise, *College Architecture,* 25.

111. Wright, "Modern Architecture" (1931), 23.

112. "Quality, Not Quantity, Seen as Big Need by Mr. Wright," 2.

113. Wright, *The Disappearing City,* 105.

114. "Quality, Not Quantity, Seen as Big Need by Mr. Wright," 2.

Chapter 3. "Out of the ground and into the light"

1. Wright to Spivey, 13 December 1938, F033 A05, FLWFA.

2. Wright to Spivey, 11 February 1939, F035 D06, FLWFA.

3. "Programme for University," no date, 1502.279.019, FLWFA.

4. FLWFA 3816.001 and 3805.008.

5. This observation was first made by Siry, "Annie M. Pfeiffer Chapel," 509.

6. This choir screen would later lead to a conflict with the college's choir leader, who asked Wright during construction to lower it so that the audience might have a better view of the singers and so that they might see him if he stood on the lower-level stage. Wright defended his decision: "For many years I have deplored the intrusion of personality with music even in the concert hall. How much more then in the house of worship. The first time I tried to do something about it was in Unity Temple, Oak Park. I put a close wooden screen in front of the choir-singers. The singers revolted—mostly women . . . the new hat was wasted, etc, etc.," he wrote. "So in this chapel I opened the screen wall so that there might be an awareness of the choir and yet not too much distraction by way of the persons involved." Wright to George Tenney, 4 October 1941, F048 B08, FLWFA.

7. Wright designed twenty-three-foot-long electric light lanterns (drawing 3816.069) to hang from the skylight, which would have served as further inducement to cast one's eyes upward; the lanterns were never built.

8. For a detailed description of the chapel's structure, see Siry, "Annie M. Pfeiffer Chapel."

9. Campus workers soon discovered that it was too difficult, if not impossible, to reach some of the plants to provide water and care, and the plants disappeared. The lack of plants created a problem: the combination of intense sunlight—without greenery to block it—and the absence of air-conditioning could create extremely uncomfortable conditions. Wright tried to promote ventilation inside the chapel with perforated concrete blocks at ground level and hollow corner piers, but the system proved inadequate. After the 1944 hurricane Spivey began a campaign to persuade Wright to redesign the chapel to include air-conditioning, but he was unsuccessful. Wright himself may have recognized the problem: he allegedly commented after one session in the chapel that he felt "like a prune being stewed in his own broth." "Through the Years," 1.

10. For photographs of the skylights before and after damage from a 1944 hurricane, see MacDonald, Galbraith, and Rogers, Jr., *The Buildings of Frank Lloyd Wright.*

11. The uppermost level of blocks was eventually stuccoed, much to Wright's chagrin and against his wishes.

12. "Frank Lloyd Wright's Newest Creation," 34.

13. This interpretation is supported by anecdotal evidence that Wright discouraged the college from planting flowers and greenery around the bases of the buildings, even attempting to chop down some vegetation around the administration building with his cane during a campus visit. Thrift, Jr., ed., *Of Fact and Fancy*, 69–70. The effect was rendered moot, however, after the upper level of the

base was stuccoed following the 1944 hurricane and the number of trees steadily diminished over time, resulting in a building that today stands in a nearly bare landscape.

14. Harris G. Sims, "Wright Views First Work on Large Program," *Lakeland Evening Ledger and Star-Telegram*, 20 December 1938.

15. Wright to Spivey, 5 March 1941, F044 E09, FLWFA.

16. Wright, "Is It Good-By to Gothic?" (1958), 227, 228.

17. On the history of American Methodist church architecture, see Tucker, *American Methodist Worship*, chapter 10, and Kilde, *When Church Became Theatre*.

18. Conover, *Building the House of God* (1928), cited in Tucker, *American Methodist Worship*, 253.

19. "Programme for University," no date, 1502.279.019, FLWFA.

20. Spivey to Wright, 8 November 1938, F032 B05, FLWFA.

21. "Cornerstone for College Chapel to Be Laid," *Lakeland Sunday Ledger and Star-Telegram*, 20 November 1938.

22. Harris G. Sims, "Jones Lays Cornerstone of New Chapel," *Lakeland Evening Ledger and Star-Telegram*, 27 November 1938.

23. Spivey to Wright, 8 November 1938, F032 B05, FLWFA.

24. Wright to Spivey, 13 December 1938, F033 A05, FLWFA.

25. Spivey to Annie M. Pfeiffer, 28 May 1938, Spivey Collection Box 2–3, Folder 13-B-00: Pfeiffer (Mrs.) Annie Correspondence 1938–1946, FSCA.

26. Haggard, *Through Three Decades*, 85; "Chapel Donor," *Lakeland Ledger*, 9 March 1941.

27. Gross, "Henry Pfeiffer and Annie Merner Pfeiffer."

28. Spivey to Wright, 20 January 1939, F035 A08, FLWFA.

29. The details of Wright's textile block system are explained in Ford, *Details of Modern Architecture*, 325–31. Kenneth Frampton offers an evaluation of the system in "Modernization and Mediation," 67–69. For a more extensive discussion of the Florida Southern College block system, see Patterson, *Wright and the Meaning of Materials*, 119–24.

30. The reminiscences of some student laborers can be found in "Through the Years."

31. Spivey had suggested using cypress blocks in early January 1939, but Wright rejected the idea. According to Nils Schweizer, a Taliesin apprentice who supervised construction on the campus in the 1950s, the original block mix was four parts coquina shell, one part white trinity cement, and a little water. By 1950, however, the recipe had changed to one-half part light gray cement, one-half part white trinity cement, four parts davenport sand, some Horne's raw sienna color, and water. Schweizer wrote these formulas on some drawings for the restoration of the Pfeiffer Chapel in 1979. I thank Jeff Baker of Mesick, Cohen, Wilson, Baker Architects for this information.

32. Wright, "In the Cause of Architecture: The Third Dimension" (1925), 213.

Wright intended to use local soil for the blocks of the San Marcos in the Desert project as well.

33. Wright to Spivey, 11 February 1939, F035 D06, FLWFA.

34. Spivey to Wesley Peters, 23 May 1939, F037 A05, FLWFA.

35. Spivey to Wright, 20 June 1939, F037 D01, FLWFA.

36. Wright to Spivey, 18 April 1939, F036 C06, FLWFA.

37. C. W. Palmore to Wright, 4 August 1939, F038 A07, FLWFA.

38. Wright to Spivey, 14 August 1939, F038 B05, FLWFA.

39. "Blocks Are in the Making," *Southern*, 8 September 1939; "Crew of Men Busy Making Bricks for New Jones Chapel," *Southern*, 30 September 1939.

40. Frederick M. Babcock to Russell V. Tinney, 9 January 1940, 1502.279.024, FLWFA.

41. Russell V. Tinney to John L. Wright, 2 February 1940, 1502.279.032, FLWFA.

42. Wright to Spivey, 13 February 1940, FSCA.

43. Spivey discussed the program's patriotic goals in "10 Objectives for Chair of Democracy to Be Established on Campus Combating Un-American Trends Are Outlined by Dr. Ludd M. Spivey," *Southern*, 22 October 1938.

44. See, e.g., "European War to Come, Dr. Spivey Says," *Southern*, 16 September 1936; "Church Here Must Combat Communism," *Southern*, 3 October 1936; and "Professor Spivey Lectures Thrice about Russians," *Southern*, 17 April 1937.

45. See *The Bill of Rights*.

46. The quote is from "A Plan for a Major in 'The American Idea,' Department of American Culture, 1954–1955," Spivey Collection Box 3–2, Folder 13-H-00: American Culture Department Correspondence 1951–1954, FSCA.

47. J. C. Peel and Dr. John C. Glenn, "A Plan for a Major in 'The American Idea,' Department of American Culture, 1954–1955," Spivey Collection Box 3–2, Folder 13-H-00: American Culture Department Correspondence 1951–54, FSCA.

48. Gordon Halstead to E. Stanley Jones, 22 November 1939, Jones Archives, Asbury Seminary.

49. Dana F. Robinson to Spivey, 15 November 1939, Spivey Collection Box 6–2, Folder 13-A-00: Correspondence 1938, 1939, 1940, 1941, FSCA.

50. See Peters to Wright, 1 November 1939, F039 D08, FLWFA. For the board's perspective, see Mary Lowe West to Bishop Paul Kern, 11 December 1939, Spivey Collection Box 5–4, Folder 13-C-00: West, Mary L.—Correspondence—1938–1949, FSCA. The archives contain several letters of encouragement regarding the situation, written by Spivey's colleagues and friends in November and December 1939.

51. See Thomas P. Chalker to P. A. Roy, S.J., 20 August 1940, Spivey Collection Box 6–1, Folder 13-D-56: Chalker, Thomas Correspondence April–October 1940, FSCA.

52. For correspondence on the Chalker charges and their resolution, see the following in the Florida Southern College Archives: Spivey to Bishop Arthur Moore, 6 September 1940, Spivey Collection Box 5–3, Folder 13-G-00: Moore, Arthur J.

(Bishop) Correspondence, 1939–1950; Spivey to Dr. John Frazier, 13 September 1940, Spivey Collection Box 6–1, Folder 13-D-56: Chalker, Thomas Correspondence April–October 1940; A. Fred Turner to E. Stanley Jones, 16 October 1940, Spivey Collection Box 6–1, Folder 13-D-56: Chalker, Thomas Correspondence April–October 1940; Spivey to Bishop Arthur Moore, 19 October 1940, Spivey Collection Box 5–3, Folder 13-G-00: Moore, Arthur J. (Bishop) Correspondence, 1939–1950; and Bishop Arthur Moore to Spivey, 28 October 1940, Spivey Collection Box 5–3, Folder 13-G-00: Moore, Arthur J. (Bishop) Correspondence, 1939–1950.

53. Spivey to Wright, 18 April 1940, 1502.279.051, FLWFA.

54. Rogers, "The Architect and the Academician," 3.

55. Haggard, *The First 100 Years*, 52.

56. Peters to Wright, 1 November 1939, F039 D08, FLWFA.

57. Peters to Wright, 14 December 1946, 1502.279.317, FLWFA.

58. Rogers, "The Architect and the Academician," 3.

59. Thrift, Jr., ed., *Of Fact and Fancy*, 104.

60. Wright quoted in "Frank Lloyd Wright," *Architectural Forum* 102 (April 1955), 116.

61. Wright quoted in "Frank Lloyd Wright," *Architectural Forum* 88 (January 1948): 129.

62. Levine, *Architecture of Frank Lloyd Wright*, 308.

63. FLWFA 3805.008.

64. "Programme for University," no date, 1502.279.019, FLWFA.

65. Spivey to Wright, 28 May 1940, FSCA.

66. This system would lead to problems: in a 1949 letter discussing plans for the industrial arts building, Spivey expressed some displeasure with the seminar buildings: "Let's not have any more buildings like the Seminars. The three we have are fine but I think the new buildings should have some windows or at least glass in the sides. It is very difficult in Florida to keep openings in the top from leaking." Spivey to Wright, 10 June 1949, FSCA. One can imagine that the openings also attracted a fair number of insects, reptiles, and other unwanted visitors.

67. *Insuring Our Destiny.*

68. "Spivey Cites College Aims and Purposes," *Southern*, 29 October 1938.

69. Florida Southern College, *Florida Southern College Bulletin* 66 (April 1950): 56.

70. Ibid., 22.

71. Wright to Spivey, 11 January 1940, FLWFA. On the unbuilt house Wright designed for Spivey in Ft. Lauderdale, see Henning, "Wright's Other Florida Designs."

72. Spivey to Wright, 31 January 1940, FSCA. It is nearly impossible to determine the veracity of Spivey's statements without further documentation. An intriguing document in the Frank Lloyd Wright Foundation Archives, however, on Spivey's letterhead, lists E. Stanley Jones Educational Foundation income for the period May 1–15, 1940, at $10,656.75 and expenditures at $4,747.70, implying that, at least for the beginning of May, the foundation was making money. Untitled document 1502.279.055, FLWFA. The financial relationship between

Florida Southern College and the Jones Educational Foundation was never clear, however, and the lack of accurate bookkeeping would become a serious problem after Wright's death. See chapter 6.

73. Peters to Wright, 1 November 1939, F039 D08, FLWFA.

74. Peters to Svetlana Wright Peters, 13 November 1939, FLWFA.

75. Peters to Wright, 29 November 1939, F039 E03, FLWFA.

76. Spivey to Wright, 1 April 1940, 1502.279.047, FLWFA.

77. Robert Crosse to Wright, 24 January 1952, 1502.279.575, FLWFA.

78. Wright to Spivey, 26 June 1945, 1502.279.248, FLWFA.

79. See former student laborers' reminiscences in "Through the Years."

80. Peters to Wright, 14 December 1946, 1502.279.317, FLWFA.

81. Wright's first constructed library was the Lawrence Memorial Library, Springfield, Illinois (1905)—a simple rectangular room.

82. See, e.g., Van Slyck, *Free to All*, 105–7, 119–22.

83. Wright, "The Japanese Print: An Interpretation" (1912), 118; Levine, *Architecture of Frank Lloyd Wright*, 301.

84. FLWFA 4118.004.

85. Wright alluded to these intended design similarities when he wrote Spivey: "We are working on the Library now which promises to be a fine companion for the chapel." Wright to Spivey, 5 March 1941, F044 E09, FLWFA.

86. Quoted in Diane Lacey Allen, "Frank Lloyd Wright," *Lakeland Ledger*, 24 September 1989.

87. Burchard, David, and Boyd, *Planning the University Library Building*, vii. On the change in collegiate libraries, see Gyure, "The Heart of the University."

88. Walter, "The University Library Building," 315.

89. Quoted in Allen, "Frank Lloyd Wright." The "Programme for University" called for a 50,000-book library.

90. See, e.g., Spivey to Wright, 11 October 1943, FLWFA (100,000); Spivey to Dr. B. A. Whitmore, 15 January 1944, Spivey Collection Box 4–4, Folder 13-A-00: Roux Library Correspondence, "Correspondence 1938–1951," FSCA (150,000); and "Interior View of Roux Library," *Southern*, 30 March 1945 (200,000).

91. "Students at Florida Southern Work in 'Functional Library,'" unknown newspaper article, 30 October 1949, FSCA.

92. Nils Schweizer to Wright, 14 December 1957, FLWFA.

93. Wright to Spivey, 5 March 1941, F044 E09, FLWFA.

94. Quoted in Haggard, *First 100 Years*, 82.

95. "College Chapel Is Dedicated," *Lakeland Ledger*, 10 March 1941.

Chapter 4. The War Years, 1942–1945

1. Spivey to Wright, 30 December 1941, FSCA.

2. Spivey to Wright, 20 January 1942, F053 D10, FLWFA.

3. Spivey to Wright, 31 March 1942, F055 B05, FLWFA.

4. Wright to Spivey, 26 May 1942, F056 C03, FLWFA.

5. Ibid.

6. Wright to Spivey, 1 July 1942, F057 A01, FLWFA.

7. Spivey to Wright, 11 February 1943, 1502.279.123, FLWFA.

8. Spivey to Wright, 11 October 1943, FSCA.

9. In March, Spivey reported to Wright: "I have someone interested in the Music Building," but did not name Whitney. By late May she had been identified, because Wright had attempted unsuccessfully to meet her in New York to show her sketches of the music building. Spivey to Wright, 31 March 1942, F055 B05, FLWFA; Wright to Spivey, 26 May 1942, F056 C03, FLWFA.

10. Wright to Spivey, undated telegram, 1502.279.144, FLWFA. The telegram is with other 1943 correspondence in the Wright Archives.

11. "Programme for University," no date, 1502.279.019, FLWFA.

12. Quoted in Kaufmann, ed., *Wright: An American Architecture*, 182. For discussions of Wright's theater designs, see Cole, "The Theatre Projects of Frank Lloyd Wright," and Bridgeman, "The Development of a Theatre Concept."

13. A perspective drawing for this building (3817.004), which probably dates to 1938, was resurrected in the 1950s as a proposed auditorium for the Florida Methodist Conference. See *Southern*, 3 November 1950, and "Construction Planned for Tenth Wright Building," *Southern*, 15 January 1954.

14. Spivey to Wright, 15 November 1943, 1502.279.136, FLWFA.

15. He also mistakenly referred to Whitney in two letters—and at least one drawing—as "Gloria Vanderbilt Whitney," confusing the artist and mother-in-law of Eleanor (Gertrude Vanderbilt Whitney) with her famous niece (Gloria Vanderbilt). Wright to Spivey, 6 December 1943, 1502.279.138, FLWFA.

16. The quote is from Wright to Spivey (copy to Whitney), 29 December 1943, FLWFA.

17. Ibid.

18. Ibid.

19. Whitney to Spivey, 26 January 1944, 1502.279.151, FLWFA.

20. Spivey to Wright, 7 February 1944, 1502.279.155, FLWFA.

21. Wright to Spivey, 9 February 1944, 1502.279.158, FLWFA.

22. Spivey to Wright, 15 February 1944, 1502.279.160, FLWFA.

23. Spivey to Wright, 19 February 1944, 1502.279.162, FLWFA.

24. "Unless you do something right away she will give up the whole plan. I can't over exaggerate the necessity of your doing something about this matter at once." Spivey to Wright, 21 April 1944, 1502.279.172, FLWFA. After two weeks without a response, Spivey pleaded with Wright: "I wish that you would re-read my letter about the music building, and I want you to make another try at making the change which Mrs. Whitney wants. After all, you can make some very minor changes and please her . . . We cannot afford to displease these people. If you would make just a little pencil sketch and send it to her, this would answer all purposes. I hope that you will do this because there is so much involved for the college and for yourself." Spivey to Wright, 4 May 1944, 1502.279.174, FLWFA.

25. Wright to Whitney, 12 June 1944, 1502.279.180, FLWFA.

26. Ibid.

27. Wright to Whitney, 28 July 1944, 1502.279.187, FLWFA.

28. Ibid.

29. Spivey to Wright, 5 August 1944, 1502.279.189, FLWFA.

30. Spivey to Wright, 21 August 1944, 1502.279.191, FLWFA.

31. Wright to Spivey, 27 September 1944, 1502.279.199, FLWFA.

32. Spivey to Wright, 2 November 1944, 1502.279.210, FLWFA.

33. "Programme for University," no date, 1502.279.019, FLWFA.

34. Ibid.

35. Wright to Spivey, 12 March 1944, FLWFA.

36. Wright to Spivey, 12 March 1944, FLWFA.

37. On Milles see Liden, *Between Water and Heaven*, and Clark and Belloli, eds., *Design in America*.

38. Wright, *Autobiography*, 516.

39. Wright to Carl Milles, 14 June 1938, M077 C08, FLWFA.

40. Carl Milles to Wright, date unknown, M080 E05, FLWFA.

41. A typescript fundraising speech in the Ludd Spivey files at Florida Southern College, entitled "A True Story," contains a list of costs for constructed and proposed projects that includes "Statues of Boy" and "Statue of Three figures" at $10,000 each.

42. Wright to Spivey, 12 March 1944, FLWFA.

43. One of Wright's drawings for the unbuilt Nakoma Country Club (1924) included notes suggesting "stone memorials" to "Nakoma-Warrior (domestic)" and "Nakomis-Plateau-Nakomis warrior (dramatic)," suggesting abstract rather than figural depictions.

44. According to Anne Whitson Spirn, "Wright had a fascination and much experience with dams, ponds, and falling water." Spirn, "Wright: Architect of Landscape," in De Long, ed., *Designs for an American Landscape*, 148.

45. For a drawing and brief description of the Nakoma sculptures, see Futagawa, ed., *Frank Lloyd Wright Monograph, vol. 5*, text by Bruce Brooks Pfeiffer, 21.

46. Wright to Spivey, 30 October 1944, FLWFA. This statement must be evaluated in light of the national news coverage devoted to disastrous hurricanes in Florida in 1926 (almost 400 killed and thousands injured) and 1928 (nearly 2,000 killed).

47. Spivey to Wright, 19 October 1944, FSCA. Wright ignored the request, but on May 25, 1945, Spivey reiterated this point: "Here are a few observations I want you to remember when you make up the plans for the re-building of the chapel: (1) You must try to keep in mind that the sun in Florida for at least nine months out of the year is very hot. One of the sharpest criticisms that has come to me about the chapel is the sun shining down on the audience from the skylight during the service. It is impossible for people to bear it. We have to stop the meeting and ask the people to move out of the sun. Then, before the service is over, the sun has moved over into another portion of the audience. I hope you will devise a plan to take care of this criticism. Perhaps this can be taken care of by certain kinds

of glass . . . (2) The second thing I hope you will do is to re-build it in such a way that we can ventilate it, or else suggest an air-conditioning plant. This, of course, cannot be done until after the war. Let me remind you again that for nine months out of the year in Florida the weather is hot—very hot. When the sun beats down upon this concrete for a few hours the inside of the building becomes boiling heat." Spivey to Wright, 25 May 1945, 1502.279.247, FLWFA. But no air-conditioning was added nor alterations made.

Spivey, however, was not finished pleading. Almost four years later he wrote to Wright about the chapel conditions again: "I want you to keep in mind that the chapel is not usable during eight months of the year in its present condition. The heat is terrific. This year, we are planning to entertain our Methodist Conference. We have no other place for them to meet other than in the chapel. It is utterly impossible to have them there without the air-conditioning . . . With the proper air-conditioning in this chapel, we can use it the whole year. Since we are not planning to erect a large auditorium, we must find a way to put this chapel into use." Spivey to Wright, 16 March 1949, FSCA. Wright adamantly refused to budge on the air-conditioning issue. According to historian Bruce Brooks Pfeiffer, former Taliesin apprentice, "Wright disliked most forms of artificial air conditioning because he believed them harmful. 'Just think what happens to the "old pump" (the heart) when you come into an icy cold room after being out in the hot sun, or vice versa.' The flow of natural air was always more desirable, even if the temperature of that moving air is higher than the cold blasts from excessive air conditioning." Pfeiffer, in Futagawa, ed., *Wright Monograph, vol. 5*, 99.

48. Although there were two separate structures with distinct names, all of the drawings and correspondence from the project refer to the "administration building" in the singular, and I will follow that usage.

49. Spivey to Wright, 16 October 1947, F072 A01, FLWFA.

50. Spivey to Wright, 24 October 1947, FSCA.

51. Spivey to Wright, 7 February 1949, FSCA.

52. "Florida Southern College Revisited for Glimpses of the Administration Group in Wright's Organic Campus."

53. Schweizer to Wright, 8 February 1958, F132 B04, FLWFA. In 1953 a small area in front of the entryway to the E. T. Roux Library had been glassed in as a memorial to a Florida Southern professor who died of polio, but this did not affect the building's interior.

Chapter 5. A "Florida Form"

1. Peters to Wright, no date (1946), 1502.279.283, FLWFA.

2. There is no evidence that Todd ever looked at the plans. In late May, Spivey sent an angry letter to Todd's assistant, stressing the importance of Todd's seeing the plans; there is no response from Todd or his office in the Frank Lloyd Wright or Florida Southern College archives. Interestingly, Todd and Wright began a

friendship around this time (early 1946). Hession and Pickrel, *Frank Lloyd Wright in New York*, 137, note 53. In 1958 Wright designed some schemes for a cinema for Todd to house a new method of widescreen projection, but none was ever built. Pfeiffer, *Treasures of Taliesin*, 156–57.

3. Lee Simonson to Spivey, 25 January 1947, FSCA; Spivey to Wright, 24 February 1947, FSCA.

4. Wright to Spivey, 1 March 1947, FSCA. Wright's four-page response to the "desired changes" concluded with the following: "No grand opera house, I take it, should be a part of the Florida Southern College Group of Modern Buildings. If an antique is desired it should be built in the village by some ham architect."

5. Philip Johnson to Wright, 2 May 1947, M162 A07, FLWFA.

6. Johnson to Wright, 20 May 1947, M162 A04, FLWFA.

7. Wright to "To whom it may concern," 6 September 1947, 1502.279.374, FLWFA.

8. Quoted in Thrift, Jr., ed., *Of Fact and Fancy*, 53.

9. See "Architecture of Robert Law Weed, A.I.A., at Florida Southern College," 1, 5.

10. Neil Levine has commented on the relationship between Thomas Jefferson's University of Virginia Rotunda and Wright's Water Dome. Levine, *Architecture of Frank Lloyd Wright*, 309.

11. Wright continued: "We have it everywhere in Usonia. We have it for the nation's Capitol and for the state house and for the county court houses. Even the district likes a dome up on its pilastered offices and big business has tried to steal it although getting along very well, thank you, with medieval mass." Wright, "An Organic Architecture" (1939), 306.

12. Wright, *Autobiography*, 333.

13. As Neil Levine points out, the Monona Terrace glass hemispheres rise from the ground rather than appearing atop a tower, reinforcing them as symbols of "social gathering and cultural activity" rather than government authority. Levine, *Architecture of Frank Lloyd Wright*, 307–8.

14. See Nute, *Wright and Japan*. For an account of Wright's unsuccessful attempt to create structures for the 1933–34 World's Fair, see Schrenk, *Building a Century of Progress*.

15. Jeff Baker, of Mesick, Cohen, Wilson, Baker Architects, telephone conversation with author, 10 September 2009.

16. "Programme for University," no date, 1502.279.019, FLWFA.

17. Ibid.

18. Spivey to Wright, 23 March 1946, F067 A07, FLWFA.

19. "I am making this suggestion because here in Florida it is almost impossible to keep a swimming pool from being contaminated." Spivey to Wright, 8 May 1947, FSCA. Correspondence in the Frank Lloyd Wright Foundation Archives from the Florida Department of Health and Sanitation to Kenn Lockhart in 1947 stated that swimming was forbidden in all of Lakeland's lakes, and its one public pool was closed because of high bacteria counts. The department also informed Wright that

he would need to use a Florida-registered engineer to design a filtering system for the pool, and that his design was unacceptable because there was no safety fence and no circulation route to force swimmers to leave the swimming area through the shower room.

20. Wright quoted in Levine, *Architecture of Frank Lloyd Wright*, 307.

21. "Swimming Pool Construction Resumed," *Southern*, 21 April 1950.

22. Wright, *A Testament* (1957), 190.

23. Wright and Brownell, *Architecture and Modern Life* (1937), 228; Wright, *A Testament*, 190–91.

24. Wright to *Magazine of Art*, reprinted in Tselos, "Wright and World Architecture," 72. Wright was responding to Tselos, "Exotic Influences." See also Weisberg, "Wright and Pre-Columbian Art," and Kirk, "Sources of Pre-Columbian Influences."

25. The plausibility of Florida Southern as a modern Mayan temple and the similarities in climate were raised by Braun, *Pre-Columbian Art*.

26. Although there are actually two administration buildings, I will refer to them in the singular, as did Wright.

27. Spivey to Wright, 16 October 1947, F072 A01, FLWFA, and 24 October 1947, FSCA.

28. Spivey to Wright, 24 October 1947, FSCA.

29. Peters to Wright, 1946 (no date), 1502.279.283, FLWFA.

30. Spivey to Mrs. George Grimes, 7 May 1949, FSCA.

31. Spivey to Wright, 28 May 1940, FSCA. Spivey's hopes were high: in addition to this building, he also wanted to begin work on two seminar rooms and a faculty house and to finish the chapel that summer.

32. Peters to Spivey, 20 February 1942, F054 C04, FLWFA.

33. Spivey to Wright, 10 June 1949, FSCA.

34. Quoted in Meehan, *Truth against the World*, 163, 167.

35. Quoted in Meehan, *Truth against the World*, 171.

36. Minutes of the board of trustees meeting of Florida Southern College, 1 June 1951, FSCA.

37. Spivey to Wright, 4 October 1952, FSCA. See also Spivey to Wright, 17 May 1952, 1502.279.597, FLWFA, and 23 May 1952, FSCA.

38. Spivey to Wright, 2 July 1953, 1502.279.657, FLWFA.

39. "Frank Lloyd Wright," *Architectural Forum* 102 (April 1955): 116.

40. "Frank Lloyd Wright Completes a Long, Low Industrial Arts Building for Florida Southern University," 116. In an interview with the *Southern*, Taliesin apprentice Kenn Lockhart said the building would have 127 columns and be "almost a forest of walkways." "Lockhart Gives New Facts on Industrial Arts Building," *Southern*, 14 April 1950.

41. "Wright Reveals FSC's Flaws," *Southern*, 11 November 1955.

42. Ludd M. Spivey and Boris Blai, interview by Dr. Juliana Jordan, *Sags Auf Deutsch*.

43. "Florida Southern—New Building," *New York Times*, 31 May 1953.

44. "Frank Lloyd Wright Completes a Long, Low Industrial Arts Building for Florida Southern," 116.

45. See Sweeney, *Wright: An Annotated Bibliography.*

46. "Frank Lloyd Wright," *Architectural Forum* 88 (January 1948): 65–156; "A Four-Color Portfolio of the Recent Work of the Dean of Contemporary Architects, with His Own Commentary on Each Building"; "Florida Southern College Revisited for Glimpses of the Administration Group in Wright's Organic Campus."

47. Prior to that issue *Architectural Record* had been Wright's ardent supporter and had a long history of publishing his work, dating back to the early 1900s. On the January 1938 *Architectural Forum* issue, see Toker, *Fallingwater Rising.*

48. "Frank Lloyd Wright," *Architectural Forum* 88 (January 1948): 129.

49. "Frank Lloyd Wright's Newest Creation"; Chambers, Jr., "Innovation in College Chapel Architecture"; "Florida Southern College, Designed by Frank Lloyd Wright"; Stoddard, "Wright Designs a College"; "Wright Campus Blooms in Fla."; "The Architecture of Frank Lloyd Wright at Florida Southern College"; "Frank Lloyd Wright: A Selection of Current Work."

50. Stoddard, "Wright Designs a College," 12, 23.

51. Harris G. Sims, "New Project Links Science, Religion," *New York Times,* 22 May 1938; "A New Chapel for Florida Southern College," *New York Times,* 9 March 1941; Sims, "Modernistic College Chapel," *New York Times Magazine,* 14 September 1941; "Florida Southern—Housing," *New York Times,* 11 May 1947; "Florida Southern—Housing," *New York Times,* 19 December 1948.

52. Wright to Spivey, 31 August 1942, F057 D01, FLWFA.

53. "Southern Receives $45,000 Donation for Small Chapel," *Southern,* 31 March 1947.

54. Spivey to Wright, 6 April 1954, FSCA. Danforth lived long enough to attend the building's dedication in March 1955, then passed away six months later.

55. "Wright Reveals FSC's Flaws," *Southern,* 11 November 1955.

56. Spivey to Wright, 31 March 1942, F055 B05, FLWFA. The reason Spivey pluralized the building is unknown, as nothing in the previous drawings or correspondence suggests more than one structure.

57. Frank Corrigan, "Polk Pledges $350,000 to New Science Building," *Southern,* 16 February 1951.

58. Russ Fee, "Spivey Enlists Student Aid in Science Bldg. Campaign," *Southern,* 6 April 1951.

59. Spivey to Wright, 28 October 1953, FSCA.

60. "Polk County Science Building," *Southern,* 9 March 1951. The drawing appeared again in "Florida Southern College Will Break Ground for $500,000 Frank Lloyd Wright Designed Polk County Science Building," *Southern,* 29 February 1952.

61. Untitled document, 1502.279.564, FLWFA.

62. According to Bruce Brooks Pfeiffer, nearly one-third of Wright's lifetime commissions were received between 1949 and 1959. Pfeiffer, "Frank Lloyd Wright, A Biographical Sketch: 1949–1959," in *Wright Collected Writings, vol. 5,* 19.

63. Hilla Rebay to Wright, June 1943, cited in Pfeiffer, ed., *Wright: The Guggenheim Correspondence*, 4.

64. On Rebay's involvement and the Guggenheim Museum in general, see Levine, *Architecture of Frank Lloyd Wright*, chapter 10.

65. Rebay to Wright, 23 March 1944, cited in Lukach, *Hilla Rebay*, 207.

66. Rebay to Wright, 5 April 1955, R091 B04, FLWFA.

67. Spivey to Wright, 16 April 1955, F116 A05, FLWFA.

68. Spivey to Wright, 1 December 1955, FSCA.

69. Spivey to Wright, 7 October 1955, FSCA.

70. Spivey, "Huge Building Program Continues," *Southern*, 20 October 1950. See also "New Conference Auditorium Slated for Campus by '52," *Southern*, 27 October 1950.

71. *Southern*, 3 November 1950.

72. "Construction Planned for Tenth Wright Building," *Southern*, 15 January 1954.

73. "Music Building Is in FSC Spring Program," *Southern*, 12 October 1956.

74. "Frank Lloyd Wright to Be FSC Guest Founders' Week," *Southern*, 18 January 1957.

75. "Frank Lloyd Wright: A Selection of Current Work."

76. Spivey to Wright, 10 January 1956, FSCA.

77. Quoted in Dave Watson, "Noted Architect Says FSC Only 'American' Campus," *Tampa Tribune*, 8 March 1957.

78. "Dr. Ludd M. Spivey's Retirement Marks the End of an Era," *Southern*, 27 September 1957.

Chapter 6. A New Era

1. Schweizer to Wright, 13 July 1957, 1502.279.761, FLWFA.

2. Schweizer to Wright, 28 September 1957, F129 C04, FLWFA.

3. Schweizer to Peters, 6 July 1958, F135 B09, FLWFA.

4. Wright to Spivey, 20 October 1958, 1502.279.777, FLWFA; Wright to Spivey, 2 December 1958, 1502.279.779, FLWFA; Olgivanna Wright to Thrift, Jr., 9 May 1959, FSCA.

5. Farr, "Frank Lloyd Wright: Defiant Genius," 83.

6. See "Frank Lloyd Wright's Work Is Carried On."

7. Spivey to Thrift, Jr., 3 January 1959, FSCA.

8. Spivey to Wright, 16 December 1949, FSCA.

9. Wright to Spivey, 20 December 1949, FSCA.

10. Spivey to Wright, 30 December 1949, FSCA.

11. "We are in such shape we cannot see squandering much of our resources on him at the present time. When we get around to it, we may figure more closely on it." Thrift, Jr., to Spivey, 21 January 1959, FSCA.

12. "This is the first letter the College has received about any supposed obligation to your late husband during my two year tenure as president, so I am com-

pletely unaware of the facts in the matter." Thrift, Jr., to Olgivanna Wright, 18 May 1959, FSCA.

13. Peters to Thrift, Jr., 19 August 1961, FSCA.

14. Thrift, Jr., to Tolle, 13 March 1963, FSCA.

15. Peters to Thrift, Jr., 19 March 1963, FSCA.

16. A letter from Thrift to Corning Tolle, who was traveling in Oregon after his visit to Taliesin, reveals that the president even had a model in mind for the new auditorium: he suggested Tolle again visit Willamette University or at least try to get pictures, blueprints, or sketches of their auditorium. "Am convinced that Herbert Smith built about as versatile a bldg. at rock bottom price as can be built anywhere," Thrift wrote. Thrift, Jr., to Tolle, 11 August 1959, FSCA.

17. Thrift, Jr., to Peters, 22 August 1961, FSCA.

18. Peters to Thrift, Jr., 19 August 1961, FSCA.

19. Thrift, Jr., ed., *Of Fact and Fancy*, 134.

20. I am grateful to Jeff Baker of Mesick, Cohen, Wilson, Baker Architects for these details.

21. Stowell, "Education's New Demands," 649. See also Stubbins, Jr., "College Dormitories."

22. Hudnut, "On Form in Universities," 90, 92.

Bibliography

Primary Sources

Ackerman, Frederick L. "The Planning of Colleges and Universities." *Architectural Forum* 54 (June 1931): 691–96.

"The Architecture of Frank Lloyd Wright at Florida Southern College; Architecture of Robert Law Weed, A.I.A., at Florida Southern College." *National Architect* (Detroit) 7 (April 1951): 1, 4–6.

Barney, Maginel Wright. *In the Valley of the God-Almighty Joneses*. New York: Appleton-Century, 1965.

The Bill of Rights, 150 Years After: The Story of Civil Liberty, 1938–1939. New York: American Civil Liberties Union, 1939.

Burchard, John E., Charles W. David, and Julian P. Boyd. *Planning the University Library Building*. Princeton: Princeton University Press, 1949.

Chambers, William S., Jr. "Innovation in College Chapel Architecture." *Architectural Concrete* 8 (January 1942): 16–17.

Chase, Mary Ellen. *A Goodly Fellowship*. New York: Macmillan Company, 1947.

Clark, Elmer T. *An Immortality of Remembrance*. Lakeland, Fla.: Southern College, 1926.

Crowson, E. H. "The Betrayal of Southern College. A Study in the Technique of Modern Infidelity." Unpublished manuscript, 1933, Emory University Library.

Dewey, John. "The School and Society" (1899). In *Dewey on Education: Selections*. Introduction and notes by Martin S. Dworkin, 33–90. Teachers College Classics in Education No. 3. New York: Teachers College Press, 1959.

Edgell, George H. *The American Architecture of To-Day*. New York: Charles Scribner's Sons, 1928.

Emerson, Ralph Waldo. "Art," "Nature," and "The Young American." In *The Complete Prose Works of Ralph Waldo Emerson*, 87–91, 310–28, 396–404. Whitefish, Mont.: Kessinger Publishing, 2006.

Farr, Finis. "Frank Lloyd Wright: Defiant Genius." *Saturday Evening Post*, 7 January 1961, 17–21, 83, 85–86.

Federal Writers' Project of the Work Projects Administration for the State of Florida. *Florida: A Guide to the Southernmost State*. New York: Oxford University Press, 1939.

"Florida." *Architectural Forum* 69 (December 1938): 449–64.

Florida: Empire of the Sun. Tallahassee: Florida State Hotel Commission, 1930.

Florida Southern College. *The E. Stanley Jones Educational Foundation*. Lakeland, Fla.: Florida Southern College, 1938.
———. *E. Stanley Jones for Christian Education*. Lakeland, Fla.: Florida Southern College, c. 1938.
———. *Florida Southern College Bulletin*. Lakeland, Fla.: Florida Southern College, 1938.
———. *Florida Southern College Bulletin* 66 (April 1950).
"Florida Southern College, Designed by Frank Lloyd Wright." *Architect's Journal* 106 (December 25, 1947): 559–61.
"Florida Southern College Revisited for Glimpses of the Administration Group in Wright's Organic Campus." *Architectural Forum* 97 (September 1952): 120–27.
"A Four-Color Portfolio of the Recent Work of the Dean of Contemporary Architects, with His Own Commentary on Each Building." *Architectural Forum* 94 (January 1951): 73–108. "Frank Lloyd Wright Completes a Long, Low Industrial Arts Building for Florida Southern University . . . and Begins a Civic Center for the Capital of His Home State." *Architectural Forum* 102 (April 1955): 114–21.
"Frank Lloyd Wright." *Architectural Forum* 68 (January 1938): entire issue.
"Frank Lloyd Wright." *Architectural Forum* 88 (January 1948): 65–156.
"Frank Lloyd Wright." *Architectural Forum* 102 (April 1955): 114–19.
"Frank Lloyd Wright: A Selection of Current Work." *Architectural Record* 123 (May 1958): 167–90.
"Frank Lloyd Wright's Newest Creation: A College Chapel Designed to Express the Significance of a Name—Florida." *Architect & Engineer* 146 (July 1941): 34–36.
Futagawa, Yukio, ed. *Frank Lloyd Wright Monograph.* Vol. 5, *1924–1936*. Text by Bruce Brooks Pfeiffer. Tokyo: A.D.A. Edita, 1990.
Hamlin, A.D.F. "The Educational Influence of Collegiate Architecture." *Architectural Forum* 43 (December 1925): 321–26.
Hitchcock, Henry-Russell. "Frank Lloyd Wright at the Museum of Modern Art." *Art Bulletin* 23 (March 1941): 73–76.
———. *In the Nature of Materials: 1887–1941, the Buildings of Frank Lloyd Wright.* New York: Duell, Sloan, and Pearce, 1942.
Hudnut, Joseph. "On Form in Universities." *Architectural Record* 102 (December 1947): 88–96.
Hurt, Huber William, and Harriet Hurt. *The 1939 College Blue Book*. DeLand, Fla.: The College Blue Book, 1940.
Insuring Our Destiny. New York: T. W. Willard Motion Picture Company, c. 1937.
"Into College Plants Has Poured $2,250,000,000." *Life* (7 June 1937): 52–57.
Johnson, Franklin W. "Some Factors Involved in Planning a New College Campus." *American School and University* 10 (1938): 23–26.
Journal of the Florida Annual Conference of the Methodist Church, South. Lakeland, Fla.: Southern Printing Company, 1931.
Klauder, Charles Z., and Herbert L. Wise. *College Architecture in America and Its Part in the Development of the Campus*. New York: Charles Scribner's Sons, 1929.

Larson, Jens F., and Archie M. Palmer. *Architectural Planning of the American College.* New York: McGraw-Hill, 1933.

Lukach, Joan M. *Hilla Rebay: In Search of the Spirit in Art.* New York: George Braziller, 1983.

Pfeiffer, Bruce Brooks, ed. *Frank Lloyd Wright Monograph.* Vol. 5, *1924–1936.* Tokyo: A.D.A. Edita, 1986.

"Programme for University," no date, 1502.279.019. Frank Lloyd Wright Foundation Archives.

Sags Auf Deutsch. Tampa, Fla.: WEDU-TV, 1962.

"Spivey Enthusiastic over Prospects of Support for Rich Foundation." Undated newspaper article, Box MH4–2, Folder M-00-Jones, E. Stanley Educational Foundation: "Proposed E. Stanley Jones Educational Foundation, Late 1930s." Florida Southern College Archives.

Spivey, Ludd M. "The Authority of Social Intelligence." 10–13, in Spivey Collection, Folder 13-A-00: "Lectures & Speeches—Spivey Lectures and Speeches—Various, 1 of 2." Florida Southern College Archives.

———. *Good News! A Progress Report about the E. Stanley Jones Educational Foundation* (Florida Southern College, 1939), in Spivey Collection, Box MH4–2, Folder M-00-Jones, E. Stanley Educational Foundation: "Proposed E. Stanley Jones Educational Foundation, Late 1930s." Florida Southern College Archives.

Stoddard, Donna M. "Frank Lloyd Wright Designs a College." *Design* 50 (June 1949): 12–13, 23.

Stowell, Kenneth Kingsley. "Education's New Demands." *Architectural Forum* 54 (June 1931): 649–51.

Stubbins, Hugh, Jr. "College Dormitories: What Do the Colleges Really Want?" *Architectural Record* 99 (April 1946): 107–8.

Sullivan, Louis H. "What Is Architecture? A Study in the American People of Today" (1906). In *Kindergarten Chats and Other Writings,* 17–174. New York: Dover Publications, 1979.

"Tampans Raise $10,000 to Open College Drive." *Tampa Morning Tribune,* 17 May 1938.

Thoreau, Henry David. *Walden* (1854). New York: Thomas Y. Crowell, 1910.

Walker, C. Howard. "Expression—And the Collegiate Style." *Architectural Forum* 54 (June 1931): 653–56.

Walter, Frank K. "The University Library Building," *American School and University* 13 (1941): 307–15.

"Where Is Modern Now?" *Architectural Forum* 68 (June 1938): 465–70.

Whitman, Walt. "By Blue Ontario's Shore" (1856; 1881). In *The Complete Poems of Walt Whitman,* 310–24. Ware, Hertfordshire: Wordsworth Editions, 1995.

———. "Democratic Vistas" (1871). In *Complete Prose Works,* 203–57. Philadelphia: David McKay, 1892.

The Works and Aims of the Department of New Testament and Early Christian Literature of the University of Chicago (unknown publisher, 1931).

"Wright Campus Blooms in Fla." *Art Digest* 24 (15 April 1950): 13.

Wright, Frank Lloyd. *Ausgefuhrte Bauten und Entwurfe von Frank Lloyd Wright* (1910). In *Frank Lloyd Wright Collected Writings, Vol. 1, 1894–1930*, edited by Bruce Brooks Pfeiffer, 101–15. New York: Rizzoli International Publications and Frank Lloyd Wright Foundation, 1992.

———. *An Autobiography.* New York: Duell, Sloan, and Pearce, 1932.

———. "Books That Have Meant Most to Me" (1932). In *Frank Lloyd Wright Collected Writings, Vol. 3, 1931–1939*, edited by Bruce Brooks Pfeiffer, 156–66. New York: Rizzoli International Publications and Frank Lloyd Wright Foundation, 1995.

———. *The Disappearing City* (1932). In *Frank Lloyd Wright Collected Writings, Vol. 3, 1931–1939*, edited by Bruce Brooks Pfeiffer, 70–112. New York: Rizzoli International Publications and Frank Lloyd Wright Foundation, 1993.

———. "Frank Lloyd Wright Speaks Up" (1953). In *Frank Lloyd Wright Collected Writings, Vol. 5, 1949–1959*, edited by Bruce Brooks Pfeiffer, 66–69. New York: Rizzoli International Publications and Frank Lloyd Wright Foundation, 1995.

———. "In the Cause of Architecture" (1908). In *Frank Lloyd Wright Collected Writings, Vol. 1, 1894–1930*, edited by Bruce Brooks Pfeiffer, 84–100. New York: Rizzoli International Publications and Frank Lloyd Wright Foundation, 1992.

———. "In the Cause of Architecture: The Third Dimension" (1925). In *Frank Lloyd Wright Collected Writings, Vol. 1, 1894–1930*, edited by Bruce Brooks Pfeiffer, 209–14. New York: Rizzoli International Publications and Frank Lloyd Wright Foundation, 1992.

———. "Is It Good-By to Gothic?" (1958). In *Frank Lloyd Wright Collected Writings, Vol. 5, 1949–1959*, edited by Bruce Brooks Pfeiffer, 227–33. New York: Rizzoli International Publications and Frank Lloyd Wright Foundation, 1995.

———. "The Japanese Print: An Interpretation" (1912). In *Frank Lloyd Wright Collected Writings, Vol. 1, 1894–1930*, edited by Bruce Brooks Pfeiffer, 116–25. New York: Rizzoli International Publications and Frank Lloyd Wright Foundation, 1992.

———. "The Language of an Organic Architecture." *The Future of Architecture.* New York: Horizon Press, 1953.

———. "Letter to the Editor." *Magazine of Art* 31 (June 1938): 368.

———. Letter to *Magazine of Art* (1953), reprinted in Dmitri Tselos, "Frank Lloyd Wright and World Architecture." *Journal of the Society of Architectural Historians* 28 (March 1969): 58–72.

———. *The Living City* (1958). In *Frank Lloyd Wright Collected Writings, Vol. 5, 1949–1959*, edited by Bruce Brooks Pfeiffer, 251–344. New York: Rizzoli International Publications and Frank Lloyd Wright Foundation, 1995.

———. "Living in the Desert." *Arizona Highways* 25 (October 1949): 12–15.

———. "Modern Architecture, Being the Kahn Lectures" (1931). In *Frank Lloyd Wright Collected Writings, Vol. 2, 1930-1932*, edited by Bruce Brooks Pfeiffer, 19–79. New York: Rizzoli International Publications and Frank Lloyd Wright Foundation, 1992.

———. "An Organic Architecture" (1939). In *Frank Lloyd Wright Collected Writ-*

ings, Vol. 3, 1931–1939, edited by Bruce Brooks Pfeiffer, 299–334. New York: Rizzoli International Publications and Frank Lloyd Wright Foundation, 1993.

———. "Sixty Years of Living Architecture" (1951). In *Frank Lloyd Wright Collected Writings, Vol. 5, 1949–1959*, edited by Bruce Brooks Pfeiffer, 31–39. New York: Rizzoli International Publications and Frank Lloyd Wright Foundation, 1995.

———. *The Taliesin Fellowship* (1933). In *Frank Lloyd Wright Collected Writings, Vol. 3, 1931–1939*, edited by Bruce Brooks Pfeiffer, 156–66. New York: Rizzoli International Publications and Frank Lloyd Wright Foundation, 1995.

———. *A Testament* (1957). In *Frank Lloyd Wright Collected Writings, Vol. 5, 1949–1959*, edited by Bruce Brooks Pfeiffer, 155–226. New York: Rizzoli International Publications and Frank Lloyd Wright Foundation, 1995.

——— and Baker Brownell. *Architecture and Modern Life* (1937). In *Frank Lloyd Wright Collected Writings, Vol. 3, 1931–1939*, edited by Bruce Brooks Pfeiffer, 335–50. New York: Rizzoli International Publications and Frank Lloyd Wright Foundation, 1993.

Secondary Sources

Alofsin, Anthony. *Frank Lloyd Wright—The Lost Years, 1910–22: A Study of Influence*. Chicago: University of Chicago Press, 1993.

Biemiller, Lawrence. "Echoes of Jefferson in a Campus Designed by Frank Lloyd Wright." *Chronicle of Higher Education* (15 April 1992): B4–5.

Braden, Susan R. *The Architecture of Leisure: The Florida Resort Hotels of Henry Flagler and Henry Plant*. Gainesville: University Press of Florida, 2002.

Braun, Barbara. *Pre-Columbian Art and the Post-Columbian World: Ancient Sources of American* Art. New York: Harry N. Abrams, 1993.

Bridgeman, Frieda Estes. "The Development of a Theatre Concept as Reflected in the Theatrical Architecture of Frank Lloyd Wright." PhD dissertation, University of Wisconsin, 1971.

Clark, Robert Judson, and Andrea P. A. Belloli, eds. *Design in America: The Cranbrook Vision, 1925–1950*. New York: Harry N. Abrams, in association with the Detroit Institute of Arts and the Metropolitan Museum of Art, 1984.

Cole, Wendell. "The Theatre Projects of Frank Lloyd Wright." *Educational Theatre Journal* 12 (May 1960): 86–93.

Collins, Christiane C., and George R. Collins. "Monumentality: A Critical Matter in Modern Architecture." *Harvard Architecture Review* 4 (Spring 1984): 14–35.

Cronon, William. "Inconstant Unity." In *Frank Lloyd Wright: Architect*, edited by Terrence Riley, 8–31. New York: Museum of Modern Art, 1994.

Curl, Donald W. *Mizner's Florida: American Resort Architecture*. New York, Cambridge, and London: Architectural Foundation and MIT Press, 1987.

De Long, David, ed. *Frank Lloyd Wright: Designs for an American Landscape, 1922–1932*. New York: Harry N. Abrams, in association with the Canadian Centre for Architecture, the Library of Congress, and the Frank Lloyd Wright Foundation, 1996.

Doremus, Thomas. *Frank Lloyd Wright and Le Corbusier: The Great Dialogue.* New York: Van Nostrand Reinhold, 1992.

Dorrien, Gary. *The Making of American Liberal Theology: Idealism, Realism, and Modernity, 1900–1950.* Louisville and London: Westminster John Knox Press, 2003.

Duberman, Martin. *Black Mountain: An Exploration in Community.* New York: E. P. Dutton, 1972.

Farish, Hunter Dickinson. *The Circuit Rider Dismounts: A Social History of Southern Methodism, 1865–1900.* 1938. Reprint, New York: Da Capo Press, 1969.

Fitch, James Marston. "Facsimiles and Reality: On Vincent Scully's American Architecture and Urbanism." *Journal of Aesthetic Education* 5 (October 1971): 154.

Ford, Edward R. *The Details of Modern Architecture.* Vol. 1. Cambridge and London: MIT Press, 1990.

Frampton, Kenneth. "Modernization and Mediation: Frank Lloyd Wright and the Impact of Technology." In *Frank Lloyd Wright: Architect,* edited by Terrence Riley. New York: Museum of Modern Art, 1994.

Friedland, Roger, and Harold Zellman. *The Fellowship: The Untold Story of Frank Lloyd Wright and the Taliesin Fellowship.* New York: Harper Perennial, 2007.

Futagawa, Yukio, ed. *Frank Lloyd Wright Monograph, 1924–1936.* Vol. 5. Text by Bruce Brooks Pfeiffer. Tokyo: A.D.A. Edita, 1985.

———, ed. *Frank Lloyd Wright Monograph, 1937–1941.* Vol. 6. Text by Bruce Brooks Pfeiffer. Tokyo: A.D.A. Edita, 1986.

———, ed. *Frank Lloyd Wright Monograph, 1942–1950.* Vol. 7. Text by Bruce Brooks Pfeiffer. Tokyo: A.D.A. Edita, 1988.

———, ed. *Frank Lloyd Wright Monograph, 1951–1959.* Vol. 8. Text by Bruce Brooks Pfeiffer. Tokyo: A.D.A. Edita, 1988.

Gannon, Michael, ed. *The New History of Florida.* Gainesville: University Press of Florida, 1993.

Gill, Brendan. *Many Masks: A Life of Frank Lloyd Wright.* New York: Da Capo Press, 1998.

Green, Aaron G., with Donald P. DeNevi. *An Architecture for Democracy: The Marin County Civic Center.* Edited by Ben Raeburn and Nancy Klein. San Francisco: Grendon Publishing, 1990.

Gross, John O. "Henry Pfeiffer and Annie Merner Pfeiffer." In *Encyclopedia of World Methodism,* vol. 2, edited by Nolan B. Harmon, 1893. Nashville: United Methodist Publishing House, 1974.

A Guide to Florida's Historic Architecture. Gainesville: University Presses of Florida, 1989.

Gyure, Dale Allen. "The Heart of the University: A History of the Library as an Architectural Symbol of American Higher Education." *Winterthur Portfolio* 42 (Summer/Autumn 2008): 107–32.

Haggard, Theodore M. *Florida Southern College, Lakeland, Florida: The First 100 Years, An Illustrated History, 1985.* Lakeland, Fla.: Florida Southern College Press, 1985.

Hanna, Paul R., and Jean S. Hanna. *Frank Lloyd Wright's Hanna House, The Clients' Report.* New York: Architectural History Foundation and Cambridge: MIT Press, 1981.

Hatton, Hap. *Tropical Splendor: An Architectural History of Florida.* New York: Alfred A. Knopf, 1987.

Henning, Randolph C. "Frank Lloyd Wright's Other Florida Designs." *Frank Lloyd Wright Quarterly* 13 (Winter 2002): 4–21.

Hertz, David Michael. *Frank Lloyd Wright in Word and Form.* New York: G. K. Hall, 1995.

Hession, Jane King, and Debra Pickrel. *Frank Lloyd Wright in New York: The Plaza Years, 1954–1959.* Salt Lake City: Gibbs Smith, 2007.

Horwitz, Hattie S. "The West Campus at Florida Southern College, Lakeland, Florida, and Its Builders." M.A. thesis, University of Miami, 1976.

Hynes, William J. *Shirley Jackson Case and the Chicago School: The Socio-Historical Method.* Chico, Ca.: Scholars Press, 1981.

Johnson, Donald Leslie. *Frank Lloyd Wright versus America: The 1930s.* Cambridge: MIT Press, 1994.

Johnson, Martin Ross. "The Christian Vision of E. Stanley Jones: Missionary Evangelist, Prophet, and Statesman." PhD dissertation, Florida State University, 1978.

Joncas, Richard. "Buildings for Learning." In *Frank Lloyd Wright and the Living City,* edited by David G. De Long, 114–29. Weil am Rhein, Germany: Vitra Design Museum and Milan, Italy: Skira, 1998.

———. "'Pure Form': The Origins and Development of Frank Lloyd Wright's Non-Rectangular Geometry." PhD dissertation, Stanford University, 1991.

Kaufmann, Edgar, ed. *Frank Lloyd Wright: An American Architecture.* New York: Barnes and Noble, 1998.

Kilde, Jean Halgren. *When Church Became Theatre: The Transformation of Evangelical Architecture and Worship in Nineteenth-Century America.* New York: Oxford University Press, 2005.

Kirk, Terry R. "The Sources of Pre-Columbian Influences on Frank Lloyd Wright." M.A. thesis, Columbia University, 1986.

Kirwin, Koby. "Florida Southern College: A Frank Lloyd Wright Campus, Lakeland, Florida." M.L.A. thesis, University of Florida, 1995.

Kjellmark, Eric. "Vegetation History of the Lake Hollingsworth Area: Past Landscapes and Present Restoration." In *Lake Hollingsworth: Reflections and Studies on a Florida Landmark,* edited by John Haldeman and Bernard Quetchenbach. Charleston S.C.: History Press, 2005.

Kornwolf, James D. *Modernism in America, 1937–1941.* Williamsburg, Va.: Joseph and Margaret Muscarelle Museum of Art, College of William and Mary, 1985.

Laseau, Paul, and James Tice. *Frank Lloyd Wright: Between Principle and Form.* New York: John Wiley and Sons, 1991.

Levine, Neil. *The Architecture of Frank Lloyd Wright.* Chicago: University of Chicago Press, 1996.

———. "Frank Lloyd Wright's Diagonal Planning." In *In Search of Modern Architecture*, edited by Helen Searing, 232–63. New York: Architectural History Foundation and Cambridge and London: MIT Press, 1982.

Liden, Elisabeth. *Between Water and Heaven: Carl Milles' Search for American Commissions*. Stockholm: Almqvist and Wiksell International and Montclair, N.J.: Abner Schram, 1986.

MacDonald, Randall M., Nora E. Galbraith, and James G. Rogers, Jr. *The Buildings of Frank Lloyd Wright at Florida Southern College*. Charleston, S.C.: Arcadia Publishing, 2007.

MacDonald, William L., and John A. Pinto. *Hadrian's Villa and Its Legacy*. New Haven and London: Yale University Press, 1995.

Marty, Myron A. *Communities of Frank Lloyd Wright: Taliesin and Beyond*. DeKalb, Ill.: Northern Illinois University Press, 2009.

——— and Shirley L. Marty. *Frank Lloyd Wright's Taliesin Fellowship*. Kirksville, Mo.: Truman State University Press, 1999.

McCarter, Robert. *Frank Lloyd Wright*. London: Phaidon Press, 1997.

Meehan, Patrick J., ed. *Frank Lloyd Wright Remembered*. Washington, D.C.: Preservation Press, 1991.

———, ed. *Truth against the World: Frank Lloyd Wright Speaks for an Organic Architecture*. New York: John Wiley and Sons, 1987.

Menocal, Narciso G. "Frank Lloyd Wright's Concept of Democracy: An American Architectural Jeremiad." In *Frank Lloyd Wright in the Realm of Ideas*, edited by Bruce Brooks Pfeiffer and Gerald Nordland, 149–64. Carbondale and Edwardsville, Ill.: Southern Illinois University Press, 1988.

The National Cyclopedia of American Biography. Vol. 58. Clifton, N.J.: James T. White, 1979.

Nute, Kevin. *Frank Lloyd Wright and Japan: The Role of Traditional Japanese Art and Architecture in the Work of Frank Lloyd Wright*. London and New York: Routledge, 2000.

Olsberg, Nicholas. Introduction. In *Frank Lloyd Wright: Designs for an American Landscape, 1922–1932*, edited by David De Long, 9–14. New York: Harry N. Abrams, in association with the Canadian Centre for Architecture, the Library of Congress, and the Frank Lloyd Wright Foundation, 1996.

Patterson, Terry L. *Frank Lloyd Wright and the Meaning of Materials*. New York: Van Nostrand Reinhold, 1994.

Paul, Sherman. *Louis Sullivan: An Architect in American Thought*. Englewood Cliffs, N.J.: Prentice-Hall, 1962.

Pfeiffer, Bruce Brooks, ed. *Frank Lloyd Wright: His Living Voice*. Fresno, Cal.: Press at California State University, 1987.

———, ed. *Frank Lloyd Wright: The Guggenheim Correspondence*. Fresno, Cal.: Press at California State University and Edwardsville, Ill.: Southern Illinois University Press, 1986.

———. *Treasures of Taliesin: Seventy-Seven Unbuilt Designs*. 2nd ed. Rahnert Park, Cal.: Pomegranate Communications, 1999.

Riley, Terrence. "The Landscapes of Frank Lloyd Wright: A Pattern of Work." In *Frank Lloyd Wright: Architect*, edited by Terrence Riley, 96–107. New York: Museum of Modern Art, 1994.

Ringenberg, William C. "Eli Stanley Jones." In *American National Biography*, vol. 12, edited by John A. Garaty and Mark C. Carnes, 192–93. New York: Oxford University Press, 1999.

Roche, John F. "Building for Democracy: Organic Architecture in Relation to Progressive Education." *Educational Theory* 40 (Summer 1990): 295–307.

Rogers, Steven B. "The Academician and the Architect: Ludd M. Spivey and Frank Lloyd Wright and the Creation of a Florida Architecture." Paper presentation, Florida Historical Society, Ft. Myers, Fla., 20 May 1994. Florida Southern College Archives.

———. "The Frank Lloyd Wright Campus at Florida Southern College: A Child of the Sun." *Frank Lloyd Wright Quarterly* 12 (Summer 2001): 4–23.

Schrenk, Lisa D. *Building a Century of Progress: The Architecture of Chicago's 1933–34 World's Fair*. Minneapolis and London: University of Minnesota Press, 2007.

Scully, Vincent, Jr. *Frank Lloyd Wright*. New York: George Braziller, 1960.

Secrest, Meryl. *Frank Lloyd Wright: A Biography*. New York: Harper Perennial, 1992.

Sherwood, Patricia, and Joseph Michael Lasala. "Education and Architecture: The Evolution of the University of Virginia's Academical Village." In *Thomas Jefferson's Academical Village: The Creation of an Architectural Masterpiece*, edited by Richard Guy Wilson, 9–46. Charlottesville, Va.: Bayley Museum of the University of Virginia, 1993.

Siry, Joseph M. "Frank Lloyd Wright's Annie M. Pfeiffer Chapel for Florida Southern College: Modernist Theology and Regional Architecture." *Journal of the Society of Architectural Historians* 63 (December 2004): 498–539.

———. "Wright's Baghdad Opera House and Gammage Auditorium: In Search of Regional Modernity." *Art Bulletin* 87 (June 2005): 265–311.

Sledge, Robert Watson. *Hands on the Ark: The Struggle for Change in the Methodist Episcopal Church, South, 1914–1939*. Lake Junaluska, N.C.: Commission on Archives and History, The United Methodist Church, 1972.

Spirn, Anne Whitson. "Frank Lloyd Wright: Architect of Landscape." In *Frank Lloyd Wright: Designs for an American Landscape, 1922–1932*, edited by David De Long, 135–69. New York: Harry N. Abrams, in association with the Canadian Centre for Architecture, the Library of Congress, and the Frank Lloyd Wright Foundation, 1996.

Storrer, William Allin. *The Frank Lloyd Wright Companion*. Chicago: University of Chicago Press, 1993.

Summerson, John. "The Mischievous Analogy" (1941). In *Heavenly Mansions*, 159–218. London: Cresset Press, 1949.

Sweeney, Robert L. *Frank Lloyd Wright: An Annotated Bibliography*. Los Angeles: Hennessey and Ingalls, 1978.

Tafel, Edgar, ed. *Frank Lloyd Wright: Recollections by Those Who Knew Him*. New York: Courier Dover, 2001.

Tebeau, Charlton W. *A History of Florida*. Coral Gables: University of Miami Press, 1971.

Thrift, Charles T., Jr., ed. *Of Fact and Fancy . . . at Florida Southern College*. Lakeland, Fla.: Florida Southern College Press, 1979.

———. *Through Three Decades, at Florida Southern College, Lakeland, Florida*. Lakeland, Fla.: Florida Southern College Press, 1955.

"Through the Years: Reflections on Frank Lloyd Wright." Transcript of a discussion held 20 February 1985, photocopy, Florida Southern College Archives.

Toker, Franklin. *Fallingwater Rising: Frank Lloyd Wright, E.J. Kaufmann, and America's Most Extraordinary House*. New York: Alfred A. Knopf, 2003.

Tselos, Dmitri. "Exotic Influences on Frank Lloyd Wright." *Magazine of Art* 47 (April 1953): 160–69, 184.

Tucker, Karen B. Westerfield. *American Methodist Worship*. New York: Oxford University Press, 2001.

Turner, Paul Venable. *Campus: An American Planning Tradition*. Cambridge: MIT Press, 1984.

———. "The Collaborative Design of Stanford University." In *The Founders and the Architects: The Design of Stanford University*, 9–68. Stanford, Cal.: Department of Art, 1976.

Twombly, Robert C. *Frank Lloyd Wright: His Life and His Architecture*. New York: John Wiley and Sons, 1979.

———. "Organic Living: Frank Lloyd Wright's Taliesin Fellowship and Georgi Gurdjieff's Institute for the Harmonious Development of Man." *Wisconsin Magazine of History* 58 (Winter 1974–75): 126–39.

Van Slyck, Abigail A. *Free to All: Carnegie Libraries and American Culture*. Chicago and London: University of Chicago Press, 1995.

Weisberg, Gabriel. "Frank Lloyd Wright and Pre-Columbian Art: The Background for His Architecture." *Art Quarterly* 30 (March 1969): 58–72.

Westbrook, Robert B. *John Dewey and American Democracy*. Ithaca, N.Y., and London: Cornell University Press, 1991.

Wilson, Richard Guy. "Jefferson's Lawn: Perceptions, Interpretations, Meanings." In *Thomas Jefferson's Academical Village: The Creation of an Architectural Masterpiece*, edited by Richard Guy Wilson, 47–73. Charlottesville, Va.: Bayley Museum of the University of Virginia, 1993.

Wright, John Lloyd. *My Father, Frank Lloyd Wright*. New York: Dover Publications, 1992.

Index

The Florida History and Culture Series
Edited by Raymond Arsenault and Gary R. Mormino

Al Burt's Florida: Snowbirds, Sand Castles, and Self-Rising Crackers, by Al Burt (1997)
Black Miami in the Twentieth Century, by Marvin Dunn (1997)
Gladesmen: Gator Hunters, Moonshiners, and Skiffers, by Glen Simmons and Laura Ogden (1998)
"Come to My Sunland": Letters of Julia Daniels Moseley from the Florida Frontier, 1882–1886, by Julia Winifred Moseley and Betty Powers Crislip (1998)
The Enduring Seminoles: From Alligator Wrestling to Ecotourism, by Patsy West (1998, first paperback edition, 2008)
Government in the Sunshine State: Florida Since Statehood, by David R. Colburn and Lance deHaven-Smith (1999)
The Everglades: An Environmental History, by David McCally (1999, first paperback edition, 2001)
Beechers, Stowes, and Yankee Strangers: The Transformation of Florida, by John T. Foster Jr. and Sarah Whitmer Foster (1999)
The Tropic of Cracker, by Al Burt (1999)
Balancing Evils Judiciously: The Proslavery Writings of Zephaniah Kingsley, edited and annotated by Daniel W. Stowell (1999)
Hitler's Soldiers in the Sunshine State: German POWs in Florida, by Robert D. Billinger Jr. (2000)
Cassadaga: The South's Oldest Spiritualist Community, edited by John J. Guthrie, Phillip Charles Lucas, and Gary Monroe (2000)
Claude Pepper and Ed Ball: Politics, Purpose, and Power, by Tracy E. Danese (2000)
Pensacola during the Civil War: A Thorn in the Side of the Confederacy, by George F. Pearce (2000)
Castles in the Sand: The Life and Times of Carl Graham Fisher, by Mark S. Foster (2000)
Miami, U.S.A., by Helen Muir (2000)
Politics and Growth in Twentieth-Century Tampa, by Robert Kerstein (2001)
The Invisible Empire: The Ku Klux Klan in Florida, by Michael Newton (2001)
The Wide Brim: Early Poems and Ponderings of Marjory Stoneman Douglas, edited by Jack E. Davis (2002)
The Architecture of Leisure: The Florida Resort Hotels of Henry Flagler and Henry Plant, by Susan R. Braden (2002)
Florida's Space Coast: The Impact of NASA on the Sunshine State, by William Barnaby Faherty, S.J. (2002)
In the Eye of Hurricane Andrew, by Eugene F. Provenzo Jr. and Asterie Baker Provenzo (2002)
Florida's Farmworkers in the Twenty-first Century, text by Nano Riley and photographs by Davida Johns (2003)
Making Waves: Female Activists in Twentieth-Century Florida, edited by Jack E. Davis and Kari Frederickson (2003)
Orange Journalism: Voices from Florida Newspapers, by Julian M. Pleasants (2003)
The Stranahans of Ft. Lauderdale: A Pioneer Family of New River, by Harry A. Kersey Jr. (2003)

Death in the Everglades: The Murder of Guy Bradley, America's First Martyr to Environmentalism, by Stuart B. McIver (2003)
Jacksonville: The Consolidation Story, from Civil Rights to the Jaguars, by James B. Crooks (2004)
The Seminole Wars: The Nation's Longest Indian Conflict, by John and Mary Lou Missall (2004)
The Mosquito Wars: A History of Mosquito Control in Florida, by Gordon Patterson (2004)
Seasons of Real Florida, by Jeff Klinkenberg (2004, first paperback edition, 2009)
Land of Sunshine, State of Dreams: A Social History of Modern Florida, by Gary Mormino (2005, first paperback edition 2008)
Paradise Lost? The Environmental History of Florida, edited by Jack E. Davis and Raymond Arsenault (2005)
Frolicking Bears, Wet Vultures, and Other Oddities: A New York City Journalist in Nineteenth-Century Florida, edited by Jerald T. Milanich (2005)
Waters Less Traveled: Exploring Florida's Big Bend Coast, by Doug Alderson (2005)
Saving South Beach, by M. Barron Stofik (2005)
Losing It All to Sprawl: How Progress Ate My Cracker Landscape, by Bill Belleville (2006, first paperback edition 2010)
Voices of the Apalachicola, compiled and edited by Faith Eidse (2006)
Floridian of His Century: The Courage of Governor LeRoy Collins, by Martin A. Dyckman (2006)
America's Fortress: A History of Fort Jefferson, Dry Tortugas, Florida, by Thomas Reid (2006)
Weeki Wachee, City of Mermaids: A History of One of Florida's Oldest Roadside Attractions, by Lu Vickers (2007)
City of Intrigue, Nest of Revolution: A Documentary History of Key West in the Nineteenth Century, by Consuelo E. Stebbins (2007)
The New Deal in South Florida: Design, Policy, and Community Building, 1933–1940, edited by John A. Stuart and John F. Stack Jr. (2008)
Pilgrim in the Land of Alligators: More Stories about Real Florida, by Jeff Klinkenberg (2008)
A Most Disorderly Court: Scandal and Reform in the Florida Judiciary, by Martin A. Dyckman (2008)
A Journey into Florida Railroad History, by Gregg M. Turner (2008)
Sandspurs: Notes from a Coastal Columnist, by Mark Lane (2008)
Paving Paradise: Florida's Vanishing Wetlands and the Failure of No Net Loss, by Craig Pittman and Matthew Waite (2009, first paperback edition 2010)
Embry-Riddle at War: Aviation Training During World War II, by Stephen G. Craft (2009)
The Columbia Restaurant: Celebrating a Century of History, Culture, and Cuisine, by Andrew T. Huse, with recipes and memories from Richard Gonzmart and the Columbia restaurant family (2009)
Ditch of Dreams: The Cross Florida Barge Canal and the Struggle for Florida's Future, by Steven Noll and David Tegeder (2009)
Manatee Insanity: Inside the War over Florida's Most Famous Endangered Species, by Craig Pittman (2010)
Frank Lloyd Wright's Florida Southern College, by Dale Allen Gyure (2010)

Dale Allen Gyure is associate professor of architecture at Lawrence Technological University and adjunct associate professor of historic preservation at Goucher College. He specializes in the history of American educational architecture.